PROCLAIMING
THE GOSPEL

PROCLAIMING THE GOSPEL

First-Century Performance of Mark

WHITNEY SHINER

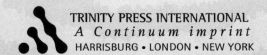
TRINITY PRESS INTERNATIONAL
A Continuum imprint
HARRISBURG · LONDON · NEW YORK

Trinity Press International, P.O. Box 1321, Harrisburg, PA 17105

Trinity Press International is a member of the Continuum International Publishing Group.

The Bible text is sometimes translated by the author but is chiefly from the *New Revised Standard Version Bible,* copyright 1989, by the Division of Christian Education of the National Council of the Churches of Christ in the USA, and is used by permission.

Cover art: Aulus Metellus (L'Arringatore): Roman orator. Copyright Scala/Art Resource, NY. Museo Archeologico, Florence, Italy.

Design: Corey Kent

Library of Congress Cataloging-in-Publication Data

Shiner, Whitney Taylor.
  Proclaiming the Gospel : first-century performance of Mark / Whitney Shiner.
    p. cm.
Includes bibliographical references and index.
  ISBN 1-56338-396-9
  1. Bible. N.T. Mark—Criticism, interpretation, etc. I. Title.
  BS2585.52 .S45 2003
  226.3'066—dc21
                              2003013119

Printed in the United States of America

03 04 05 06 07 08   10 9 8 7 6 5 4 3 2 1

Contents

Acknowledgments

Scholarship is always a communal activity. Ideas are born, grow, and develop in discussion with colleagues, reading their works, and hearing their papers. I have benefitted especially from the responses to earlier versions of this work presented as papers at the Society of Biblical Literature annual meetings, meetings of the Mid-Atlantic Region of the Society of Biblical Literature, and *Rhetorics and Hermeneutics: A Conference Honoring the Work of Wilhelm Wuellner*, sponsored by The Rhetorical New Testament Project of the Institute for Antiquity and Christianity at Claremont. The members of the Bible in Ancient and Modern Media Group of the Society of Biblical Literature and the participants in Claremont Conference have been very helpful. Joanna Dewey, Thomas Boomershine, and David Rhoads, all masters of the issues of orality and textuality, have been particularly helpful with their encouragement and advice, as was Wilhelm Wuellner and James Hester.

I would like to thank the Mathy family and the George Mason University College of Arts and Science for the Mathy Junior Faculty Award, which provided a semester sabbatical from teaching for work on this book. The Department of Philosophy and Religious Studies at George Mason University provided money for travel to conferences at which much of this book was orally performed. The Institute for Antiquity and Christianity at Claremont provided assistance for attending the conference which they sponsored. My colleagues in the Department of Philosophy and Religious Studies at George Mason University have provided a great deal of encouragement and many valuable insights. My children, Nicole, Daniel, and Gabrielle have displayed a good-natured tolerance of their dad's preoccupation with the book, and their constant love and affection made its writing possible.

Portions of this book appear in "Applause and Applause Lines in the Gospel of Mark," which is appearing in *Rhetorics and Hermeneutics:*

Wilhelm Wuellner and His Influence, edited by James D. Hester, to be published by Trinity Press International. Those portions are reprinted here with the gracious permission of Trinity Press. I would like to thank Prof. Carol Mattusch of George Mason University for assistance in locating art work related to oral performance. Carol Swistak performed yeoman service in securing copyright permission for the use of photographs. I would like to thank Henry Carrigan of Trinity Press International for his interest in the project and the editors at Trinity Press for many improvements in the text.

Abbreviations

AB	Anchor Bible
AGSS	Access Guide for Scripture Study
AJP	*American Journal of Philology*
AmAnth	*American Anthropologist*
ANF	*Ante-Nicene Fathers*
ANRW	*Aufstieg und Niedergang der rümischen Welt: Geschichte und Kultur Roms im Spiegel der neueren Forschung.* Edited by H. Temporini and W. Haase. Berlin, 1972–
APQ	*American Philosophical Quarterly*
ApSem	Approaches to Semiotics
ASNP	*Annali della Scuola normale superiore di Pisa*
BalS	*Balkan Studies*
BICSSup	Bulletin of the Institute of Classical Studies Supplement
BJRL	*Bulletin of the John Rylands University Library of Manchester*
BKP	Beitröge zur klassischen Philologie
BTB	*Biblical Theology Bulletin*
CAASMem	Connecticut Academy of Arts and Sciences, New Haven. Memoirs
CBA	Catholic Biblical Association
CBQ	*Catholic Biblical Quarterly*
CFLUM	Collection de la Faculte des Lettres de l'Universte de Montpellier
CGTC	Cambridge Greek Testament Commentary
CJ	*Classical Journal*
ClBul	*The Classical Bulletin*
ClWeek	*The Classical Weekly*

CP	*Classical Philology*
CQ	*Classical Quarterly*
CSASE	Cambridge Studies in Anglo-Saxon England
CSOLC	Cambridge Studies in Oral and Literate Culture
CSSA	Cambridge Studies in Social Anthropology
EHKSL	Europüische Hochschulschriften, Klassische Sprachen und Literaturen
ETSSS	Evangelical Theological Society Studies Series
ExpTim	*Expository Times*
FF	Foundations and Facets
GRBS	*Greek, Roman, and Byzantine Studies*
GSIA	Greek Studies: Interdisciplinary Approaches
Gym	*Gymnasium*
HSCP	*Harvard Studies in Classical Philology*
HvTS	*Hervormde Teologiese Studies*
ICSBSup	*Institute of Classical Studies Bulletin Supplement*
JAAR	*Journal of the American Academy of Religion*
JBL	*Journal of Biblical Literature*
JEGP	*Journal of English and Germanic Philology*
JHS	*Journal of Hellenic Studies*
JLSP	Janua Linguarum, Series Practica
JRASup	Journal of Roman Archaeology Supplementary Series
JRH	*Journal of Religious History*
JSJ	*Journal for the Study of Judaism in the Persian, Hellenistic, and Roman Periods*
JSNT	*Journal for the Study of the New Testament*
JSNTSup	Journal for the Study of the New Testament: Supplement Series
JSOTSup	Journal for the Study of the Old Testament: Supplement Series
JTS	*Journal of Theological Studies*
Kühn	Kühn, K. G. *Claudii Galeni Opera Omnia*. Vol. 1–20 of *Medicorum Graecorum Opera Quae Exstant*. Hildesheim, 1964–65.
LCL	Loeb Classical Library
LireB	Lire la Bible
LSJ	Liddell, H. G., R. Scott, and H. S. Jones. *A Greek-English Lexicon*. 9th ed. With revised supplement. Oxford, 1996.

MidFolk	*Midwest Folklore*
MnemSup	Mnemosyne, Bibliotheca Classica Batava, Supplementum
NEAEHL	*The New Encyclopedia of Archaeological Excavations in the Holy Land.* Edited by E. Stern. 4 vols. Jerusalem, 1993.
Neot	*Neotestamentica*
NICNT	New International Commentary on the New Testament
NovT	*Novum Testamentum*
NRSV	New Revised Standard Version
OCD	*Oxford Classical Dictionary.* Edited by S. Hornblower and A. Spawforth. 3d ed. Oxford, 1996.
PG	Patrologia graeca [= Patrologiae cursus completus: Series graeca]. Edited by J.-P. Migne. 162 vols. Paris, 1857–86.
Phil	*Philologus*
Phoenix	*Phoenix*
PL	Patrologia latina [= Patrologiae cursus completus: Series latina]. Edited by J.-P. Migne. 221 vols. Paris, 1844–65
PNTC	Pelican New Testament Commentaries
PW	Pauly, A. F. *Paulys Real-encyclopdëdie der classischen Altertumswissenschaft.* New edition, G. Wissowa. 49 vols. Stuttgart, 1894–1919.
QJS	*The Quarterly Journal of Speech*
QJSE	*The Quarterly Journal of Speech Education*
Rabe	Rabe, H. *Prolegomenon sylloge.* Rhetores Graeci, 14. Leipzig, 1931.
REG	*Revue des études grecques*
RevAnt	Revealing Antiquity
RhMus	*Rheinisches Museum für Philologie*
SBL	Society of Biblical Literature
SBLDS	Society of Biblical Literature Dissertation Series
SBLEJL	Society of Biblical Literature Early Judaism and Its Literature
SBLGRRS	Society of Biblical Literature Graeco-Roman Religion Series
SBLSymS	Society of Biblical Literature Symposium Series

SBLTT   Society of Biblical Literature Texts and Translations
Semeia   *Semeia*. Atlanta: Scholars Press.
SemeiaSup   Semeia Supplements
SIG   *Sylloge inscriptionum graecarum*. Edited by W.
        Dittenberger. 4 vols. 3rd ed. Leipzig, 1915–24.
SNTSMS   Society for New Testament Studies Monograph
         Series
Spengel   Spengel, L. *Rhetores Graeci*. 3 vols. Leipzig, 1853–56.
Spengel-   Hammer, C. *Rhetores Graeci ex Recognitione*
Hammer   *Leonardi Spengel*. 2d ed. of vol. 1/2 of L. Spengel,
         Rhetores Graeci. Leipzig, 1894.
SPHS   Scholars Press Homage Series
SpMon   *Speech Monographs*
SSCJ   *Southern Speech Communication Journal*
Str-B   Strack, H. L., and P. Billerbeck. *Kommentar zum
        Neuen Testament aus Talmud und Midrasch*. 6 vols.
        Munich, 1922–61.
StPatr   Studia Patristica
STRev   *Sewanee Theological Review*
TAPA   *Transactions of the American Philological Association*
Walz   Walz, C. *Rhetores graeci*. 9 vols. Stuttgart: 1832–36.
WCA   Written Communication Annual
WJSC   *Western Journal of Speech Communication*
WS   *Wiener Studien*
WUNT   Wissenshaftliche Untersuchungen zum Neuen
       Testament
YCS   Yale Classical Studies
ZNW   *Zeitschrift für die neutestamentliche Wissenschaft und die
        Kunde der älteren Kirche*

Abbreviations of Works of Ancient Authors

Titles in brackets are attributed to the author under whom they are listed, but the attribution is rejected by many scholars. Nevertheless, they are often found in collections of that author's work and are generally catalogued by libraries under that author's name.

Achilles Tatius
Leuc. Clit.	*Leucippe et Clitophon*	*The Adventures of Leucippe and Cleitophon*

Alciphron
Ep.	*Epistulae*	*Letters*

Aphthonius
Pros.	*Progymnasmata*	*Progymnasmata*

Apostolic Church Order

Apuleius
Metam.	*Metamorphoses*	*The Golden Ass*

Aristides
Or.	*Orationes*	*Orations*

Aristotle
Poet.	*Poetica*	*Poetics*
Rhet.	*Rhetorica*	*Rhetoric*
[Rhet. Alex.]	*Rhetorica ad Alexandrum*	*Rhetoric to Alexander*

Athanasius
Prol.	*Prolegomenon*	*Prolegomenon*

Athenaeus
Deipn.   *Deipnosophistae*   *Deipnosophists*

Augustine
Doctr. chr.   *De doctrina christiana*   *On Christian Doctrine*

Aulus Gellius
Noct. att.   *Noctes atticae*   *Attic Nights*

b   Babylonian Talmud (followed by name of tractate)

Callimachus
Epigr.   *Epigrammata*   *Epigrams*

Cicero
Ad Attic.   *Epistulae ad Atticum*   *Letters to Atticus*
Brut.   *Brutus or De claris*   *Brutus*
                         oratoribus
De or.   *De oratore*   *On the Making of*
                                                        an Orator
Fin.   *De finibus*   *On Limits*
Inv.   *De inventione rhetorica*   *On Invention*
Lig.   *Pro Ligario*   *For Ligario*
Mil.   *Pro Milone*   *For Milone*
Off.   *De officiis*   *On Duties*
Or. Brut.   *Orator ad M. Brutum*   *Orator*
Parad.   *Paradoxa Stoicorum*   *Paradox of the Stoics*
Sest.   *Pro Sestio*   *For Sestio*
Tusc.   *Tusculanae disputationes*   *Tusculan Disputations*

Clement of Alexandria
Ecl.   *Eclogae propheticae*   *Extracts from the Prophets*
Paed.   *Paedagogus*   *Christ the Educator*
Strom.   *Stromata*   *Miscellanies*

Cyprian
Ep.   *Epistulae*   *Letters*

Demosthenes
Cor.   *De corona*   *On the Crown*

Did.	*Didache*	*Didache/Teaching*

Dio Cassius
Hist.	*Historia romana*	*Roman History*

Dio Chrysostom
Or.	*Orationes*	*Orations*

Diodorus Siculus
Bib. hist.	*Bibliotheca historica*	*Historical Library*

Diogenes Laertius
De vita	*De vita et moribus philosophorum*	*The Lives and Opinions of Eminent Philosophers*

Dionysius of Halicarnassus
Lys.	*De Lysia*	*Lysias*

Dionysius Thrax
Ars gram.	*Ars grammatica*	*Grammar*

Epictetus
Diatr.	*Diatribai (Dissertationes)*	*Discourses*

Eunapius
Vit. soph	*Vitae sophistarum*	*Lives of the Philosophers and Sophists*

Eusebius
Hist. eccl.	*Historia ecclesiastica*	*Ecclesiastical History*

Galen
De comp. med.	*De compositione medicamentorum secundum locum*	*Treatise on the Preparation of Medicine*
De libr. propr.	*De libris propriis*	*On My Own Books*
Gos. Thom.	*Gospel of Thomas*	

Herodotus
Hist.	*Historiae*	*Histories*

Hesychius
Serm.   *Sermones*   *Sermons*

Hippolytus
Trad. ap.   *Traditio apostolica*   *The Apostolic Tradition*

Homer
Il.   *Ilias*   *Iliad*

Horace
Ars   *Ars poetica*   *Art of Poetry*
Ep.   *Epistulae*   *Letters*
Sat.   *Satirae*   *Satires*

Isocrates
Or.   *Orationes*   *Orations*

Jerome
Comm. Ezech.   *Commentariorum in*   *Commentary on Ezekiel*
                   Ezechielem
Ep.   *Epistulae*   *Letters*

John Chrysostom
Adv. Jud.   *Adversus Judaeos*   *Discourses against*
                                                 Judaizing Christians
Exp. Ps.   *Expositiones in Psalmos*   *Interpretation of*
                                                 the Psalms
Hom. Jo.   *Homiliae in Joannem*   *Homilies on John*

Josephus
B.J.   *Bellum judaicum*   *Jewish War*

Julius Pollux
Onom.   *Onomastikon*   *Vocabulary*

Justin
1 Apol.   *Apologia i*   *First Apology*

Juvenal
Sat.   *Satirae*   *Satires*

Libanius
Ep.	*Epistulae*	*Letters*
Or.	*Orationes*	*Orations*

Longinus
Rhet. Graeci	*Rhetorica Graeci*	*Greek Rhetoric*
[Subl.]	*De sublimitate*	*On the Sublime*

Longus
Daphn.	*Daphnis and Chloe*	

Lucian
[Am.]	*Amores*	*Affairs of the Heart*
Apol.	*Apologia*	*Apology*
Bis. acc.	*Bis accusatus*	*The Double Indictment*
Demon.	*Demonax*	*Demonax*
Dom.	*De domo*	*The Hall*
Fug.	*Fugitivi*	*The Runaways*
Gall.	*Gallus*	*The Dream,* or *The Cock*
Herod.	*Herodotus*	*Herodotus*
Ind.	*Adversus indoctum*	*The Ignorant Book-Collector*
Merc. cond.	*De mercede conductis*	*Salaried Posts in Great Houses*
Nigr.	*Nigrinus*	*Nigrinus*
Peregr.	*De morte Peregrini*	*The Passing of Peregrinus*
Pro imag.	*Pro imaginibus*	*Essays in Portraiture Defended*
Pseudol.	*Pseudologista*	*The Mistaken Critic*
Rhet. praec.	*Rhetorum praeceptor*	*A Professor of Public Speaking*
Salt.	*De saltatione*	*The Dance*
Symp.	*Symposium*	*The Carousal,* or *The Lapiths*

m	Mishna (followed by name of tractate)

Macrobius
Sat.	*Saturnaliorum Conviviorum*	*Saturnalia*

Martial
Ep.   *Epigrammata*   *Epigrams*
Meg.   *Megillah*   *Mishna Megillah*

Origen
Cels.   *Contra Celsum*   *Against Celsus*

Ovid
Fast.   *Fasti*   *Fasti*

Pausanias
Descr.   *Graeciae description*   *Description of Greece*

Persius
Sat.   *Satirae*   *Satires*

Petronius
Sat.   *Satyrica*   *Satyricon*

Philo
Contempl.   *De vita contemplativa*   *On the Contemplative Life*
Prob.   *Quod omnis probus liber sit*   *That Every Good Person
                                                  Is Free*

Philodemus
Rhet.   *Rhetorica*   *Rhetoric*

Philostratus
Vit. Apoll.   *Vita Apollonii*   *Life of Apollonius
                                                   [of Tyana]*
Vit. soph.   *Vita sophistarum*   *Lives of the Sophists*

Pindar
Ol.   *Olympionikai*   *Olympian Odes*
Pyth.   *Pythionikai*   *Pythian Odes*

Plato
Hipp. maj.   *Hippias major*   *Greater Hippias*
Hipp. min.   *Hippias minor*   *Lesser Hippias*
Ion   *Ion*   *Ion*

Leg.	Leges	Laws
Menex.	Menexenus	Menexenus
Phaedr.	Phaedrus	Phaedrus
Resp.	Respublica	Republic

Plautus

Amph.	Amphitruo	Amphitryon
Aul.	Aulularia	The Pot of Gold
Most.	Mostellaria	The Haunted House
Poen.	Poenulus	The Little Carthaginian
Trin.	Trinummus	Three Bob Day

Pliny the Elder

| Nat. | Naturalis historia | Natural History |

Pliny the Younger

| Ep. | Epistulae | Letters |

Plutarch

Amat.	Amatorius	On Love
Cic.	Cicero	Cicero
Comp. Dem. Cic.	Comparatio Demosthenis et Ciceronis	Comparison of Demosthenes and Cicero
Def. orac.	De defectu oraculorum	On the Obsolescence of Oracles
Dem.	Demosthenes	Demosthenes
Phoc.	Phocion	Life of Phocion
Pomp.	Pompeius	Pompey
Pyth. orac.	De Pythiae oraculis	Why the Pythia No Longer Gives Oracles in Verse
Quaest. conv.	Quaestionum convivialum	Table Talk
Rect. rat. aud.	De recta ratione audiendi	On Listening to Lectures
[Reg. imp. apophth.]	Regum et imperatorum apophthegmata	Sayings of Kings and Commanders
Sept. sap. conv.	Septum sapientum convivium	The Dinner of the Seven Wise Men
[Vit. X orat.]	Vitae decem oratorum	Lives of the Ten Orators

Polybius
Hist. | *Historiae* | *Histories*

Quintilian
Inst. | *Institutio oratoria* | *The Education of the Orator*
Rhet. Her. | *Rhetorica ad Herennium* | *Rhetoric to Herennium*

Seneca the Elder
Controv. | *Controversiae* | *Declamations*
Suas. | *Suasoriae* | *Suasoriae*

Seneca the Younger
Apol. | *Apolocyntosis* | *The Pumkinification of Claudius*
Dial. | *Dialogi* | *Dialogues*
Ep. | *Epistulae morales* | *Moral Epistles*
Ira | *De ira* | *On Wrath*

Sextus Empiricus
Math. | *Adversus mathematicos* | *Against the Professors*
Sop. | *Soperim* | *Soferim*

Suetonius
Aug. | *Divus Augustus* | *Augustus*
Cal. | *Gaius Caligula* | *Caligula*
Claud. | *Divus Claudius* | *Claudius*
Galb. | *Galba* | *Galba*
Gramm. | *De grammaticis* | *On Grammarians*
Jul. | *Divus Julius* | *Julius*
Nero | *Nero* | *Nero*
Poet. | *De poetis* | *On Poets*
Rhet. | *De rhetoribus* | *On Rhetoricians*
Vita Terenti | *Vita Terenti* | *Terence*
Vita Verg. | *Vita Vergili* | *Virgil*

Tacitus
Ann. | *Annales* | *Annals*
Dial. | *Dialogus de oratoribus* | *Dialogue on Orators*

Terence
Ad.	*Adelphi*	*The Brothers*
Andr.	*Andria*	*The Lady of Andros*
Eun.	*Eunuchus*	*The Eunuch*
Haut.	*Hauton timorumenos*	*The Self-Tormentor*
Hec.	*Hecyra*	*The Mother-in-Law*
Phorm.	*Phormio*	*Phormio*

Tertullian
| *Spect.* | *De spectaculis* | *The Shows* |

Theon
| *Prog.* | *Progymnasmata* | *Progymnasmata* |

Valerius Maximus
| *Fact. dict.* | *Facta et dicta memorabila* | *Memorable Deeds and Sayings* |
| *Vit. Aes.* | *Vita Aesopi* | *Life of Aesop* |

Xenophon
| *Sym.* | *Symposium* | *Symposium* |

Introduction

The world in which Jesus lived and the world in which the Gospels were written was a world much different from our own. We are separated by nearly two thousand years of technological development and population movements. Political, social, economic, and family structures have been transformed. Religions arose and religions have died. Great areas of wilderness have been settled, the natural world transformed by our own creations. And people communicate differently. We think of the written word differently.

First-century literary works were almost always heard in a communal setting rather than read silently by individuals. This is generally accepted today, but we have only begun to grasp its importance for understanding the Gospels in their first-century settings The experience of oral recitation or performance is much different from silent reading. Silent reading involves eye and brain. An oral performance involves the ear, the eye, and whole body. The meaning of the Gospel in its original setting would not be found in the text. It would be found in its performance within a community. This book is an attempt to recover the experience of a Gospel performance in its first-century setting.

The anthropologist Bronislaw Malinowski observed the importance of performance contexts in his studies of storytelling among the Trobriand Islanders:

> The text, of course, is extremely important, but without the context it remains lifeless. As we have seen, the interest of the story is vastly enhanced, and it is given its proper character by the manner in which it is told. The whole nature of the performance, the voice and the mimicry, the stimulus and the response of the audience mean as much to the natives as the text; and the sociologist should take his cue from the natives. The performance,

again, has to be placed in its proper time setting—the hour of the day, and the season, with the background of the sprouting gardens awaiting future work, and slightly influenced by the magic of the fairy tales. We must also bear in mind the sociological context of private ownership, the sociable function, and the cultural role of amusing fiction. All these elements are equally relevant; all must be studied as well as the text. The stories live in native life and not on paper, and when a scholar jots them down without being able to evoke the atmosphere in which they flourish, he has given us but a mutilated bit of reality.[1]

Since the first-century Christians were not very good anthropologists, they forgot to record the contexts in which the writings of the New Testament were performed. Biblical scholars try to reconstruct those contexts as well as they can. A great deal of effort has been expended in reconstructing the situations to which the writings refer. This study tries to reconstruct the performance of one New Testament writing, the Gospel of Mark. It is an attempt to understand the manner in which it is told, the whole nature of the performance, the voice and the mimicry, the stimulus and the response of the audience. I have concentrated on the Gospel of Mark, but many of the observations would apply to the other books of the New Testament as well.

The great difference between reading to oneself and listening to a public recitation was clear to those in the first century who experienced the oral performances of that culture. Quintilian, a famous orator and teacher of rhetoric in the first century C.E., provides a good description:

The advantages conferred by reading and listening are not identical. The speaker stimulates us by the animation of his delivery, and kindles the imagination, not by presenting us with an elaborate picture, but by bringing us into actual touch with the things themselves. Then all is life and movement, and we receive the new-born offspring of his imagination with enthusiastic approval. We are moved not merely by the actual issue . . . , but by all that the orator himself has at stake. Moreover his voice, the grace of his gestures, the adaptation of his delivery (which is of supreme importance in oratory), and, in a word, all his excellences in combination, have their educative effect. In reading, on the other hand, the critical faculty is a surer guide, inasmuch as the listener's judgment is often swept away by his preference for a particular speaker, or by the applause of an enthusiastic audience. . . . Reading, however, is free, and does not hurry past us with the speed of oral delivery; we can reread a passage again and again if we are in doubt about it or wish to fix it in the memory. We must return to what we have read and reconsider it with care, while, just as we do not swallow our food till we have chewed it . . . , so what we read must not be committed to the memory for subsequent imitation while it is still in a crude state, but must be softened and, if I may use the phrase, reduced to a pulp by frequent re-perusal.[2]

The delivery of a speaker moves our imagination in a different way. It presents us a more realistic portrayal of actual events. It is itself an actual event. We experience a living person before us, one who has something at stake in the performance. We are affected by the speaker's presence. We are affected by his emotions. We have an opinion of the speaker. That affects how we receive the performance. We are surrounded by other people in the audience. They make their opinion clear. Their expressions of opinion affect our experience of the performance.

There are a great variety of oral literatures and oral performance styles. The performance styles of one culture are different from those of any other. Each culture has a variety of performance styles, each suited for a different situation. The style of performance deeply affects the meaning of an oral presentation. So we need to define as clearly as possible the style in which the Gospel would be presented if we are to understand its meaning in performance. Obviously enough, oral performances are fleeting, and no two performances are exactly alike. We have no way of recovering the particular oral style of those who performed Mark. We have no way of knowing how they inflected every phrase, every place they raised their voice or spoke softly, what gestures they used to accompany each phrase, and all the other particulars of a specific performance. Nevertheless, we can determine the general nature of the delivery style of the time.

There are two lines of evidence that can be used for recovering the performance style for a presentation of the Gospel. The first is historical evidence through which we can reconstruct an ideal delivery style for the time and culture. We can fairly successfully recover the style of delivery that would win applause in the first-century Mediterranean world. This we can consider the ideal performance style. It is likely that any performer of Mark would try to approximate that style, although actual performers may have fallen short. The second line of evidence is found in the Gospel itself. Sometimes the text tells us Jesus spoke in a loud voice. That suggests a loud performance voice for the line as well. If the text tells us Jesus looked around in anger, that suggests to me as a performer to look around as well.

Of course, we have no way of knowing whether Mark or other early performers of the Gospel would have been judged competent performers by their peers. Nor can we tell how well their performance mirrored the performance style implied by the Gospel itself. Still, if the ideal performance style and the style implied by the text converge, it is probable that actual performances at least tended in the same direction. Judging from the way Mark's Gospel is composed, he is a gifted storyteller. That gift was most likely developed through the performance of Gospel stories rather than through the writing of narratives. One does not have many opportunities to tell stories if one has no talent. Mark has a keen eye for audience effects. I expect his performances would be very engaging. He might not have been the greatest performer, but he could approximate the cultural ideal.

Some Conclusions

This investigation of oral performance in the world of the New Testament has led me to a number of conclusions:

1. The ancient Mediterranean cultures valued oral performance much more highly than our culture, and the ideal for literary performance was to approximate purely oral performance as closely as possible. As a result, texts were generally memorized for performance, and the text was recited rather than read. This did not always mean verbatim memorization. It could mean simply memorization of the general arrangement.

2. Oral performance of narrative was in a semi-dramatic style. Dialogue was spoken in character and inflected to indicate emotional meanings. Recitation was accompanied by nearly constant gesturing. The same Greek word, *hypokrinō*, was used for acting on a stage, the delivery of an oration, and expressive reading. That is what I mean by the delivery or performance of the Gospel.

3. Recitation emphasized emotional impact. Audiences were frequently moved to tears or anger. The performer was expected to feel

the emotions of the characters and convey those emotions to the audience.

4. The accepted style of delivery was quite bombastic by contemporary standards. There was lots of yelling. Sometimes speakers came close to singing some passages. Audiences loved vocal gymnastics that added to the emotional tone of the recitation.

5. First-century audiences were equally bombastic. They frequently interrupted with applause of different types, including waving hands, loud exclamations, and rhythmic clapping. Listeners leaped from their seats and thumped the floor with their feet. They were just as boisterous in condemning what they did not like. Listeners applauded not only for the content of a performance, but also for stylistic niceties and the quality of a speaker's delivery.

Performances of the Gospel such as are described in this book would not have survived for long in the early church. Once the Gospels became *Scripture*, the manner of their use would have changed greatly. As scripture their delivery was most likely modeled on the delivery of Scripture in Jewish synagogues. Although the book of Esther was read through on Purim, it was more normal practice to deliver a fairly short passage from Torah and for a speaker to comment on its meaning. The books disintegrated into a series of readings and individual episodes. They became objects of learned commentary and interpretation. They became schoolbooks and holy artifacts, source books for theological wrangling, collections of familiar quotations.

As mentioned above, the most probable style of Gospel delivery emphasized the emotional impact of the Gospel. That is the most important point to understand. We are not hearing the Gospel through first-century eyes if we do not hear the emotions. The emotions conveyed by the Gospel have been largely overlooked. I hope that this study leads others to investigate how the Gospel leads and shapes the emotions of its audience.

Sources

Most of the written evidence from the New Testament period is from aristocratic literary circles. Nevertheless, there is good reason for taking it, with some caution, as evidence for the nature of oral performance in the less aristocratic circles of the early Christians. Often these writers comment on the reactions of the common people. Much of the high culture was available in performances attended by people

not included in the aristocratic elite. There were many cultural attitudes common to both the aristocracy and the common people.[3]

For stylistic reasons I have often reported stories about historical
figures and events as if they were true. Many of the sources have axes
to grind. Others are satirical. Still others are written so long after the
events that their reliability is suspect. The truth of many of these stories should be taken with a grain of salt. For our purposes, it is usually
not important whether a specific event occurred or not. Descriptions
of performers and audiences reflect the expectations of the time, so
bogus facts can still provide good evidence.

I have often drawn on the rhetorical handbooks, written as guidance for budding orators, to help illuminate the delivery of the book
of Mark. This does not mean that Mark the evangelist had a rhetorical
education. Given his literary style, that is highly unlikely. He may have
been exposed to some of the preliminary rhetorical exercises used in
the intermediate stages of education. These handbooks are extremely
valuable in reflecting the types of appeals and styles of performance
found effective in that culture. The handbooks often prescribe proper
ways of doing things, but they also record the abominable taste of
common folk, who were not interested in the prescriptions. The techniques of rhetoric found in the handbooks could be learned even if
one never attended a rhetorical school. Indeed, Augustine says it is
easier to learn eloquence by reading and hearing eloquent men than
by studying rules.[4]

One cannot understand the Gospel in oral performance without
actually experiencing it performed. Many of my observations about
the Gospel in performance are based on my own performances of
Mark for classes, church groups, and student organizations. I have
noticed the interaction between the audience and myself, types of
audience responses, and ways that the act of performance modifies my
own understanding of the Gospel. My performance is quite imperfect
by first-century standards. Unlike a good first-century performer, I
have not memorized the Gospel. Instead, I hold a sheaf of papers in
one hand, while doing my best to perform rather than read the text. As
I have learned more ancient performance style, I have tried to make my
performances reflect the ancient ideal. My performance has become
increasingly emotional, increasingly animated, and increasingly loud.

In addition to my own performances, I have some opportunities to
be in the audience experiencing the performances of others. I was
lucky enough to see the Gospel of Mark presented on stage by Alec

McCowen, who has performed the Gospel for years as a one-man show, both on and off Broadway. McCowen's style is decidedly modern, but the success of his show is eloquent testimony to the dramatic nature of the Gospel narrative.[5] The biblical scholar David Rhoads has also performed Mark for years, and I have seen his performance of parts of the Gospel. Both McCowen's and Rhoads's performances are available on videotape, though the taped performances are a very pale reflection of their live presentations. Other videotaped presentations of the Gospel are available by Max McLean and Frank Runyeon. There are also audiotapes available, either of the entire Gospel or of selected portions. One interesting presentation is that of another biblical scholar, Thomas Boomershine.[6] None of the performances with which I am familiar comes close to the emotional and bombastic style of the first-century Mediterranean world. Performance styles change, and the first-century style may not appeal to many people today. Throughout history Gospel stories have been adapted for presentation in a variety of forms. When Christianity enters a new culture, it is presented in familiar forms. For example, in Japan biblical stories have been turned into traditional Japanese Noh dramas.[7] Such adaptations are certainly in keeping with the spirit of oral performance.

Just as each production of a play is different and brings out different aspects of the text, each performer will have his or her own interpretation of a text like Mark. Particular performances by the same performer may also vary greatly. The performer may understand the same passage in different ways over time. Performers also respond to their audiences. I am more likely to present passages as humorous when an audience has already seen earlier passages as humorous. Whenever I suggest particular ways of performing passages in Mark, it should not be taken as a claim that Mark himself performed the passage that way or that it is the one correct way to understand the Gospel.[8] As I edited the book, I often threw out older interpretations and ran in a different direction. Sometimes I thought the new interpretations were more insightful; sometimes they only reflect a different mood. The examples of how passages might be performed are intended only to suggest possible interpretations and the range of effects available in performance. The living voice is subject to change. This book is but the dead, fossilized remains of my living voice as I attempted to resurrect the fossilized remains of the living voice of a first-century evangelist.

As a performer of the text, I quickly learned that performance requires one to interpret every passage of a text. Every line of dialogue

must given some inflection. Is Jesus angry? Annoyed? Compassion-
ate? Are Jesus' opponents obnoxious? Do I present them with dignity
or mock them mercilessly? What is the woman feeling when she
sneaks up behind Jesus to touch his hem? How do I portray the scene
so the audience understands her feelings? If I have not thought through
an episode, I have to interpret it on the spot. This makes the dramatic
recitation of the text a wonderful teaching tool. I would encourage
teachers, whether of Sunday school groups or university classes, to get
their students to recite the stories with feeling or to act them out as
dramas. Excellent advice on using Gospel recitation in this way can be
found in Thomas Boomershine's *Story Journey*, and Elizabeth Struthers
Malbon's *Hearing Mark*.[9] An excellent translation for oral performance can be found in Reynolds Price's book *The Three Gospels*.[10]
Price has used his talents as a novelist to reproduce the rough-and-
ready style of the original Greek of the Gospel. Another excellent
performance translation is included in *Mark as Story*, by David Rhoads,
Joanna Dewey, and Donald Michie.[11]

Recent years have brought many studies of the oral nature of New
Testament writings. Several of those studies include excellent summaries of scholarship on the subject, and interested readers may con-
sult them for discussions of many points.[12] I have been careful to
document the ancient sources from which the evidence for oral performance is taken and to indicate studies through which the reader
may find more information on particular topics. I have not attempted
to relate my interpretations of the Gospel to debates about the meaning of passages, to document the source of every interpretation of
Mark included here, nor to consistently document earlier studies in
which similar points have already been made. I trust that specialists
will recognize the sources of familiar ideas and that nonspecialists will
be thankful that the book contains no more notes than it does.

Notes

1. Bronislaw Malinowski, *Magic, Science and Religion and Other Essays* (Boston:
Beacon Press, 1948), 104; quoted by Barbara Kirshenblatt-Gimblett, "A Parable in
Context: A Social-Interactional Analysis of Storytelling Performance," in *Folklore:
Performance and Communication* (eds. D. Ben-Amos and K. S. Goldstein; The Hague:
Mouton, 1975), 105.

2. Quintilian, *Inst.* 10.1.16–19 (Butler, LCL).

3. F. Gerald Downing, "À bas les aristos: The Relevance of Higher Literature for
the Understanding of the Earliest Christian Writings," *NovT* 30 (1988): 212–30.

4. Augustine, *Doctr. chr.* 4.3.4–5.

5. For reviews, see Janet Karsten Larson, "St. Alec's Gospel," *Christian Century* 96 (1979): 17–19; John Koenig, "St. Mark on the Stage: Laughing All the Way to the Cross," *Theology Today* 36 (1979): 84–88. For the actor's personal reflections on performing Mark, see Alec McCowen, *Personal Mark* (London: H. Hamilton, 1984).

6. Alec McCowen, *St. Mark's Gospel: King James Version* (videotape; produced by Arthur Cantor Films, 2112 Broadway, Suite 400, New York, NY 10023; distributed by the American Bible Society, 1865 Broadway, New York, NY 10023); David Rhoads, *Dramatic Presentation of the Gospel of Mark* (videotape; distributed by SELECT, c/o Lutheran Seminary, 2199 E. Main St., Columbus, OH 43209); Max McLean, *Mark's Gospel as Told by Max McLean* (videotape; produced by Fellowship for the Performing Arts, P.O. Box 230, Convent Station, NJ 07961-0230); Frank Runyeon, *AFRAID! The Gospel of Mark* (videotape; distributed by Runyeon Productions, P.O. Box 6393, Thousand Oaks, CA 91359); Thomas E. Boomershine, *Story Journey: An Invitation to the Gospel as Storytelling* (two audiocassettes; Nashville: Abingdon, 1988; available at NOBS Business Office, Becky Schram, Office Manager, 1810 Harvard Blvd., Dayton OH 45406). For descriptions of most of these, see Elizabeth Struthers Malbon, *Hearing Mark: A Listener's Guide* (Harrisburg, Penn.: Trinity Press International, 2002), 107–109.

7. Yuko Yuasa, "Performing Sacred Texts," in *Women's Sacred Scriptures* (ed. Kwok Pui-Lan, E. Schüssler Fiorenza, and L. S. Cahill), in *Concilium* 1998 (no. 3; London: SCM Press, 1998): 81–90.

8. For brief and insightful discussion of the issue of "correct" readings, see Susan R. Garrett, *The Temptations of Jesus in Mark's Gospel* (Grand Rapids: Eerdmans, 1998), 6–12.

9. Thomas E. Boomershine, *Story Journey: An Invitation to the Gospel as Storytelling* (Nashville: Abingdon, 1988); Elizabeth Struthers Malbon, *Hearing Mark: A Listener's Guide* (Harrisburg.: Trinity Press International, 2002), esp. 111–14.

10. Reynolds Price, *The Three Gospels* (New York: Scribner, 1996).

11. David Rhoads, Joanna Dewey, and Donald Michie, *Mark as Story: An Introduction to the Narrative of a Gospel* (2d ed.; Minneapolis: Fortress, 1999).

12. Recent summaries of oral studies as they relate to the investigation of New Testament literature are available in John D. Harvey, *Listening to the Text: Oral Patterning in Paul's Letters* (ETSSS 1; Grand Rapids: Baker Books, 1998), 1–59; Casey Wayne Davis, *Oral Biblical Criticism: The Influence of the Principles of Orality on the Literary Structure of Paul's Epistle to the Philippians* (JSNTSup 172; Sheffield: Sheffield Academic Press, 1999), 11–63; Richard A. Horsley with Jonathan A. Draper, *Whoever Hears You Hears Me: Prophets, Performance, and Tradition in Q* (Harrisburg, Penn.: Trinity Press International, 1999), 123–74. For studies related to the Gospel of Mark in particular, see Werner H. Kelber, *Oral and Written Gospel: The Hermeneutics of Speaking and Writing in the Synoptic Tradition, Mark, Paul, and Q* (Philadelphia: Fortress, 1983); Christopher Bryan, *A Preface to Mark: Notes on the Gospel in Its Literary and Cultural Setting* (Oxford: Oxford University Press, 1993); Richard A. Horsley, *Hearing the Whole Story : The Politics of Plot in Mark's Gospel* (Louisville: Westminster John Knox, 2001); and the many important contributions of Thomas Boomershine, Pieter J. J. Botha, and Joanna Dewey listed in the bibliography.

For a study of orality and scripture in a number of religious traditions, see William A. Graham, *Beyond the Written Word: Oral Aspects of Scripture in the History of Religion* (Cambridge: Cambridge University Press, 1987).

CHAPTER 1
Oral Performance in the Ancient World

Why would the Gospel have been presented in oral performance? There are two principal reasons. The first is practical. The level of literacy in the Roman Empire was nowhere near levels of literacy in modern Western cultures. Most people could not read. The only way they could experience the Gospel was through performance. The second reason is cultural. By and large, writing was understood as a representation of oral communication. This was not true for bureaucratic uses of writing, such as tax records or inventory lists. For most types of communication, however, people preferred to hear a written message rather than read it silently.[1]

Literacy in the Ancient Mediterranean World

Most people in the Greco-Roman world were illiterate. There are various estimates of literacy in our period. The most extensive and thorough study, however, is that of William V. Harris. He considers it is unlikely that even 10 percent of the population of the Roman Empire could read. The proportion would have been higher among males and in the cities, where literacy was concentrated. Harris estimates that adult male literacy was less than 5 percent in the western provinces of the Roman Empire in the first century C.E. Even in Rome it was considerably less than 20 percent. The literacy rate was considerably higher in Greek cities, though even there the overall literacy rate was probably less than 50 percent even in the heyday of education in the fourth to first centuries B.C.E.[2] Estimates of literacy among Jews in Israel range as low as 3 percent of the population.[3] These estimates of literacy are based on a combination of ancient evidence and comparative studies of literacy. Preindustrial, agricultural societies for which accurate estimates of literacy are available universally have very low literacy rates. Although some scholars argue for higher literacy rates, none has undertaken the type of thoroughgoing study that would be necessary to refute Harris.[4] Recent studies of the social position of early Christians indicate that Christianity was primarily an urban phenomenon and that it did not draw from the lowest social strata.[5] Thus the level of literacy might have been higher among Christians than the general level of society. Still, if the Gospel was to reach all members of the church, it would have to be recited aloud. There is no agreement about the geographical location in which Mark was written. Rural Syria-Palestine and Rome are the locations most often suggested. Literacy would have been much lower in rural areas than in Rome, so much so that a rural location for the composition of the Gospel is unlikely.

"Literacy" in the ancient world generally meant a rudimentary ability to read and write, only enough to get by in one's trade. Those who wrote graffiti on the walls of Pompeii and other cities were not necessarily literate in the modern sense. One did not learn to read fluently and expressively until the secondary level of schooling, a level that only a few achieved. Even then writings were memorized for delivery rather than performed from a text.[6] One reason that few people could read fluently is found in the "typography" of ancient texts. The texts were written by hand, and the legibility of individual letters in handwritten texts varies from superb to abysmal. Greek texts had none of the reading aids that we take for granted. Usually the entire text was written in capital letters. There was little or no punctuation.[7] Words were not separated by spaces. Instead, the letters of the text ran together in unbroken lines. Divisions between lines of text were determined by the length of the line, and words were divided at arbitrary points when the scribe ran out of room. Word divisions did not necessarily correspond with syllables. No hyphens were used to alert the reader to words divided between different lines. Texts looked something like this:

MOSTPEOPLEINTHEGRECOROMANWORLD
WEREILLITERATETHEREAREVARIOUSESTIMATES
OFLITERACYINOURPERIODTHEMOSTEXTENSIVE
ANDTHOROUGHSTUDYHOWEVERISTHATOF
WILLIAMVHARRISHECONSIDERSITISUNLIKELY
THATEVENTENPERCENTOFTHEPOPULATIONOF
THEROMANEMPIRECOULDREADTHEPROPORTION

WOULDHAVEBEENHIGHERAMONGMALESANDIN
THECITIESWHERELITERACYWASCONCENTRAED
HARRISESTIMATESTHATADULTMALELITERACY
WASLESSTHANFIVEPERCENTINTHEWESTERN
PROVINCESOFTHEROMANEMPIREINTHEFIRST
CENTURYCEEVENINROMEITWASCONSIDERABLY
LESSTHANTWENTYPERCENTTHELITERACYRATE
WASCONSIDERABLYHIGHERINGREEKCITIES
THOUGHEVENTHERETHEOVERALLLITERACY
RATEWASPROBABLYLESSTHANFIFTYPERCENT
EVENINTHEHEYDAYOFEDUCATIONINTHE
FOURTHTOFIRSTCENTURIESBCE

How did you do? It should have been easy, since you have just read the same paragraph in modern typography. I think you will agree that texts such as that are very hard to read, let alone to sight-read with expressive delivery.[8] Some papyri, perhaps reflecting school exercises, have had strokes added to separate words or syllables and make reading easier. In Latin texts of this period it was more common for words to be separated and for various marks of punctuation to be used, but even in Latin texts this was not a universal practice.[9]

Cost and Availability of Books

Few people in the first century read books. Books were handwritten on scrolls and were much more expensive than books today. Martial suggests five denarii as the price for the first book of his *Epigrams* in a high quality copy (approximately seven hundred lines of text, about half the length of the Gospel of Mark), one and one-half to two and one-half denarii for a cheap edition, and one denarius for the price of book thirteen (274 lines).[10] Since a denarius was a day's wage for a laborer, these prices represent a considerable expense for most people. At similar rates, a copy of Mark would cost the average person several days' wages.

A recent study of the book trade in the city of Antioch during fourth century C.E. shows that only a small minority, even among the upper class, bought books. Both a Christian writer, John Chrysostom, and a Gentile orator, Libanius, complain about the lack of good literature in upper-class homes. Even the books that people owned were seldom read.[11] Libanius criticizes parents who do not provide students with enough money to purchase needed books.[12] One did not need to own a book for the elementary level of education. These parents were among the small group of wealthy people who could afford the higher levels of education. The study concludes, "The number of copyists was small, and the number of customers for whom they catered was also small, as was their output."[13]

It was quite unlikely that one could buy the Gospel of Mark or any other Christian book from a bookseller. Most books were not purchased from book dealers but circulated as private copies among friends. The aristocrats who made up the bulk of the reading population generally had their slaves making copies for themselves or friends.[14] Undoubtedly, Christian books circulated the same way, with copies produced either by slaves or scribes who were Christian.[15] The private circulation of books, however, did not solve the problem of expense, since the materials for writing were expensive. Papyrus was the least expensive material. Even in Egypt, the source of the material, a roll of papyrus cost four drachmas in the first century C.E., at a time when a skilled laborer could earn a drachma a day and an unskilled laborer only half that amount.[16] That means that Paul would have to work four days to buy papyrus for one of his longer letters.

The Preference for Oral Delivery

In addition to considerations of literacy and expense, people in the ancient Mediterranean world understood the relationship between writing and oral communication much differently than we do today. In our world writing is an independent form of communication. Most of what we read and write is never spoken. Writing is often preferred as a means of communication because it is usually more exact and more permanent. In the ancient Mediterranean world, writing was largely understood as representing oral speech. In most cases it was understood as a poor substitute for oral speech. In bureaucratic functions such as making inventories and collecting taxes, writing was not necessarily connected with speech, but in most other areas it was.[17]

Although it was once believed that most, if not all, reading in antiquity was done aloud,[18] more careful studies have shown that individual silent reading of letters and other material was common, and that even literary texts could be read silently.[19] Nevertheless, it was much more common for literary texts to be read aloud. For example, the treatise *On the Sublime* attributed to Longinus assumes that the audience of literature is listening to texts, not reading for themselves.[20] The writer assumes that both poetry and history would be orally performed, since in discussion of passages from Homer, Aratus, and Herodotus he speaks of those listening to the passages.[21] In another place he says that historians pay close attention to choosing words to move their listeners.[22] Apuleius includes references to both hearing and the written text in the opening sentence to his novel, *The Golden Ass.* "But I would like . . . to caress your ears into approval with a pretty whisper, if only you will not begrudge looking at Egyptian papyrus inscribed with the sharpness of a reed from the Nile."[23] The ancients appreciated the sound of words, as is abundantly clear from the amount of time devoted to the discussion of aural effects in both rhetorical handbooks and works of literary criticism.

Even those who could read and afford books preferred hearing a text rather than reading for themselves. Upper-class Romans had reading specialists, generally slaves or freedmen, known as *lectores* in Latin, to read to them.[24] Augustus, for example, would summon readers or storytellers when he had trouble sleeping.[25] In counseling a statesman interested in developing his rhetorical abilities, Dio Chrysostom emphasizes the importance of hearing literary works.

> I would counsel you to make it your first priority to converse with Menander of the writers of comedy, and Euripides of the writers of tragedy, and to do so, not casually by reading them to yourself, but (by hearing them) through others, preferably those who know how to deliver the lines (*hypokrinasthai*), pleasurably, but at least so as not to cause pain. For the sense perception is greater when one avoids the trouble of reading.[26]

Dio implies that reading to oneself is not serious reading. To be truly familiar with a piece of literature, it should be heard with correct delivery. If you remember the example of ancient typography, you have a sense of what is meant by "the trouble of reading." Authors preferred the oral performance of texts as much as audiences. In the city of Antioch during the fourth century C.E., the orator Libanius restricted the number of written copies of his works so that his oral presentation of the material might remain more important than the text.[27]

Because most "reading" took the form of hearing someone else read the text aloud, when we find the term "reader" in ancient texts, it does not always mean what "reader" means in our culture. When an author addresses the reader, as Apuleius does in his prologue, "Pay attention, reader, and you will find delight," the "reader" is not the one we would think of as *reading* the novel, but the ones who are *hearing* the novel being read to them. That is why Apuleius can say to the reader that he wants "to caress your ears into approval."[28] The novel is eleven books long, meaning it would fill eleven rolls of papyrus or parchment. A work of that length would cost the equivalent of thousands of dollars in terms of the earning power of those living in the United States today. If I can afford to spend thousands of dollars to have myself and my guests entertained for a week or two, I can afford a slave to read the book aloud. If I am a Roman aristocrat, and I hear my slave read, "Pay attention, reader, and you will find delight," I am not going to think for a minute that Apuleius is addressing my slave. He is addressing *me* and my guests. I am the one who paid thousands of dollars so that we could read the book by hearing it through *my slave*.

Writing by Dictation

The connection between the written word and oral delivery was strengthened by the fact that much writing was composed by dictating to a scribe who wrote the words down. The process of dictation and revision of the Roman poet Virgil is described by Suetonius. The poet would dictate a large number of lines in the morning and spend the rest of the day editing them.[29] Horace, another Roman poet, pokes fun at a rival who would dictate two hundred lines in an hour.[30] Horace considers the rapid pace a fault because it does not allow time for careful composition. Julius Caesar was said to be able to dictate four, or even seven, letters at once by using multiple scribes.[31] One of Paul's scribes sends his greetings at the end of Romans (16:22). As a result of the dictation process, the author composes with an awareness of the aural effect, and writers often "wrote" by speaking in a manner that would approximate the intended oral delivery.

High Valuation on Oral Performance in the Ancient World

From as early as Homer, we have evidence of the high value placed on oral performance in the ancient Mediterranean world. In the *Iliad*, Phoenix taught Achilles to be a "speaker of words and doer of deeds," and Achilles is praised as ready and cunning of speech.[32] A speaker in Tacitus's *Dialogue on Orators*, written about 100 C.E., says eloquence allows one to make and preserve friendships, extend connections, and take care of whole provinces. There is no profession, he states, "more productive of practical benefits, or that carries with it a sweeter sense of satisfaction, or that does more to enhance a man's personal standing, or that brings more honour and renown here in Rome, or that secures a more brilliant reputation throughout the Empire and in the world at large."[33] Dio Chrysostom, writing about the same time, presents a similar picture of the value of the ability to speak:

> A statesman needs experience and training in public speaking and in eloquence. For it is true that this will prove of very great help toward making him beloved and influential and esteemed instead of being looked down upon. For when men are afraid, what does more to inspire them than the spoken word? And when they wax insolent and uplifted in spirit, what more effectively brings them down and chastens them? What has greater influence in keeping them from indulging their desires? Whose admonitions do they endure more meekly than the man's whose speech delights them? Time and again, at any rate, there may be seen in our cities one group of men spending, handing out largess, adorning their city with dedications, but the orators who support these measures getting the applause, as though they and not the others had brought these things about. For this same reason the poets of the earliest times, who received their gift of poetry from the gods, never spoke of either the strong or the beautiful as being "looked upon as gods," but reserved this praise for the orators.[34]

The principal form of higher education was training in rhetoric because the ability was perceived to be of such great value in the success of men in the upper class. The first century B.C.E. historian Diodorus Siculus says it is by the power of speech that Greeks are superior to barbarians and the educated to the uneducated. By the power of speech one man gains power over the many.[35] It was one of the few ways that men could advance their social position. For example, an orator satirized by Lucian is said to come from poor parents. His father was a slave or freedman, his mother a seamstress in the slums. Yet through the appearance of ability in speaking, he achieved fortune and status.[36] The *Rhetoric to Alexander* indicates that one should follow its rules for speaking not only in situations of formal debate but also in general social intercourse.[37]

Another indication of the connection between power and rhetorical ability is the number of portrayals of emperors in rhetorical poses. A statue of the Emperor Tiberius now in the Louvre is typical. The statue follows the usual iconography of an orator. Tiberius holds a rolled scroll in his left hand while he gestures with his right. In many statues of public officials as orators, the official gestures with both hands. As will be shown in chapter 5, most orators spoke without referring to notes or a written speech, so such a pose is more realistic. The scroll is often included, however, to indicate the importance of words. The pose is intended to convey the idea of the emperor speaking rather than to accurately record him as a speaker. Another common representation of emperors shows them, often with an outstretched right arm, addressing a crowd of citizens or soldiers. Such scenes are found on many imperial coins, and Trajan's Column contains five such scenes.[38]

There was a clear preference for oral over written communication in the early Christian churches as well as in the surrounding culture.[39] Early in the second century C.E., Papias writes that he had spoken to the followers of the original disciples of Jesus whenever he had a chance. "For," he says, "I did not suppose that information from books would help me so much as the word of a living and surviving voice." He wrote the material he collected this way in five books of interpretations of the words of the Lord.[40] Clement of Alexandria's apology for writing down the teaching of the church in his *Stromateis* shows that many Christians had similar attitudes later in the century as well.[41] Written notes, Clement says, are feeble compared to original discourses, but they can serve to revive the memory and prevent the loss of important teaching through forgetfulness.[42] The oral teacher is better able to test his students, but the writer can better test himself by checking his motivation for teaching.[43] Nevertheless, some teachings must be handed on orally, and it would be wrong and dangerous to write them down.[44] Elsewhere he says that the early church elders did not write because they were too busy with oral teaching.[45]

There were proverbial sayings in both Greek and Latin concerning the superiority of the living voice over written communication. Galen, the physician, says, "There may well be truth in the idiom current among most craftsmen, that reading out of a book is not the same as, or even comparable to, learning from the living voice." Quintilian, the teacher of rhetoric, says, "The living voice, as the saying goes, provides more nourishment." Pliny, orator and statesman, writes, "The living voice, as the common saying has it, is much more effective." The philosopher Seneca writes, "You will gain more from the living voice and from sharing someone's daily life than from any treatise."[46] This is the cultural value that is reflected in Paul's statement "The letter kills, but the Spirit gives life" (2 Cor 3:6). Writing, not even "the writing" (the literal meaning of "Scripture") or "the book" (the literal meaning of "Bible"), is by itself an adequate means of communication. It is the human interpreter, through whom the Spirit works, who is the vehicle for true understanding. This same value lies behind the ancient and medieval mania for spiritual interpretations of texts that moderns find so hard to fathom. It is assumed that the text itself does not carry the full meaning. The text is only a partial communication of meaning. The full meaning is found only in the living voice commenting upon the text.

Competitive Nature of Ancient Oral Performance

Public oral performance in the ancient Mediterranean world was marked by a considerable degree of competition and combativeness, and the ability to perform well was essential to success in most social situations. Aristotle emphasizes the combative nature of much rhetoric by labeling one style of rhetoric agonistic (*agōnistikē*), or fit for combat.[47] The writer of the *Rhetoric to Alexander* makes the same distinction between speaking in a contest (*agōn*), and for display (*epideixis*).[48] Eulogy and vituperation are the two forms of epideictic that he discusses. Clearly, vituperation has an agonistic aspect, since it is used to discredit our opponents, and eulogy is used to praise those we favor. Thus epideictic often functions within the broader struggle of political and social life even if its immediate context is not structured as a contest.

Martial metaphors appear in other descriptions of rhetoric. In Tacitus's *Dialogue on Oratory*, one speaker calls rhetoric

an art which gives you an ever ready weapon with which to protect your friends, to succour those to whom you are a stranger, to strike fear and terror into the hearts of malignant foes—while you yourself have no anxiety, entrenched as you are behind a

rampart of inalienable authority and power. . . . When danger
hurtles round your own head, then surely no sword or buckler
in the press of arms gives stouter support than does eloquence
to him who is imperilled by a prosecution; for it is a sure de-
fence and a weapon of attack withal, that enables you with equal
ease to act on the defensive or to advance to the assault, whether
in the law courts, or in the senate house, or in the Emperor's
cabinet council.[49]

Quintilian also makes use of martial metaphors in describing orators:

We indeed stand armed in the line of battle, decide the most
important matters, and exert ourselves to win the victory. And
yet I would not have our weapons defaced by mould and rust,
but would have them shine with a splendor that shall strike terror to the heart of the foe, like the flashing steel that dazzles
heart and eye at once.[50]

Rhetorical training concentrated on combative situations, forensic
oratory for the lawcourt, and deliberative oratory for the political
sphere. The third branch of oratory, epideictic, which included speeches
of praise or blame often presented in a ceremonial context, was not
necessarily delivered in a competitive situation, but the level of implied
competition between speakers was high.

Competitions among performers of both poetry and prose had
long been part of the games held as part of religious festivals in
Greece, and that practice was continued into Roman times.[51] There is
a report of a poetry contest in the funeral games for the mythological
king Pelias, who had been cut into pieces and boiled by his daughters.[52]
According to some ancient text critics, Homer includes speaking contests in the funeral games for Patroclus in the *Iliad*.[53] The reading is
probably wrong, but it shows an attempt to provide such contests with
the venerable authority of Homer. Rhapsodes (stitchers of song, rhap-
sodists), who were professional performers of the Homeric poems,
competed at many festivals. In Plato's *Ion* the rhapsode Ion has come
to Athens to compete in the contest that was part of the Panathenaia,
one of the most important festivals held in the city. Previously, he had
competed at the festival honoring the healing god Asclepius, which
was held in Epidaurus.[54] Herodotus also refers to contests between
rhapsodes in the city-state of Sikyon.[55] Plutarch describes contests of

poets and prose writers at Delphi.[56] Inscriptions from the Amphi-
areion of Oropos near Athens show that by the second century B.C.E.
the games included a number of contests in rhetoric, drama, and
recitation, including performances of encomia (eulogies), poetic comedy, rhapsodic exercises, and the recitation of drama. The number of
such contests increased during the period of Roman domination, and
evidence from other sites indicates that they continued into the third
century C.E.[57] Playwrights would compete in their performances of
tragedies and comedies. In Rome, the competition between pantomimes, who performed a type of narrative and expressive dance, was
so intense that riots between the partisans of rival dancers frequently
broke out in the audience.[58]

When participation in meaningful political or legal combat was not
possible because of changed political realities, artificial competitive
situations were set up to provide a venue for oral conflict. In the first
century C.E., the practice of disputation was common.[59] Orators would
argue opposing sides of questions, often fantastic legal situations or
legal issues based on mythological themes. Though the practice is
almost universally decried as decadent by modern critics, it was well
suited for ancient audiences, who understood oral performance to be
largely a matter of combat. Since the questions were imaginary, one
won not by being more persuasive but by other measures of performance skill, such as the quality of one's delivery and one's skill in creating artistic imagery or other verbal embellishment.

It was natural for those in the ancient world to think of literary
activity as competition, even when no specific competition existed. For
example, the essay On the Sublime attributed to Longinus describes Plato's
use of Homeric imagery in agonistic terms:

> Plato would never have reared so many of these flowers to bloom
> among his philosophic tenets, never have wandered so often
> with Homer into the regions and phrases of poetry, had he not
> striven, yea with heart and soul, to contest the prize with
> Homer like a young antagonist with one who had already won
> his spurs, perhaps in too keen emulation, longing as it were to
> break a spear, and yet always to good purpose. For as Hesiod
> says, "Good is this strife for mankind." Fair indeed is the crown,
> and the fight for fame well worth the winning, where even to be
> worsted by our forerunners is not without glory.[60]

He describes the superiority of Homer, Demosthenes, and Plato as being awarded the crown of victory, a metaphor taken from the competitions at the games.[61] "Longinus" proposes that his addressees imagine Homer or Demosthenes listening to their words. "Great indeed the contest," he says, "if we propose such a jury and audience as this to listen to our own utterances."[62] It is a common opinion, he says in another place, that the decline in literature in recent times was caused by the loss of democracy: "With freedom there spreads the spirit of mutual rivalry and eager competition for the foremost place of honor."[63] Without competition, it was thought, there was no motivation to excel.

The combative nature of oral performance in the ancient Mediterranean world is closely related to the importance of honor and shame as cultural values.[64] Honor refers both to one's own valuation of oneself and to the acknowledgment of that value by others in society.[65] Lucian gives a good example of the way in which honor/shame battles were conducted in relation to public speaking. Two of his essays, *The Mistaken Critic* and *The Ignorant Book-Collector*, were personal attacks on critics of his. One dispute arose because Lucian had laughed at a sophist for the poor quality of his speech, leading to a state of war between the two. The sophist seized an opportunity to laugh at Lucian for an apparent mistake in the use of a word. Lucian retaliates in *The Mistaken Critic* by composing a scathing attack on the sophist, charging him with a multitude of offenses. From the bitterness of this attack it is clear that the struggle is taken very seriously.[66]

One frequently finds such personal disputes being carried out in rhetors' speeches and other forms of oral performance. For example, in Aelius Aristides's *Oration* 28, the orator replies to a critic who had objected to his praise of himself in an earlier speech. The Roman playwright Terence, in the prefaces to his plays, carried on a dispute with Luscius Lavinius, a critic whom he terms a malevolent old poet.[67] One is almost reminded of the ritualized prefight insults that form such an important part of the hype of professional wrestling and boxing matches. The audience may well have found the plays more enjoyable when placed in an explicitly agonistic context.

The competitive nature of public speaking is also indicated by Lucian in his satirical *Professor of Public Speaking*. The successful speaker, he states, must constantly praise himself and denigrate the speaking of others. He should claim to be better than Demosthenes, the greatest of the Greek orators. He should laugh at all other contemporary speakers, claiming they stole their material from others, and refuse them anything but the most perfunctory applause. Jealousy and hatred of others, he claims to be part of the character of public speakers. They expressed these feelings by heaping abuse on others.[68] Those who had no stomach for such abuse ought to avoid public speaking. Seneca counsels against making speeches at the bar because, as with any other pursuit that attracts attention to oneself, it creates enemies.[69] In a competitive world where one man's honor necessarily came at the expense of others, any means of claiming honor for oneself means making enemies.

Rhetorical ability also played a part in the disputes between Paul and his opponents at Corinth. It is hard to judge whether such competition was present among the performers of Gospels.

Authority of the Speaker

One of the most important differences between oral and written communication is the close connection between oral communication and the persona of the speaker.[70] The persona of the speaker is a major part of the communication, and the message cannot be abstracted from the messenger. Thus writings on rhetoric often refer to the importance of a speaker's character. Aristotle includes this as one of the three kinds of proofs furnished by a speech, along with emotional tone and logical deduction. "We believe fair-minded people," he states, "to a greater extent and more quickly on all subjects in general and completely so in cases where there is not exact knowledge but room for doubt." In fact, character is almost the controlling factor in persuasion. The opinion that the audience already holds of the speaker is not itself a part of rhetoric, but it is important for a speech to make the speaker appear to be fair-minded.[71] We trust people who exhibit good judgment, virtue, and goodwill.[72] The *Rhetoric to Alexander* also explores the connection between character and persuasion. A speaker must be careful about his conduct since one's manner of life contributes to one's powers of persuasion as well as to one's general reputation.[73] In discussing the speaking style of Phocion, who was recognized for his brevity, Plutarch asserts that his effectiveness was largely due to his character, "since a word or a nod merely from a good man is of more convincing weight than any number of elaborate phrases."[74]

Cicero includes the character of the speaker as one of the factors that secure the goodwill of the audience. The audience will consider a person's merit, achievement, and reputable life. The speech should present these to the audience as well, but, he says, qualifications are easier to establish if they are real.[75] Quintilian says much the same:

> But what really carries greatest weight in *deliberative* speeches is the authority of the speaker. For he, who would have all men trust his judgment as to what is expedient and honourable, should both possess and be regarded as possessing genuine wisdom and excellence of character.[76]

Quintilian urges speakers to use the opening portion of forensic speeches to establish their own authority and especially their character as reliable witnesses who have undertaken the case for a high moral purpose.[77] It is important, he says, that an orator be a man of good character in order to convincingly argue for the good character of his client.[78] While a speaker's authority derives largely from his character, it can be increased by a dignified and serious style.[79] The confidence of the orator is of particular importance in establishing his authority.[80]

When one writes a speech for another, Quintilian says, it is important to adapt the speech to the position and character of the one who will deliver it, so that the speech will be congruent with his character.[81] Different forms of eloquence are suitable for different speakers, and a speaker should be careful to adopt an appropriate style.[82] Augustine reflects the same idea in arguing that the writers of Scripture had a particular kind of eloquence suitable to those inspired by God.[83]

Advising listeners rather than speakers, Plutarch warns against accepting philosophical doctrines from speakers on the basis of the goodwill and confidence the listener feels toward them. It is easy for the inexperienced listener to be carried away by an empty show of authority, the speaker's gray hair, his formality, his serious brow, his self-assertion, and the applause of the audience. Nevertheless, he cites with approval an account of Spartan officials, who, after accepting a proposal made by a man of low character, appointed a man of good character to present the proposal to the people. It is correct to thus encourage the people to pay attention to the character of their counselors.[84]

Among the moral philosophers, it was a commonplace that a man should lead a philosophic life before he attempted to speak about philosophy. For example, Epictetus reviles those who speak about the principles of Stoic philosophy, analyze arguments and syllogisms, and exegete difficult passages without having lived a long life according the Stoic principles and having received a calling from God. He also attacks those who speak on philosophy as a form of display rhetoric.[85]

Among Christians, the insistence on the connection between the speaker's character and his words continued. Likely the one who read in Christian worship was generally accorded some authority.[86] In 1 Tim 4:13, Timothy, appointed as bishop, is told to attend to reading, preaching, and teaching. Clement of Alexandria compared teaching, the distribution of the word, to the Eucharist, the distribution of bread. One who teaches in the church should have clean hands and a clean heart, just as those who distribute the Eucharist.[87] The reader became a formal office by the late second century, considered one of the minor offices in the West but a major office, conferred by the laying on of hands, in the East. Readers were required to be of good moral character and the *Apostolic Church Order* states that the reader should be "mindful that he functions in the place of the evangelist." Cyprian appointed the confessor Celerinus as reader so that the congregation might imitate his faith.[88] Although there is no direct evidence for the first century, for which reading practice is largely unknown, it is likely that from the beginning there was some connection between reading in church and authority.

This means that in the reception of the Gospel, the performer's character and authority would play an important role. We cannot know with certainty what position in the church the writer or performers of the Gospel would have had. The traditional ascriptions of the Gospels to disciples or prominent followers of apostles reflects an expectation that the Gospel should be connected to someone with considerable authority. Certainly, if Mark was Peter's interpreter, as Papias states, he would have considerable authority and stature in the church.[89] Given the concern of the church with the authority of the authors of Gospels, it is quite unlikely that a Gospel written by someone with no position of authority, or at least the backing of someone with authority, would be received and gain a position of general circulation in the church.

It is likely that the author of the Gospel would give the first recitations, but once a written text of the Gospel had been produced, it could be presented by someone other than the author. It would not be necessary for the performer of the Gospel to have the same level of authority as the author, but likely the one who recited a Gospel in a first-century church would have a certain amount of authority within the local church. Probably a leader within the local church would do the recitation if any of the church leaders had the ability to do so. Given the low level of literacy in the Hellenistic world, it is far from certain that any of the leadership could read or recite a text like Mark fluently. On the other hand, as much of the reading in upper-class households was done by slaves, it is possible that the reading was done by the slave of one of the more affluent members of the church. The possession of such specialized slaves may have been restricted to the highest levels of society, however, and it is not clear that any early church member was affluent enough, or had enough interest in literary pursuits, to have had such a slave. On the other hand, it is not necessary that the Gospel performer know how to read. The performer could learn the Gospel from hearing oral performances or by hearing another read it.

If the task of performance fell to one who was not otherwise in a leadership position, a certain amount of authority would likely accrue to that person simply from the ability to perform the Gospel. If the Gospel was recited by an itinerant Gospel reciter, the same sort of authority would probably accrue to the itinerant. Since much of the Gospel consists of the words of Jesus, the Gospel performer becomes in some sense a stand-in for Jesus during the performance and would gain a certain amount of authority as a result. Thus issues of authority would be much more complex than would be the case for literary readings, where a slave doing a reading is not likely to have authority conferred upon him as a result.

Audience Specificity

Richard Bauckham has argued quite persuasively that the Gospels were most probably written for wide dissemination throughout the international Christian community rather than for specific local communities.[90] Given the amount of communication between Christian churches in various cities and the speed with which some Christian writings are known to have been disseminated, the Gospel authors could expect their works to be widely circulated. The network among Christian churches was much like the networks through which books ordinarily came into circulation in the ancient world.[91] As a result,

Gospel writers most likely thought in terms of the general international Christian community as their audiences rather than specific communities with their specific situations and problems.

Oral performance, however, tends to be much more audience specific than the written word.[92] Plato in the *Phaedrus* indicates the importance of an orator's knowing the different types of souls, their emotional affinities, and which kinds of speech will affect which types of soul.[93] Dionysius of Halicarnassus praises Lysias for his ability to tailor his arguments to fit both the speaker and the audience for which they are intended.[94] Quintilian indicates that it is important in oral performance to tailor one's performance to the particular audience before one. It is important to know the character of the judge and how to fit our presentation to his character, as well as to know whether the judge favors our case or that of our opponent or whether his own interests are involved.[95] In forensic rhetoric this meant primarily considering the nature of the judge and the types of arguments that would appeal to him.[96] Quintilian includes among the first points to consider before making a jest the people involved in the performance situation, the speaker himself, the judge, and the victim.[97] He also suggests paying close attention to which arguments impress a judge, following up on those that do, and abandoning those that prove to be less successful.[98] The tone of the speech should also fit the audience, as should the use of gestures.[99] Other circumstances surrounding the speech, such as the occasion for the speech, its location (e.g., in one's home city or not), or whether or not a man is defending himself, also require special consideration.[100] Such adaptation to the audience had its pitfalls as well. Clement of Alexandria claims that one who writes is less liable to flattery and corruption because his audience is not present.[101]

Oral performance of a written text allows the performer to tailor his performance to his specific audience to a significant degree because the written word allows for a great range of specific performance. Moreover, it is far from certain that the text would have been considered sacrosanct in the early years of its existence. As we will see, speakers were often quite free with their texts. There is certainly no reason to believe that a speaker would adhere to the text word for word. The most likely situation for the performance of the Gospel is a gathering in a house church. That means that the audience for any particular reading is unlikely to have been larger than fifty persons. If a member of the local church performed the reading, he or she would have been familiar with the general situation of the local church and would have known the personalities and situations of most members of the audience. If, on the other hand, a visiting leader (perhaps the author himself) presented the reading, his knowledge of the audience would be less, but it is reasonable to expect that he would have become aware of the general situation of the church and to have been familiar with at least some of the members of the audience. Thus, depending on the situation, the performer would be able to tailor the reading more or less well to the particular interests, needs, and concerns of the specific audience.

That means that particular passages would gain extra stress or a particular emotional tone based on the situation of the audience. If there are struggles over leadership, the presentation of passages on discipleship, such as 8:34–9:1 and 10:41–45, would inevitably reflect the performer's understanding of the church's situation. If the church is facing persecution, the persecution and martyrdom passages such as 8:34–9:1 and 13:9–13 could take on a coloring that would reflect the performer's understanding and concern for that situation.

The performer also has the ability to direct particular passages toward particular individuals or groups. The house setting is fairly intimate, and the performer can make eye contact with individuals. As we will see later, the performer would probably have been rather mobile and could stride from one part of the audience to another. One could easily use the presentation of the Gospel in a polemical way. By addressing certain passages to one side or the other in a dispute, the performer can make his own position clear, and the audience would have the experience of the narrative Jesus taking sides.

In my own performances I have found a natural tendency to start looking for particular people in the audience whenever I think a passage may have special relevance for them. All dialogue in oral performance is directed at the audience, and in intimate settings dialogue may be particularly directed at individuals whom the performer faces and with whom he makes eye contact. Again, in my own performances I have found that it is natural to pick members of the audience to represent dialogue partners whenever there is direct speech addressed to an individual. By directing my own speech to an individual, the scene becomes slightly dramatized and the audience gets more of a sense of intimate address in the dialogue or of the forcefulness of a particular passage. For example, it is my sense that the line "Get behind me, Satan!" (8:33) addressed to Peter, is delivered loudly and sharply by Jesus and is experienced by Peter as having a demon cast out from him. The shocking vehemence of the line, coming as it does so closely on Peter's recognition of Jesus and his apparently heartfelt concern for his teacher's welfare, is particularly clear when it is directed at an individual, and the audience is moved to sympathy for Peter through their natural sympathy for one of their own members who is being so sternly rebuked. Sympathy for the individual chosen to "play" Peter clearly registers on the face of the audience whenever I have shouted the line in someone's face. The effect of the line can be so unnerving for the recipient that I feel obliged to pick a "Peter" who can (at least in my best estimation) weather that kind of abuse relatively well.

A similar dynamic between performer and audience is recorded by John Miles Foley in his description of a traditional performance by a Serbian guslar. The guslars of the Balkan region are singers of traditional oral epic poetry, which is accompanied by a stringed instrument called the gusle. These singers have been much studied as a modern analogy through which the composition and transmission of the Homeric epics might be understood.[102]

> At one point during the proceedings, in the midst of a description of some of the major wars in which Serbs have participated in this century, the poet intoned a line that was particularly moving for the old man to his immediate right. As he sang, he looked toward him for approval and received affirmation in the form of a nod. As I watched and reflected on the collective nature of what was taking place, my companion leaned toward me to point out the reaction. When the old man saw our reaction, he looked up at me and proudly thrust aside his lapel to reveal a handsome collection of medals.[103]

Here, in a traditional setting, the performer centers a part of the performance around a particular individual in the audience because of the relevance of the passage to that person. In this case the entire group understands the interaction and approves of the interaction as a way of honoring the old man for his contribution to the events being described. One suspects that the interaction has become an expected part of the performance and that failure to direct the passage to the war hero would be understood as a slight by all present. Certainly, Foley's informant thinks that the interaction should be recorded by the collector of songs from overseas. It is a part of the meaning of the song.

A study of singers of a Turkish tale shows other ways in which an oral performance may be focused on particular members of the audience. In one case, a singer changed the particular songs contained in the performance to fit the situation of one of his listeners. The focus of his attention was a nobleman who had lost his wealth through a tragedy in his life, and the singer sang only tragic songs in the introductory portion of his performance because he thought more joyful songs would be disrespectful to the nobleman's situation. In another performance, a singer improvised a song to honor a person he saw in the audience. The oral performer could also relate his material to his audience by placing the action of the narrative within the locality of the performance. The study also found that the amount and content of traditional formulaic material differed in two performances by the same singer as the singer adapted the song to different audiences.[104]

Similarly, a significant part of the meaning of any first-century performance of Mark would be found in the particular interactions between the performer and audience that would vary with each setting and performance. In large measure, the Gospel is recreated by each community, even if the wording remains relatively stable. Stories and sayings receive meaning according to the community context in which they are performed. There is an interaction between the relatively stable story of the Gospel shared by many communities and the particularity of meaning created in a particular performance. Thus the performance is simultaneously a celebration of common Christian identity found in understanding of the story of Jesus shared by many Christian communities, and the specific meanings related to specific individuals and situations that may be embodied in a particular performance.

Notes

1. For an insightful discussion of the interaction between orality and writing in the New Testament world, see Vernon K. Robbins, "Oral, Rhetorical, and Literary Cultures: A Response," *Semeia* 65 (1994): 75–91. See also Tony M. Lentz, *Orality and Literacy in Hellenic Greece* (Carbondale: Southern Illinois University Press, 1989). Lentz concentrates on an earlier period of Greek history, but much of what he says about the interaction between orality and literacy holds true for the New Testament period as well.

2. William V. Harris, *Ancient Literacy* (Cambridge: Harvard University Press, 1989), 22, 272, 259. See also the collection of responses to Harris's book in J. H. Humphrey, ed., *Literacy in the Roman World*, (JRASup 3; Ann Arbor: Journal of Roman Archaeology, 1991). Significantly, though the articles challenged various

assertions made by Harris, there was general agreement on his conclusions concerning the levels of literacy in the ancient world. For the extent of literacy among early Christians, see Harry Y. Gamble, *Books and Readers in the Early Church: A History of Early Christian Texts* (New Haven: Yale University Press, 1995), 2–10. For a discussion of reading and writing in Palestine in particular, see Meir Bar-Ilan, "Illiteracy in the Land of Israel in the First Centuries C.E.," in *Essays in the Social Scientific Study of Judaism and Jewish Society* (ed. S. Fishbane and S. Schoenfeld with A. Goldschläger; vol. 2; Hoboken, N.J.: Ktav, 1992), 46–61; Alan Millard, *Reading and Writing in the Time of Jesus* (Washington Square, N.Y.: New York University Press, 2000). For literacy among women, see Susan Guettel Cole, "Could Greek Women Read and Write?" in *Reflections of Women in Antiquity* (ed. H. F. Foley; New York: Gordon and Breach, 1981), 219–45. For a summary of significant findings about literacy in relation to the New Testament, see Joanna Dewey, "From Storytelling to Written Text: The Loss of Early Christian Women's Voices," *BTB* 26 (1996): 73.

3. Bar-Ilan, "Illiteracy in the Land of Israel," 55. For schools in first-century C.E. Palestine, see Pieter J. J. Botha, "Schools in the World of Jesus: Analysing the Evidence," *Neot* 33 (1999): 225–60. Botha provides an extensive review of the literature; references to other studies, including many that argue for the more general availability of schooling, can be found in his notes.

4. Millard argues for higher literacy rates in Palestine, but his primary evidence is the later claims of the rabbis, *Reading and Writing*, 154–84. For a critical discussion of the rabbinic evidence, see Botha, "Schools," 236–45. Millard also tends to collapse various levels of literacy and thus overestimates the number of "literates" capable of reading and writing fluently.

5. Abraham J. Malherbe, *Social Aspects of Early Christianity* (2d, enlarged ed.; Philadelphia: Fortress, 1983), 29–91; Wayne A. Meeks, *The First Urban Christians* (New Haven: Yale University Press, 1983), 9–73.

6. H. I. Marrou, *Education in Antiquity* (trans. G. Lamb; New York: New American Library of World Literature, 1964), 230 and 526–27, n. 13; 375 and 559, n. 30; Stanley F. Bonner, *Education in Ancient Rome: From the Elder Cato to the Younger Pliny* (Berkeley: University of California Press, 1977), 220–22; Bernard Brandon Scott and Margaret E. Dean, "A Sound Map of the Sermon on the Mount," *SBL Seminar Papers, 1993* (SBLSP 32; Atlanta: Scholars Press, 1993), 674.

7. On the question of how much punctuation was used in ancient texts, see E. G. Turner, *Greek Papyri: An Introduction* (Oxford: Clarendon, 1968), 90–92; Rudolf Pfeiffer, *History of Classical Scholarship from the Beginnings to the End of the Hellenistic Age* (Oxford: Clarendon, 1968), 178–81; Marrou, *Education*, 230, 375; Bonner, *Education*, 220–22.

8. Gamble, *Books and Readers*, 203–4.

9. E. Otha Wingo, *Latin Punctuation in the Classical Age* (JLSP 133; The Hague: Mouton, 1972).

10. Marital, *Ep.* 1.66.4; 1.117.17; 13.3.2.

11. John Chrysostom, *Hom. Jo.* 11.1 (PG 59:78) and Libanius, *Or.* 35.25.

12. Libanius, *Ep.* 428.3.

13. A. F. Norman, "The Book Trade in Fourth-Century Antioch," *JHS* 80 (1960): 126.

14. Raymond J. Starr, "The Circulation of Literary Texts in the Roman World," *CQ* 37 (1987): 213–23.

15. Loveday Alexander, "Ancient Book Production and the Circulation of the Gospels," in *The Gospels for All Christians: Rethinking the Gospel Audiences* (ed. R. Bauckham; Grand Rapids: Eerdmans, 1998), 71–111.

16. Harris, *Ancient Literacy*, 195.

17. For a superb study of the relationship between oral and written of communication, see Lentz, *Orality and Literacy*. While Lentz concentrates on the Archaic and Classical eras, much of what he says is still valid for our period as well.

18. Josef Balogh, "Voces Paginarum," *Phil.* 82 (1927): 84–109, 202–40; G. L. Hendrickson, "Ancient Reading," *CJ* 25 (1929): 182–96.

19. W. P. Clark, "Ancient Reading," *CJ* 26 (1931): 698–700; Eugene S. McCartney, "Notes on Reading and Praying Audibly," *CP* 43 (1948): 184–87; Bernard M. W. Knox, "Silent Reading in Antiquity," *GRBS* 9 (1968): 421–35; Frank D. Gilliard, "More Silent Reading in Antiquity: *Non omne verbum sonat,*" *JBL* 112 (1993): 689–96; A. K. Gavrilov, "Techniques of Reading in Classical Antiquity," *CQ* 47 (1997): 56–73; M. F. Burnyeat, "Postscript on Silent Reading," *CQ* 47 (1997): 74–76.

20. E.g., Longinus, *[Subl.]*, *akroatēs*, translated "reader" by Fyfe, LCL, 10.1; translated "audience," 26.1, translated "hearer," 26.3; *akouontes* ἀκούοντες, translated "audience," 15.2; 30.1.

21. Longinus, *[Subl.]* 26.1–3.

22. Longinus, *[Subl.]* 31.1.

23. Apuleius, *Metam.* 1.1 (Hanson, LCL).

24. Raymond J. Starr, "Reading Aloud: *Lectores* and Roman Reading," *CJ* 86 (1991): 337–43.

25. Suetonius, *Aug.* 78.2; cited by Harris, *Ancient Literacy*, 226. Harris cites as other evidence Pliny, *Ep.* 5.19.2; 8.1.2; 9.34; 9.36.4 (and as a contrasting example *Ep.* 5.3.2).

26. Dio Chrysostom, *Or.* 18.6 (author's translation).

27. A. F. Norman, "The Book Trade in Fourth-Century Antioch," *JHS* 80 (1960): 122–26.

28. Apuleius, *Metam.* 1.1 (Hanson, LCL).

29. Suetonius, *Poet.: Vita Verg.* 22.

30. Horace, *Sat.* 1.4.9–10.

31. Pliny, *Nat.* 7.25.91–92.

32. Homer, *Il.* 9.442; 22.281; cited by George A. Kennedy, *A New History of Classical Rhetoric* (Princeton: Princeton University Press, 1994), 13.

33. Tacitus, *Dial.* 4 (Peterson/Winterbottom, LCL).

34. Dio Chrysostom, *Or.* 18.2–3 (Cahoon, LCL).

35. Diodorus Siculus, *Bib. hist.* 1.2.5–6.

36. Lucian, *Rhet. praec.* 24.

37. Aristotle, *[Rhet. Alex.]* 38, 1445b.

38. Examples and discussion are found in Richard Brilliant, *Gesture and Rank in Roman Art: The Use of Gestures to Denote Status in Roman Sculpture and Coinage* (CAAS-Mem 14; New Haven, The Academy, 1963), 68–69, 93, 119–21; Gregory S. Aldrete, *Gestures and Acclamations in Ancient Rome* (Baltimore: The Johns Hopkins University Press, 1999), 45–50. For the Column of Trajan, see Filippo Coarelli, *The Column of Trajan* (preface, P. Zanker; appendices, B. Brizzi, C. Conti, R. Meneghini; trans. C. Rockwell; Rome: Colombo, with the German Archaeological Institute, 2000); Karl Lehmann-Hartleben, *Die Trajanssäule: Ein römisches Kunstwerk zu Beginn der Spätantike* (Berlin: de Gruyter, 1926).

39. For excellent discussions of the issue, see Loveday Alexander, "The Living Voice: Scepticism towards the Written Word in Early Christian and in Graeco-Roman Texts," in *The Bible in Three Dimensions: Essays in Celebration of Forty Years of Biblical Studies in the University of Sheffield* (ed. D. J. A. Clines, S. E. Fowl, and S. E. Porter; JSOTSup 87; Sheffield: Sheffield Academic Press, 1990), 221–47; Pieter J. J. Botha, "Living Voice and Lifeless Letters: Reserve Towards Writing in the Graeco-Roman World," *HvTS* 49 (1993): 742–59.

40. Eusebius, *Hist. eccl.* 3.39.1–4 (Lake, LCL).

41. Clement of Alexandria, *Strom.* 1.1.2–16. For a fuller discussion, see E. F. Osborn, "Teaching and writing in the first chapter of the *Stromateis* of Clement of Alexandria," *JTS* n.s. 10 (1959): 335–43.

42. Clement of Alexandria, *Strom.* 1.1.14.

43. Clement of Alexandria, *Strom.* 1.1.9.

44. Clement of Alexandria, *Strom.* 1.1.14.

45. Clement of Alexandria, *Ecl.* 27.4.

46. Galen, *De comp. med.* 6.1; Quintilian, *Inst.* 2.2.8; Pliny, *Ep.* 2.3; Seneca, *Ep.* 6.5. All translations are taken from Pieter Botha, who also collected the passages ("Living Voice," 752).

47. Aristotle, *Rhet.* 3.12.1, 1413b. He contrasts this to the *graphikē* generally translated written, but more likely meaning descriptive. Later in the section, he says the epideictic style is *graphikōtatē* where the distinction is with the description of the deliberative style as *skiagraphia* like an inexact sketch made to be seen from afar (*Rhet.* 3.12.5, 1414a). For the agonistic nature of oral narrative in general, see Walter J. Ong, *Orality and Literacy: The Technologizing of the Word* (London: Methuen, 1982), 43–45.

48. Aristotle, *[Rhet. Alex]* 35, 1440b.

49. Tacitus, *Dial.* 5–6 (Peterson/Winterbottom, LCL).

50. Quintilian, *Inst.* 10.1.30–31 (adapted from Butler, LCL).

51. E.g., at Delphi (Plutarch, *Def. orac.* 15, 417f).

52. Plutarch, *Quaest. conv.* 5.2, 675a.

53. Plutarch, *Quaest. conv.* 5.2, 675a. The passage in question is Homer, *Il.* 23.886.

54. Plato, *Ion* 530a–b.

55. Herodotus, *Hist.* 5.67.

56. Plutarch, *Def. orac.* 15, 417f.

57. Richard Leo Enos, *Roman Rhetoric: Revolution and the Greek Influence* (Prospect Heights, Ill.: Waveland, 1995), 92–94.

58. E. J. Jory, "The Early Pantomime Riots," in *Maistor: Classical, Byzantine and Renaissance Studies for Robert Browning* (ed. by A. Moffat; Canberra: Australian Association for Byzantine Studies, 1984), 57–66.

59. S. F. Bonner, *Roman Declamation in the Late Republic and Early Empire* (Liverpool: University Press of Liverpool, 1949); D. A. Russell, *Greek Declamation* (Cambridge: Cambridge University Press, 1983). For examples of declamations, see Seneca, *Controversiae* and *Suasoriae*.

60. Longinus, *[Subl.]* 13.4 (Fyfe, LCL).

61. Longinus, *[Subl.]* 34.2.

62. Longinus, *[Subl.]* 14.1 (adapted from Fyfe, LCL).

63. Longinus, *[Subl.]* 44.2 (adapted from Fyfe, LCL). "Longinus" himself attributes the decline in literature to the love of wealth and luxury, which has debased the spirit of his contemporaries.

64. Jerome H. Neyrey, "Questions, *Chreiai,* and Challenges to Honor: The Interface of Rhetoric and Culture in Mark's Gospel," *CBQ* 60 (1998): 657–81.

65. Julian Pitt-Rivers, *The Fate of Shechem; or, the Politics of Sex: Essays in the Anthropology of the Mediterranean,* CSSA 19 (Cambridge: Cambridge University Press, 1977), 1. For honor and shame in the New Testament world, see Bruce J. Malina, *The New Testament World: Insights from Cultural Anthropology* (Atlanta: John Knox, 1981), 25–50; Don C. Benjamin and Victor H. Matthews, eds., *Honor and Shame in the World of the Bible, Semeia* 69 (1996).

66. Lucian, *Pseudol.,* especially 5–8.

67. Terence, *Andr.* proem. 5–7; *Haut.* proem. 16–34; *Eun.* proem. 4–19; *Phorm.* proem. 1–24; *Ad.* proem.1–21.

68. Lucian, *Rhet. praec.* 23.

69. Seneca, *Ep.* 14.11.

70. See also the discussion in Dewey, "From Storytelling," 74–75.

71. Aristotle, *Rhet.* 1.2.3–4, 1356a (Kennedy).

72. Aristotle, *Rhet.* 2.1.5, 1378a.

73. Aristotle, *[Rhet. Alex.]* 38, 1445b–1446a.

74. Plutarch, *Phoc.* 5.4 (adapted from Perrin, LCL).

75. Cicero, *De or.* 2.43.182.

76. Quintilian, *Inst.* 3.8.12–13 (Butler, LCL).

77. Quintilian, *Inst.* 4.1.7–10.

78. Quintilian, *Inst.* 6.2.18.

79. Quintilian, *Inst.* 4.2.125.

80. Quintilian, *Inst.* 5.13.51.

81. Quintilian, *Inst.* 3.8.48-51.

82. Quintilian, *Inst.* 11.1.31–38; 11.3.177–81.

83. Augustine, *Doctr. chr.* 4.6.9.

84. Plutarch, *Rect. rat. aud.* 41b–c.

85. Epictetus, *Diatr.* 3.21; 3.23.

86. Gamble, *Books and Readers,* 218–24.

87. Clement of Alexandria, *Strom.* 1.1.5.

88. *Apostolic Church Order* 3; Cyprian, *Ep.* 33.4.

89. Eusebius, *Hist. eccl.* 3.39.15.

90. Richard Bauckham, "For Whom Were Gospels Written?" in *The Gospels for All Christians: Rethinking the Gospel Audiences* (ed. R. Bauckham; Grand Rapids: Eerdmans, 1998), 9–48.

91. Loveday Alexander, "Ancient Book Production and the Circulation of the Gospels," in *The Gospels for All Christians: Rethinking the Gospel Audiences* (ed. R. Bauckham; Grand Rapids: Eerdmans, 1998), 86–105.

92. On the specific audiences and occasions for which archaic and classical poetry was written, see Bruno Gentili, *Poetry and Its Public in Ancient Greece: From Homer to the Fifth Century* (trans. A. T. Cole; Baltimore: Johns Hopkins University Press, 1988); M. Lefkowitz, "Who Sang Pindar's Odes?" *AJP* 109 (1988): 1–11; E. L. Bowie, "Early Greek Elegy, Symposium and Public Festival," *JHS* 106 (1986): 13-35; E. L. Bowie, "Miles Ludens? The Problem of Martial Exhortation in Early Greek Lyric," in *Sympotica: A Symposium on the Symposion,* 221–29 (ed. O. Murray; Oxford: Clarendon, 1990); Rosalind Thomas, *Literacy and Orality in Ancient Greece* (Cambridge: Cambridge University Press, 1992), 119–22.

93. Plato, *Phaedr.* 271b.

94. Dionysius of Halicarnassus, *Lys.* 9.

95. Quintilian, *Inst.* 4.1.17–20.

96. Quintilian, *Inst.* 5.12.11; 12.10.52–53.

97. Quintilian, *Inst.* 6.3.28.

98. Quintilian, *Inst.* 6.4.19; 12.10.56–57.

99. Quintilian, *Inst.* 11.1.43–48; 11.3.150.

100. Quintilian, *Inst.* 11.1.46–56.

101. Clement of Alexandria, *Strom.* 1.1.6.

102. See works of Albert Bates Lord, *The Singer of Tales* (Cambridge: Harvard University Press, 1960; 2d ed., ed. S. Mitchell and G. Nagy; Cambridge: Harvard University Press, 2000); cf. also *Epic Singers and Oral Tradition* (Ithaca: Cornell University Press, 1991); *The Singer Resumes the Tale* (Ithaca: Cornell University Press, 1995); and Milman Parry, *The Making of Homeric Verse: The Collected Papers of Milman Parry* (ed. Adam Parry; New York: Oxford University Press, 1987).

103. John Miles Foley, "The Traditional Oral Audience," *BalS* 18 (1977) 147.

104. İlhan Başgöz, "The Tale-Singer and His Audience," in *Folklore: Performance and Communication* (ApSem 40; ed. D. Ben-Amos and K. S. Goldstein; The Hague: Mouton, 1975), 149, 153, 155.

CHAPTER TWO
Types of Oral Performance

There were a wide variety of oral or gestural performances in the Roman world that might serve as a model for a recitation of the Gospel.[1] While some types of performances were restricted to a small group of intellectuals and others who wanted to show that they were interested in literature, a wide variety of performances were available to the general public.

Private Readings

At least among the upper class, reading was considered a highly specialized talent, and people expected a high quality of reading.[2] Readings were given even of genres that properly required a different means of delivery, such as tragedies, which should be acted on the stage, or lyric poetry, which should be accompanied by a lyre and chorus.[3] Pliny the Younger, a successful orator and politician writing early in the second century, C.E., indicates that he had a book read aloud during every dinner whether he dined privately with his wife or was accompanied by friends. The reading was followed either by lyric poetry or the performance of a comedy.[4] In his letters he mentions a number of readers. One, a freedman named Zosimus, was an actor, played the lyre, and read speeches, history, and poetry. Pliny considers acting, lyre-playing, and reading as three separate abilities, but the fact that he uses an actor as a reader indicates that the styles are related.

Private recitations were often, as is the case in Pliny's household, a part of the after-dinner entertainment of the rich intelligentsia. There were a wide variety of diversions presented at dinners. Some of them are enumerated in Plutarch's discussion of the proper way to run a dinner:

[One correctly overseeing the dinner entertainment] will not allow it to become now a rabble-ruled congress, now a sophist's school, and again a gaming-establishment, and then perhaps a stage and a dancing-floor. For do you not see men who play the politician and harangue a jury at dinner, others who declaim and quote selections from their own writings, and others who put on shows with mimes and dancers?[5]

Plutarch also mentions forms of entertainment reminiscent of the movie *Animal House*, such as ordering stammerers to sing, bald men to comb their hair, or lame men to dance on a greased wineskin.[6] It is no wonder that the Lord's Supper in Corinth could degenerate into drunken factional fighting (1 Cor 11:17–22). Plutarch himself, being more philosophically oriented, preferred erudite discussions such as those he records in his *Table Talk*.

Recitations could last several days. Pliny gave a recitation of his *Panegyricus* that lasted for three consecutive days, and he also mentions a recitation by a poet that lasted three days.[7] Two-day recitations are mentioned in other letters.[8] Juvenal also complains about a recitation of bad poetry that took up a whole day.[9] Virgil is said to have given a four-day recitation of the Georgics for the emperor Augustus. Maecenas, the poet's patron, spelled Virgil in the reading whenever his voice failed.[10]

Sometimes an author would recite from an unfinished work as a means of receiving criticism for correction. Suetonius tells us that Virgil presented portions of his unfinished *Aeneid* for that purpose.[11] Pliny followed the same practice, which he indicates is quite common.[12] Horace describes the persistent criticism of a friend to whom he read his verses.[13] Maternus also received advice from his friends on revising his play, advice that he politely refuses.[14] It is likely that the Gospel writers followed the same practice. Certainly they would get feedback from their audiences, and one would expect them to make changes in the text in response. It is quite possible that Paul presented his letters to his associates for criticism before he sent the text to its destination. This process allows for communal input into a work even though it is primarily the creation of an individual author.

It is not clear how private reading was done. Suetonius says that when Terence, the comic playwright, was sent to the house of Caecilius for the elder poet to give his judgment on the quality of his plays, he began the reading during dinner, sitting on a bench near Caecilius's couch. Suetonius suggests that this constituted poor treatment of the playwright because of his shabby clothing, though unfortunately it is not clear what constitutes the poor treatment.[15] Caecilius made amends by allowing Terence to eat dinner with him and then hearing the rest of the reading after dinner. The reading from a bench may then be typical of a slave or hired reader providing entertainment for diners. The scheduling of the reading after dinner would not only allow the reader to eat with his host but probably assures a more attentive audience.

Public Readings

From the beginning, there was a tradition of expressive public reading in Greece.[16] Many writings were composed for public readings either in halls or out of doors.[17] Generally an author would give a public reading of his work as a way of publishing it or to create interest in the book that would later become available in written form.[18] For example, Curiatius Maternus, in Tacitus's *Dialogue on Orators*, read his drama *Cato* publicly before publishing it.[19] Not all authors presented their works in this way. Horace said he feared to recite his *Satires* in public for fear of causing offense.[20]

Public performances of literature were common enough that even members of the lower classes were exposed to high quality recitations.[21] As we have seen, such recitations were often featured at the games that were part of many religious festivals. There were also many performers at the festivals who were not part of the official program. Herodotus was said to have recited his *Histories* at an Olympic festival.[22] Dio Chrysostom, an orator from the late first and early second centuries C.E., complains about those who declaim poetry or prose works at the athletic festivals. These performers are presenting their works in public spaces, since Dio says they annoy many who come for a holiday and are not interested in hearing them.[23] Presumably, he would have excepted himself from that charge, since he also delivered a speech at an Olympic festival.[24]

Other public gathering places were also the haunts of oral performers. Dio Chrysostom reports seeing a number of entertainers at one spot in the Hippodrome, including those reciting poetry and a history or story, as well as a flute player, a dancer, a stage magician, and a singer.[25] The fact that all occupied the same spot suggests that the oral performers expected to appeal to the same audience as magicians and musicians. Horace mentions poets who recite their poetry in the forum and in the baths.[26] Juvenal claims, with satirical exaggeration, that it is foolish to try to save papyrus since it will be used up anyway, seeing that one runs into poets everywhere.[27] The satirist Lucian performed his works, often in large halls.[28] Lucian describes the preachers of Cynic philosophy that could be found in the backs of temples.[29] Many people considered the speeches of orators in the lawcourts to be a form of entertainment. A popular orator could fill a theater with an admiring audience.

It was the reading of a work rather than its "publication" in written form that insured its fame. The emperor Claudius wrote a number of histories; to promote them he built a second Museum in Alexandria, and ordered that in one Museum his *Etruscan History* should be read each year from beginning to end, and in the other his *Carthaginian History*. The readings were presented "in the manner of public recitations." Because of the length of the histories, a number of readers took turns in reciting.[30] Other authors with less power and fewer resources generally had to present recitations of their works themselves. For example, Philostratus describes a young man who invites the philosopher Apollonius (of Tyana) to attend his public recitation of an oration he has written in praise of Zeus.[31] Several ancient authors mention the recitation of histories other than those of Claudius.[32] Diodorus Siculus refers to his readers but can still say he is leaving out nothing worth hearing.[33]

Inscriptions were also performed orally. Plutarch tells how guides at the temple at Delphi would read the inscriptions for visitors as well as tell various marvelous tales related to the god or the temple.[34] Even paintings were occasions for oral performance. A speaker in a dialogue attributed to Lucian speaks of paying an interpreter to explain a painting in a temple in Rhodes.[35] The narrator of Longus's novel *Daphnis and Chloe*, after admiring a painting he came upon in the grove of the nymphs in Lesbos, searches out an interpreter *(exēgētēs)* who can explain the events depicted, and the novel is ostensibly based on the interpreter's tale.[36] The relationship between painting and narrative was a convention in the romantic novels. Achilles Tatius begins *The Adventures of Leucippe and Clitophon* in a similar manner with the description of a painting. In this case a bystander relates the painting to his own experiences, which form the body of the novel.[37]

Storytelling

Perhaps the performance of the Gospel would be most analogous to a popular storytelling style.[38] Unfortunately, there is little evidence about how popular storytellers delivered their stories. Quintilian says the rude and uneducated listened to fables, such as those of Aesop, and it is obvious that the uneducated told the stories from memory rather than read them from a text.[39] Apuleius describes a traveler entertaining his companions with a tale of incredible though supposedly true happenings from the storyteller's life. His novel also includes a dinner party guest recounting an event from his life, robbers recounting to their companions events from their lives, an old woman entertaining the robbers' captive with a fictitious tale, a young man telling of the misfortunes of his kinswoman, and another old woman recounting an adultery to another woman.[40] There are a number of different situations in which these stories are told, including traveling on the road, at a dinner party, and in a house. Unspecified personal tales are also told at a dinner party in Xenophon's romance, the *Ephesian Tale*.[41] There were also professional storytellers found on the streets, who charged a small fee for a story. Pliny introduces two accounts of recent happenings with a jocular "Have your copper ready and receive a golden story."[42] Augustus is said to have frequently featured storytellers as dinner entertainment.[43] Informal storytelling was one area of oral performance in which women were able to participate, as evidenced by references to "old women's/wives' tales/fables" (1 Tim 4:7) as well as the accounts in Apuleius.[44]

Novels

It is most likely that romantic novels were read aloud in fairly small gatherings in homes. It has been suggested that village scribes were expected to read romantic novels and other "popular literature," though there is no evidence for such an arrangement, and it is unlikely that most scribes could read fluently with expressive delivery.[45] In fact, there is little evidence that such a thing as popular literature existed in antiquity. Apuleius mentions reading or readers several times in his *Metamorphoses*. This has been cited as evidence that Apuleius is thinking in terms of individual readers rather than listeners.[46] It is not clear, however, that the mention of reading excludes a listening audience. After all, the romance opens with a promise to delight your ears, which suggests a listening audience more than an individual reading aloud.[47] On the other hand, a fragment of an illustrated papyrus roll from the second century C.E. has been recovered, and this may have come from a novel.[48] The illustrations are likely for an individual reader, since one would have to view the roll itself to see them. In an intimate setting, however, it might be possible to show the illustrated scroll to a small audience gathered around a reader. It has been suggested that the romantic novel by Xenophon of Ephesus, the *Ephesian Tale,* may have served as an outline for an after-dinner drama enacted by dinner guests against the background of the wall paintings decorating the host's home.[49]

Drama

While literary readings were largely for the rich, the theater was available to everyone.[50] Tacitus complains that the Roman passion for the theater distracted young men from more serious pursuits.[51] All large cities had theaters, and their capacities were immense. In his ancient travel guide, Pausanius says that any city worth that name had a theater, and in the same passage he describes the inhabitants of noncity areas as living in hovels like mountain huts.[52] Even in Palestine, theaters were found in the Greek cities, and the remains of twenty have been found.[53] The theater of Sepphoris, three miles from Nazareth, could hold five thousand people.[54] Scythopolis, twenty miles from Nazareth, had a theater that held eight thousand.[55] We also find drama presented at the dinner parties of the rich.[56] A participant in one of Plutarch's *Table Talk* dialogues says that the plays of the New Comic poet Menander were a standard part of such parties.[57] Pliny often had comedies presented after dinner.[58] From the time of Tertullian, the theater was condemned by Christian writers, but it is clear from the continuing condemnations that many Christians during this later time attended the theater. After the empire became Christian, the theaters continued to operate.[59]

Pantomime

The Greek and Roman pantomime was a form of dance in which a single masked dancer, accompanied by music and recitation, acted out well-known mythological stories. This was somewhat like a solo ballet, though the gestures were more stylized, perhaps more like Kabuki theater or classic Indian dance.[60] Pantomime in the form familiar during the first century was only introduced in Rome in 23 B.C.E., but before the end of that century, it had become the most popular form of theatrical entertainment in the city.[61] The audiences were quite familiar with the nature of the subtleties of the dance and could recognize the dance associated with each story. In Rome and the Latin-speaking part of the Roman Empire, pantomime, from its first introduction, was included in the games at many religious festivals. Its acceptance in the Greek-speaking East was slower, and only in the late second century C.E. was it included in the games in that area.[62] Because the pantomime dancer himself did not speak, such performances would not provide a direct model for a Gospel recitation. Pantomime would provide a store of conventionalized gestures from which a performer of narrative might draw, though we cannot know whether the gestures from the different genres overlapped.

It is possible that the Gospels were performed as pantomime, with one performer reciting and a second performer acting out the narrative. The Greek and Roman religions often incorporated the chanting of exploits of gods and goddesses into the ritual for various gods. Lucian tells us that every mystery initiation included dance as well.[63] Since his main subject for the essay is the dancing of pantomimes, it is safe to assume that these dances acted out the exploits of the gods or goddesses, much the same way that pantomimes acted out mythological themes on the stage. Dio Chrysostom also reports the use of dance in the mystery initiations. He mentions in particular a rite called enthronement, where the initiates are seated and the priests dance around them.[64] Plato complains about drunken imitations of nymphs, Pans, Sileni, and Satyrs by dancers in Bacchic rites of initiation and expiation.[65] It is not clear what effect these mystery associations would have on the performance of the Gospel. Perhaps Gentile converts expected to have the Gospel acted out as the myths were done in the mystery initiations. On the other hand, such pagan associations may have inhibited the borrowing of imitative gestures specifically associated with pantomime, if the performer wanted to maintain a distance from pagan practices.

Poetry

Tacitus says it is the recitation of poetry that brings a poet fame, not the composition.[66] Such recitations were common in a variety of settings.[67]

Pliny says there were poetry readings in Rome almost every day in April of the year in which he is writing.[68] Quintilian suggests that poetry cannot be read correctly without some knowledge of music. This is especially true for lyric poetry.[69] In classical Greece, much poetry was accompanied by music from the lyre or from lyre and flute.[70] Some lyric poetry was presented chorally and might include dancing as well as music in its performance.[71] In the early second century C.E., Pliny says lyric poetry is still properly performed with lyre and chorus.[72]

Epic

Recitations of Homer were part of religious games in classical times.[73] Rhapsodes were judged by their ability to provoke emotions in their audience and displayed a great deal of emotion in their recitations, and Plato suggests a good performer does so through a type of divine possession.[74] At least in classical Greece, rhapsodes were quite specialized. Ion recited Homer but not the other poets.[75]

Reading in Worship

In Judaism, sacred texts were read aloud both in the synagogues and privately, as shown for the readings of Jesus in Luke 4:16–19 and of the Ethiopian eunuch in Acts 8:30.[76] Christian authors expect their works to be read in the community as well.[77] The author of Revelation assumed that his work would be read aloud (Rev 1:3), as did Paul and his imitators (1 Thess 5:27; Col 4:16). In addition to regular readings from Torah and Haphtarah (prophets) in morning Sabbath services (the Torah alone on other, nonfast days), the Megillot (scrolls) were read in their entirety on festival days: Song of Songs on Passover, Ruth at Pentecost, Lamentations on the Ninth of Ab, Ecclesiastes at Sukkot, and Esther at Purim.[78] The Mishnah prescribes that readings should be done by a series of readers (at least seven for Sabbath morning services), reading consecutively, but that does not reflect common first-century practice.[79] The rabbis also make a concession to accommodate literacy levels of the time. "A town in which there is only one who reads; he stands up, reads [the Torah], and sits down, he stands up, reads, and sits down, even seven times."[80] Consecutive reading of the Torah, such that the reading of one service started where the reading from the previous had left off, was probably the practice by the first century, and a specified lectionary likely was a later development.[81]

Even in the second century, readings from the Gospels or Jewish Scriptures in Christian worship services were probably much more extensive than in most modern worship services. Justin states that on Sunday assemblies, "the memoirs of the apostles or the writings of the prophets are read for as long as time permits."[82] Hippolytus indicates that Scripture was read at the beginning of the service by a succession of readers until all had gathered, and the practice lasted at least to the time of Augustine.[83] Evidence suggests that in the third century *lectio continua*, the practice of reading consecutive pieces of Scripture on successive Sundays, was the norm, and this probably reflects earlier practice.[84]

Scriptural Chant

By the fourth century, Scripture was chanted in Christian services, and probably in Jewish services as well.[85] It has been argued that Jewish chanting of Scripture was an established practice in the second century B.C.E., but the evidence for the practice is scanty and inconclusive.[86] Although the cantillation used in both Jewish and Christian worship likely broke the text according to sense units, and in that way fostered the interpretation of the text, Quintilian's objections to chantlike delivery in public speaking makes it clear that expressive inflection, which he believes is so important in oratory, is lost in chant.[87] The very fact that chant sets the reading apart as nonordinary speech necessarily reduced its ability to express ordinary meaning. Abraham's sacrifice of Isaac, for example, is changed from a riveting story to a ritualized remembrance of the story. It may be emotionally powerful in its ritualized version, but it is an emotional power of a quite different sort. The kind of expressive speaking or reading that Quintilian espouses, however, required a great deal of preparation on the part of the reader or speaker, and readers in synagogue and church may not always have had much time for preparation. The Masoretic system of indicating accents, which was not fully developed until the fifth or sixth century, would allow a relatively unprepared reader to chant the reading according to sense units. Since the expressiveness of the reading would have been lost in any case with such unprepared readers, the net result may have been an improvement in the hearers' understanding.

Even if Scripture was chanted in first-century Jewish worship, it is unlikely that Mark's Gospel would have been chanted in its early performances, since that would claim for it a status as Scripture, not likely granted by its first audiences. Only if the practice of chanting the sayings and deeds of Jesus was in place is it likely that a narrative like Mark's would have been presented in the scriptural style. If chanting of Scripture was the norm, however, it is certainly possible that scriptural quotations, such as those that open Mark's Gospel, may have been chanted to indicate the words of Scripture. A chanted scriptural quotation would give a special solemnity to the beginning of the Gospel, and the association of chant with Scripture would emphasize the connection between the story of Jesus and the stories of Scripture. One might achieve the same effect today by using King James language in the scriptural quotes.

It is possible that holy speech in the early church was performed in some other stylized manner. Preachers in some American churches, for example, adopt a manner of speaking somewhat similar to chant, but without as much tonal variation. Sentences are broken into individual phrases punctuated by repetitive ejaculations such as adding "-ah" to the final word of the phrase or a loud, forceful outbreath after the phrase. The practice is understood by some preachers to bring the power of the Holy Spirit into their extemporaneous sermons and is taken by the audience as a sign of the Holy Spirit working. Prophetic speech is often spoken with a particular mannerism and at times with an altered voice as well. These twentieth-century phenomena, however, are associated with types of ecstatic or semiecstatic speech rather than narrative, and I know of no evidence that would suggest such a technique in the original performance of the Gospel.

Early Christian Speaking Styles

From the beginnings of the church, the ability to speak well was emphasized in Christian writings. Jesus is depicted as being a charismatic speaker. The authority with which he speaks is especially emphasized (e.g., Mark 1:22, 27) as is his ability in debate. The apostles are shown as being quite persuasive in Acts, moving whole crowds to repentance and conversion. George Kennedy argues that early Christian speaking styles were often at odds with the conventions of Greco-Roman rhetoric, at least in terms of the style of argumentation. In particular, there is a stronger emphasis on the authority of God, or the Holy Spirit, speaking through the preacher, a reliance on miracle rather than logic for persuasion, and a conviction that it is only God, not the orator, who can persuade an audience. Paul, who has some familiarity with the conventions of rhetoric, can deride the "plausible words of wisdom" of conventional rhetoric and philosophy (1 Cor 2:4).[88] On the other hand, there were speakers in the early years of the church that may have been more at home with the popular oratorical styles, as indicated by Paul's admission in 2 Cor 11:6 that he, in contrast to the superapostles, is untrained in speaking. Paul is criticized for his weakness of speech by the superapostles, who rely in part on rhetorical display for their authority (2 Cor 10:10). They may be Jewish, perhaps associated with Jerusalem. Apollos is said to have been an eloquent and persuasive speaker, and since he comes from Alexandria, he may well have had formal rhetorical training (Acts 18:24–28). Paul's sarcasm aimed at philosophy and rhetoric in 1 Cor 1–4 is likely aimed at members of the Corinthian church who were impressed by Apollos's rhetorical ability.

In his *Stromateis* Clement of Alexandria sets out a theory of Christian teaching.[89] Both writers and speakers, he says, are heralds of God, who with pen and voice make faith active through love.[90] A teacher is the benefactor of those to whom he brings the saving truth.[91] He must seek only the salvation of his listeners.[92] Those who receive the word are God's cultivation and God's building.[93] The listener has a responsibility as well and must receive God's gift to be successful. We need a new heart and new spirit before we hear the words of God.[94] There is one Teacher of both the speaker and the listener, and that Teacher is the cause of both speech and understanding.[95] Teaching in the church is primarily the handing on of tradition. It is the privilege of teachers to deposit in their listeners' souls the seed of their spiritual forebears.[96]

The Social Setting for a Gospel Performance

Most proposals for the social setting of the Gospel understand it to have been used in worship, for example, as a series of lectionary readings, or for teaching.[97] A number of scholars have suggested similarities between philosophical or other schools and the early Christian church.[98] If the analogy is accurate, one might expect that one would find the Gospel presented in a physical setting similar to those of philosophical lectures.

The use of books in a teaching setting was considerably different from their use in literary settings. As shown below, literary performances of texts stressed emotion, flamboyant vocal effects, and constant gesturing. Often the text was memorized for performance, and no physical text was present. In teaching situations, on the other hand, the teacher often read from a text and interspersed the reading of the text with exposition of its meaning. Thus in a teaching situation, a book would never be presented as a continuous whole. A book like the Gospel of Thomas, made of individual sayings with no connecting narrative, may presuppose such use. The emphasis on the importance of knowing the proper interpretation of the sayings also suggests its use for teaching.[99] The book does a reader no good without a teacher to expound the meanings. The hypothetical sayings source known as Q (from *Quelle*) would likely be used in the same way. This interplay between text and authoritative interpretation found in so many teaching situations is another factor that made the spiritual interpretation of texts feel so natural in the ancient world. The meaning of the text is only fully known through the interpretation of the teacher. The text itself did not contain the full meaning.

It is unlikely that the Gospel of Mark was intended for such use, however, since it contains little teaching material, and the teaching material it presents is subordinated to the narrative. It presents a coherently developed narrative that would not be necessary in a teaching situation and would be destroyed by the alternation of reading and expounding that took place in teaching situations. The Gospels of Matthew and Luke, which combine Markan-like narrative with Thomas-like or Q-like teaching material, would make much better books for teaching. Compared to Mark, their extra lengths also make them more difficult to perform in one setting, though they certainly fall within the length of texts for which we find oral performances in the first century. It is much more likely that Matthew and Luke were intended to be books for teaching than that Mark was.

It is not at all obvious why a narrative of Jesus would be composed for use in worship. The Qumran community has left no narrative of the Teacher of Righteousness whose teaching they considered authoritative. They did not even leave us his name. Rabbinic communities were equally uninterested in narrating the lives of great rabbis. For the most part, Jewish worship did not include the recitation of entire texts. The Megillot were read in their entirety on certain feast days, but only Ruth and Esther are narratives. The reading of Esther on

Purim, the festival that celebrates her exploits, suggests a possible use for a narrative like Mark, that it was performed in conjunction with ritual reflecting the events of the Gospel. There was also an analogous use of some religious texts in Gentile settings. The Homeric "Hymn of Demeter" is related to the mysteries of Demeter celebrated at Eleusis, in which at least some of the events were surely reenacted. The Gospel's focus on the crucifixion of Jesus would certainly be appropriate for recitation during a commemoration of that event, if first-century Christians did commemorate the events of Holy Week. If baptism is understood as dying with Jesus, as in Rom 6:1–11, the emphasis on the cross of Jesus would be appropriate for a baptismal setting as well.[100] The teaching on discipleship in Mark's Gospel would be well suited to people about to make such a formal commitment, and the opening baptismal scene would connect well with their own situation.

The Physical Setting for a Gospel Performance

There are a number of possible physical settings for a performance of the Gospel. Literary readings and lectures were given in private homes, in hired halls, and even in theaters. Pliny says that his friend Titinius Capito lent his house out for literary readings.[101] Epictetus describes a philosophical lecturer inviting people to hear him speak in the house of Quadratus.[102] Nero read his poems in the theater.[103] Even people who probably had large houses often hired halls, to allow for a bigger audience. Lucian describes an elaborately decorated lecture hall that may not have been atypical of the lecture halls frequented by the upper class.[104] The halls hired for many readings, however, would have been considerably less lavish. We have a few descriptions of the process of preparing for recitations or lectures. Tacitus describes a poet hiring a house for a reading, fitting it out with chairs, and distributing programs or handbills.[105] The preparations for a literarily pretentious philosophical lecture described by Epictetus include placing a thousand benches, inviting the audience, putting on a fancy cloak or dainty mantle, and mounting the speaker's stand.[106] Juvenal describes a similar routine of fitting out a hall, underwritten by a patron, though the miserly patron of his satire provides slaves to applaud but does not pay for the chairs.[107] Since houses were commonly used as lecture halls, it may be primarily the seating arrangement on benches that allowed for a larger crowd.

There would be a significant cost in hiring out such a house transformed into a lecture hall, but it would certainly not be beyond the means of some churches, like that in Corinth. The church in Philippi, which was able to contribute a significant amount in sustaining Paul's missionary work, could also hire such a hall if they desired. In Acts 19:9, Luke says that Paul, after leaving the synagogue in Ephesus, taught in the hall of Tyrannus. This could be either a lecture hall or a guild hall.[108] Tyrannus may have acted as a patron to Paul, making the hall available without cost to Paul or the church. We cannot be certain, though, whether this reflects either the actual practice of Paul or of Christians in Luke's day, or whether it is an apologetic motif designed to make Paul's practice parallel to that of traveling philosophical teachers, who often spoke in such halls.

A craftsman's workshop, such as Paul's tentmaking shop, is another possible site for the presentation of the Gospel.[109] Such a setting was consistent with the practice of at least some Cynic philosophers, and Celsus complained in the second century that Christians met in cobblers' shops and fullers' shops.[110] We do not have detailed descriptions of the process of teaching in a craftsman's workshop, though both discussions and reading of texts are mentioned. For example, it is reported that Crates read Aristotle's *Protrepticus* aloud in a shoemaker's shop while the shoemaker was working.[111] This would be considerably before our period, but Celsus' report suggests a similar practice may have existed among some Christian groups. There is no report that Paul presented a fully developed narrative of the Gospel, but if a craftsman/evangelist such as Paul presented the Gospel in such a setting, one might imagine him reciting the Gospel to interested onlookers while he worked.[112] If so, his presentation would be considerably more constrained than what we would find in a literary reading, since his hands would be occupied and less available for gesturing. One might expect him to develop a certain rhythm of dropping his work during more emotional or emphatic parts of the narration and then resuming his work during less emotional episodes. Alternatively, one might imagine someone reciting the Gospel in a more fully developed dramatic style while others worked and onlookers listened. In this case, the workshop would function much like a small hall, but it could be used without the expense of renting a hall.

We have seen that many speakers performed their works in public spaces such as the baths or near a hippodrome. Such a situation would fit the picture of public missionary work in Acts, but we cannot assume that Mark's Gospel is largely directed toward outsiders. The nature of the demands made on followers of Jesus suggests that the Gospel is directed to insiders. Requirements like "take up [your] cross and follow me" (8:34) or talk about leaving houses and family and fields (10:29) are likely directed at those who have already made a commitment, or are seriously considering doing so. Most of the evidence suggests that Christian activity was largely done in private and that there was relatively little public evangelizing.[113] While the philosophical schools sometimes made use of public space for their teaching, Christian use of public space was problematic.[114]

The house church would be the most likely setting for the performance of the Gospel.[115] Christians normally met in private houses, and a recitation of the Gospel could take place as part of such a gathering. It would not require any expense, and it would let the community control who was present at the performance. It would also allow for the performance to be connected with other church ritual, such as the Lord's Supper, prayer, or the singing of hymns. A house-church setting would mean that the audience would be rather small and the presentation would be on a rather intimate scale. Even the largest houses of all but the top strata of society would put serious spatial constraints on a performer.[116] The narrator was forced to be close to his audience. Thus the available space would facilitate more intimate interaction, and the audience would not experience the distancing created by a stage or pulpit.

It is also possible that the Gospel would be recited in an outdoor setting, especially if it was presented in conjunction with baptism. According to the *Didache*, the preferred location for baptism would be at a lake or stream or some other form of living water.[117] By the late second century C.E., at least in some areas baptisms took place on Easter morning after an all-night vigil.[118] If that was the practice in Mark's time, the Gospel might be presented immediately before the baptisms, with the ending timed to coincide with the break of dawn. The conjunction of dawn in the narrative with dawn in the listeners' world would help the listeners to experience themselves as present in the final climactic scene. In the Gentile mystery religions quite elaborate performances of ritual and mythic material were presented at night indoors, where torches or lamps would provide the only light. Performances in dim or flickering light would be quite effective, since it would force listeners to create more of the scene in their imaginations. It would also add to the numinous effect of the performance. A location by a body of water would certainly be an effective backdrop for episodes that take place by or on the sea. It is even better if there is water and a hill, so that two of the important locations would be physically present. Orators often alluded to their physical surroundings in their speeches and even prepared their surroundings beforehand so that they could make use of them in certain ways.[119] It is certainly possible that the constant presence of the sea in the first half of the Gospel is a result of its being composed for performance in such a setting.

Notes

1. On performance of texts in classical and archaic Greece, see Eugene Bahn, "Interpretive Reading in Ancient Greece," *QJS* 18 (1932): 432–40; Eva Stehle, *Performance and Gender in Ancient Greece: Nondramatic Poetry in Its Setting* (Princeton: Princeton University Press, 1997). For developments in classical Greece and ancient Rome, see Eugene Bahn and Margaret L. Bahn, *A History of Oral Interpretation* (Minneapolis: Burgess, 1970), 1–46.

2. On private readings, see A. N. Sherwin-White, *The Letters of Pliny: A Historical and Social Commentary* (Oxford: Clarendon, 1966), 115–16.

3. Pliny, *Ep.* 7.17.3.

4. Pliny, *Ep.* 9.36.4.

5. Plutarch, *Quaest. conv.* 1.4, 621b–c (adapted from Clement, LCL).

6. Plutarch, *Quaest. conv.* 1.4, 621e.

7. Pliny, *Ep.* 3.18.4; 4.27.1.

8. Pliny, *Ep.* 8.21.4 and 9.27.1.

9. Juvenal, *Sat.* 1.4–6.

10. Suetonius, *Poet.: Vita Verg.* 27.

11. Suetonius, *Poet.: Vita Verg.* 33.

12. Pliny, *Ep.* 7.17.5–15.

13. Horace, *Ars* 438–52.

14. Tacitus, *Dial* 3.1–3.

15. Suetonius, *Poet.:Vita Terenti* 2.

16. On performance of texts in classical and preclassical Greece, see Bahn, "Interpretive Reading," 432–40. For developments in classical Greece and ancient Rome, see Bahn and Bahn, *History of Oral Interpretation*, 1–46. For later reading aloud, see Harris, *Ancient Literacy*, 226.

17. See G. Funaioli, "Recitationes," PW, vol. 1, part 1, 2d series, cols. 435–446; Sherwin-White, *Letters of Pliny*, on *Ep.* 1.13, cited by Harris, *Ancient Literacy*, 225, n. 257.

18. Harry Y. Gamble, *Books and Readers in the Early Church: A History of Early Christian Texts* (New Haven: Yale University Press, 1995), 83–84.

19. Tacitus, *Dial.* 2–3.

20. Horace, *Sat.* 1.4.23–25, 73–74.

21. For exposure to various types of reading, see Elizabeth Rawson, *Intellectual Life in the Late Roman Republic* (London: Duckworth, 1985), 50–53.

22. Lucian, *Herod.* 1–2.

23. Dio Chrysostom, *Or.* 27.6.

24. Dio Chrysostom, *Or.* 12.

25. Dio Chrysostom, *Or* 20.10.

26. Horace, *Sat.* 1.4.74–75.

27. Juvenal, *Sat.* 1.17–18.

28. Lucian, *Apol.* 3; *Dom.* 3.

29. Lucian, *Fug.* 7.

30. Suetonius, *Claud.* 42.2 (Rolfe, LCL)

31. Philostratus, *Vit. Apoll.* 4.30.

32. Athenaeus, *Deipn.* 10.432b; Seneca, *Ira* 3.23.6; Pliny, *Ep.* 9.27; Libanius, *Ep.* 188.2 (11.983, ed. Förster); citations from Arnaldo Momigliano, "The Historians of the Classical World and Their Audiences," *ASNP* ser. 3, vol. 8 (1978): 62-66.

33. Diodorus Siculus, *Bib. hist.* 1.3.5; 1.6.1.

34. Plutarch, *Pyth. orac.* 2, 395a; cited in John J. Winkler, *"Auctor" and Actor: A Narratological Reading of Apuleius's "Golden Ass"* (Berkeley: University of California Press, 1985), 234–35.

35. Lucian, *[Am.]* 8; cited in Winkler, *"Auctor" and Actor,* 235.

36. Longus, *Daphn.* proem.

37. Achilles Tatius, *Leuc. Clit.* 1.2; cited in Winkler, *"Auctor" and Actor,* 235.

38. On storytellers, see Alexander Scobie, *Aspects of the Ancient Romance and its Heritage: Essays on Apuleius, Petronius, and the Greek Romances* (BKP 30; Meisenheim am Glan: Anton Hain, 1969), 20–29; idem, "Storytellers," 229–59; Joanna Dewey, "Textuality in an Oral Culture: A Survey of the Pauline Traditions," *Semeia* 65 (1994): 45–47.

39. Quintilian, *Inst.* 5.11.19

40. Apuleius, *Metam.* 1.2–20; 2.20–30; 4.8–21; 4.28–6.24; 7.5–9; 8.1–14; 9.17–21.

41. Xenophon of Ephesus, *Ephesiaca* 5.13.5.

42. Pliny, *Ep.* 2.20.1.

43. Suetonius, *Aug.* 74. The term he uses is *aretalogus,* which Juvenal uses to refer to someone who tells incredible tales (*Sat.* 15.16).

44. Dennis R. MacDonald, "From Audita to Legenda: Oral and Written Miracle Stories," Forum 2.4 (1986): 17; Scobie, "Storytellers," 244–51; Dewey, "From Storytelling," 73–76.

45. Tomas Hägg, *The Novel in Antiquity* (Berkeley: University of California Press, 1983), 93.

46. Apuleius, *Metam.* 1.1.16; 9.30.1; 10.2.12; 11.23.19. Scobie, *Ancient Romance,* 23.

47. Apuleius, *Metam.* 1.1.

48. Hägg, *Novel in Antiquity,* 93–94.

49. Chris Shea, "Setting the Stage for Romances: Xenophon of Ephesus and the Ecphrasis," in *Ancient Fiction and Early Christian Narrative* (ed. R. F. Hock, J. B. Chance, and J. Perkins; SBLSymS 6; Atlanta: Scholars Press, 1998), 61–76.

50. There is a vast amount of literature on the Greek and Roman theater. Some studies I found particularly relevant to the issues investigated in this book are Richard C. Beacham, *The Roman Theatre and Its Audience* (Cambridge, Mass.: Harvard University Press, 1992); David Wiles, *The Masks of Menander: Sign and Meaning in Greek and Roman Performance* (Cambridge: Cambridge University Press, 1991); W. B. Stanford, *Greek Tragedy and the Emotions: An Introductory Study* (London: Routledge & Kegan Paul, 1983).

51. Tacitus, *Dial.* 29.3.

52. Pausanius, *Descr.* 10.4.1.

53. For theaters in Asia Minor, see Daria de Bernardi Ferrero, *Teatri classici in Asia Minore* (4 vols.; Rome: L'Erma di Bretschneider, 1966–74).

54. W. Schleiermacher, "Zu den sogenannten Kulttheatern in Gallien," in *Corolla Memoriae Erich Swoboda Dedicata* (ed. R. M. Swoboda-Milenović; Graz: Böhlau, 1966), 205–213; Avraham Negev and Shimon Gibson, eds., *The Archaeological Encyclopedia of the Holy Land* (rev. ed.; New York: Continuum, 2001), 455; Zeev Weiss, "Sepphoris," *NEAEHL* 4:1325.

55. On theaters in Palestine in general, see James L. Kinneavy, *Greek Rhetorical Origins of Christian Faith: An Inquiry* (Oxford: Oxford University Press, 1987), 59.

56. Christopher Jones, "Dinner Theater," in *Dining in a Classical Context* (ed. W. J. Slater; Ann Arbor: University of Michigan Press, 1991), 185–98.

57. Plutarch, *Quaest. conv.* 7.8.3, 712b.

58. Pliny, *Ep.* 9.36.4.

59. T. D. Barnes, "Christians and the Theater," in *Roman Theater and Society: E. Togo Salmon Papers I* (ed. W. J. Slater; Ann Arbor: University of Michigan Press, 1996), 164–66.

60. On pantomime and dancing, see Lucian, *Salt.*; Minos Kokolakis, *Pantomimus and the Treatise* Περὶ Ὀρχήσεως (Athens: A. Sideris, 1959) [on Lucian's treatise Salt.]; Kathryn Wylie, *Satyric and Heroic Mimes: Attitude as the Way of the Mime in Ritual and Beyond* (Jefferson, N.C.: McFarland & Company, 1994), 138–58; E. J. Jory, "The Pantomime Assistants," in *Ancient History in a Modern University* (ed. by T. W. Hillard, R. A. Kearsley, C. E. V. Nixon, and A. M. Nobbs; 2 vols.; Grand Rapids: Eerdmans, 1998), 1:217–21; Richard C. Beacham, *The Roman Theatre and Its Audience* (Cambridge, Mass.: Harvard University Press, 1992), 140–53; Ludwig Friedlaender, *Darstellungen aus der Sittengeschichte Roms: In der Zeit von Augustus bis zum Ausgang der Antonine* (rev. G. Wissowa; 4 vols.; 10th ed.; Leipzig: Hirzel, 1921–23), 2:125–47. A collection of artistic representations related to pantomime can be found in E. J. Jory, "The Drama of the Dance: Prolegomena to an Iconography of Imperial Pantomime," in *Roman Theater and Society: E. Togo Salmon Papers I* (ed. W. J. Slater; Ann Arbor: University of Michigan Press, 1996), 1–27, and figures on unnumbered pages at the back of the book.

61. Jory, "Drama of the Dance," 2–3, 19–20.

62. Jory, "Drama of the Dance," 16.

63. Lucian, *Salt.* 15.

64. Dio Chrysostom, *Or.* 12.33.

65. Plato, *Leg.* 815c.

66. Tacitus, *Dial.* 10.1–2; cited by Harris, *Ancient Literacy*, 226, n. 259. See also Tacitus, *Dial.* 3 on recitation of a newly composed tragedy.

67. Kenneth Quinn, "The Poet and His Audience in the Augustan Age," *ANRW* 30.1:75–180, esp. 83–93 and 158-65; G. P. Goold, "The Voice of Virgil: The Pageant of Rome in *Aeneid 6*," in *Author and Audience in Latin Literature* (T. Woodman and J. Powell, eds.; Cambridge: Cambridge University Press, 1992), 110–23. For the performance of poetry in archaic and classical Greece, see Stehle, *Performance and Gender.*

68. Pliny, *Ep.* 1.13.

69. Quintilian, *Inst.* 1.10.29.

70. See Pindar's description of the poet blending words with the music of the lyre and aulos (*Ol.* 3.6–9); cited in Rosalind Thomas, *Literacy and Orality in Ancient Greece* (Cambridge: Cambridge University Press, 1992), 118.

71. See Pindar, *Pyth.* 1.1–4; cited by Thomas, *Literacy and Orality*, 118.

72. Pliny, *Ep.* 7.17.3.

73. Plato, *Ion* 530a. On rhapsodes, see Richard Leo Enos, "The Hellenic Rhapsode," *WJSC* 42 (1978): 134–43; Donald E. Hargis, "The Rhapsode," *QJS* 56 (1970): 388-97; idem, "Socrates and the Rhapsode: Plato's Ion," in *Studies in Interpretation* (ed. E. M. Doyle and V. H. Floyd; 2 vols.; Amsterdam: Rodopi, 1977), 2.1–12.

74. Plato, *Ion* 535b–e; 536c.

75. Plato, *Ion* 531a.

76. Str-B, 2.687.

77. On oral presentations of Scripture in early Christianity, see Graham, *Beyond the Written Word*, 122–25.

78. Gamble, *Books and Readers*, 323, n. 14.

79. See *m. Meg.* 4.2.

80. *Sop.* 11.2; cited by Bar-Ilan, "Illiteracy in the Land of Israel," 54.

81. Gamble, *Books and Readers*, 209–11.

82. Justin, *1 Apol.* 1.67; cited by Gamble, *Books and Readers*, 205.

83. Hippolytus, *Trad. ap.* can. 20; cited by Gamble, *Books and Readers*, 326, n. 39.

84. Gamble, *Books and Readers*, 217, citing commentaries of Origen, Chrysostom, Ambrose, and Augustine, which are compiled from a series of homilies on successive readings of Scripture.

85. Gamble, *Books and Readers*, 225–26. The Babylonian Talmud attributes to Johanan a saying that suggests chanting (*b. Meg.* 32a) and to Akiba an admonition to sing the Scripture daily. The uncertainty of Talmudic attributions, however, makes it impossible to date the practice with certainty earlier than the sixth century.

86. E. J. Revell, "The Oldest Evidence for the Hebrew Accent System," *BJRL* 54 (1971-72): 214–22; and "Biblical Punctuation and Chant in the Second Temple Period," *JSJ* 7 (1976): 181-98. Followed by Gamble, *Books and Readers*, 226–27.

87. Quintilian, *Inst.* 11.3.57–59.

88. George A. Kennedy, *A New History of Classical Rhetoric* (Princeton: Princeton University Press, 1994), 120–132. The literature on Paul's use of rhetorical conventions is vast. Early important works include Hans Dieter Betz, *Galatians: A Commentary on Paul's Letter to the Churches in Galatia* (Hermeneia; Philadelphia: Fortress, 1979); Wilhelm Wuellner, "Paul's Rhetoric of Argumentation: An Alternative to the Donfried-Karris Debate," in *The Romans Debate* (ed. K. P. Donfried; Minneapolis: Augsburg, 1977), 152–74.

89. See E. F. Osborn, "Teaching and Writing in the First Chapter of the *Stromateis* of Clement of Alexandria," *JTS* n.s. 10 (1959): 335–43.

90. Clement of Alexandria, *Strom.* 1.1.4.

91. Clement of Alexandria, *Strom.* 1.1.4.

92. Clement of Alexandria, *Strom.* 1.1.6.

93. Clement of Alexandria, *Strom.* 1.1.7.

94. Clement of Alexandria, *Strom.* 1.1.8.

95. Clement of Alexandria, *Strom.* 1.1.12.

96. Clement of Alexandria, *Strom.* 1.1.11.

97. For a discussion of various proposals for the use of the Gospel in worship or teaching, see Mary Ann Beavis, *Mark's Audience: The Literary and Social Setting of Mark 4:11–12* (JSNTSup 33; Sheffield: Sheffield Academic Press, 1989), 46–66. Beavis sees

Mark as a Christian teacher and the Gospel used to instruct both Christians and potential converts (167–73).

98. The similarities were suggested by A. D. Nock, *Conversion: The Old and the New in Religion from Alexander the Great to Augustine of Hippo* (London: Oxford University Press, 1933). See also E. A. Judge, "The Early Christians as a Scholastic Community," *JRH* 1 (1960–61): 4–15, 125–37; Abraham J. Malherbe, *Social Aspects of Early Christianity* (2d, enlarged ed.; Philadelphia: Fortress, 1983), 45–54;Wayne A. Meeks, *The First Urban Christians* (New Haven: Yale University Press, 1983), 81–84; Loveday Alexander, "Luke's Preface in the Context of Greek Preface-Writing," *NovT* 28 (1986): 48–74; Loveday Alexander, "Paul and the Hellenistic Schools: The Evidence of Galen," in *Paul and His Hellenistic Context* (ed. T. Engberg-Pedersen. Minneapolis: Fortress, 1995), 60–83.

99. *Gos. Thom.* 1.

100. Benoît Herman Marguérite Ghislain Marie Standaert, *L'Evangile selon Marc: Composition et genre litteraire* (Nijmegen: Stichting Studentenpers, 1978), 496–616; idem, *L'Evangile selon Marc: Commentaire* (LireB 61; Paris: Cerf, 1983), 22–23.

101. Pliny, *Ep.* 8.12.

102. Epictetus, *Diatr.* 3.23.23.

103. Suetonius, *Nero* 10.2.

104. Lucian, *Dom.*, esp., 5–9, 22–31.

105. Tacitus, *Dial.* 9.3.

106. Epictetus, *Diatr.* 3.23.35.

107. Juvenal, *Sat.* 7.36–51.

108. For *scholē* (school) as guild hall, see the discussion in Malherbe, *Social Aspects*, 90–91.

109. Ronald F. Hock, "The Workshop as a Social Setting for Paul's Missionary Preaching," *CBQ* 41 (1979): 438–50; idem, "Paul's Tentmaking and the Problem of His Social Class," *JBL* 97 (1978): 555–64; idem, *The Social Context of Paul's Ministry: Tentmaking and Apostleship* (Philadelphia: Fortress, 1980), 37–42.

110. Origen, *Cels.* 3.55.

111.Teles, frag. IVB, 46H. For text and translation, see Edward N. O'Neil, *Teles (The Cynic Teacher)*, (SBLTT 11, SBLGRRS 3; Missoula, Mont.: Scholars Press, 1977), 48–49.

112. Though see Richard B. Hays,*The Faith of Jesus Christ: An Investigation of the Narrative Substructure of Galatians 3:1–4:11* (SBLDS 56; Chico, Calif.: Scholars Press, 1983) for the importance of narrative underlying Paul's teaching.

113. Ramsay MacMullen, *Christianizing the Roman Empire* (New Haven: Yale University Press, 1984), esp. 33–34.

114. Alexander, "Paul and the Hellenistic Schools," 79–80; Stanley K. Stowers, "Social Status, Public Speaking and Private Teaching: The Circumstances of Paul's Preaching Activity," *NovT* 26 (1984): 59–82.

115. For the house church, see Malherbe, *Social Aspects*, 60–91.

116. On the importance of private houses as a locus for Pauline and later Christian teaching see Stowers, "Social Status," 65–82.

117. Running water is preferred for baptism; *Did.* 7.

118. Standaert, *L'Evangile selon Marc: Composition*, 515–19.

119. Gregory S. Aldrete, *Gestures and Acclamations in Ancient Rome* (Baltimore: The Johns Hopkins University Press, 1999), 17–34.

CHAPTER THREE
Emotion

While much of the study of the Gospels through history has been concerned with an intellectual analysis of the texts as a basis of doctrine or ethical behavior, in the ancient Mediterranean world oral performance was generally oriented toward emotional impact.[1] This is one of the most fundamental ways in which oral performance affected the way the Gospel would be received. The extent to which oral performance concentrated on the emotions would vary, of course, with the type of communication. Presumably the proclamation of a law would not emphasize emotional delivery, and some classroom situations may have emphasized intellectual content over emotion, but most forms of verbal art emphasized emotional impact as did most forms of oratory.

There are two related reasons for this emphasis on emotion. The first is aesthetic, the second more practical. Emotional impact was considered an essential aspect, if not the central purpose, of verbal performance in Greek culture ever since classical times. The success of verbal art was often judged by the way it affected the emotions of the listeners. Thus any speaker striving after artistic effect would pay particular attention to the way his or her performance affected the listeners. Second, it was recognized that emotional appeals are extremely important in the shaping of opinion, so rhetoricians concentrated on the emotional impact of their speeches in both the courts and deliberative bodies like the Roman Senate.

The church's apparent preference for narrative Gospels over sayings collections for use in the church probably reflects their interest in the emotional impact of the narrative. Certainly, individual sayings of Jesus can be expected to create an emotional reaction, and the organization of sayings into longer discourses such as the Sermon on the Mount would allow for more sustained emotional development. Nevertheless, the narrative Gospels are clearly a more successful vehicle for creating emotional impact than are Gospels that consist primarily of sayings of Jesus, such as the Gospel of Thomas found in the ancient Christian library recovered at Nag Hammadi in Egypt, or the hypothetical sayings source designated Q that many scholars believe was used as a source by the writers of Matthew and Luke.[2]

On the Artistic Description of Emotion

From the time of classical Greek culture, the importance of emotion was stressed both by literary theorists and by writers who describe contemporary practice. The emotional emphasis of performance is found throughout the performance arts. Emotion was so important in drama that the philosopher Aristotle defined tragedy in terms of emotion. Emotional release or catharsis, he states, is the very purpose of tragic drama.[3] Tragedy represents men in action, does not use narrative, and through pity and fear effects relief to these emotions.[4] The success that tragedy achieved in creating those emotions is indicated by a ancient commentator on the Roman satirist Juvenal, who says that it became the practice "among the ancients" to introduce comic after-pieces at the ends of tragedies, "and the laughter of this entertainment expunged the sadness and tears caused by the tragedy."[5] The Greek philosopher Plato, who wanted to expel all poets from his ideal city, brings as the chief accusation against the poets their ability to make the audience participate in emotions that a good man ought to avoid.[6]

Plato's condemnation would have included both the dramatic playwrights and the epic poets. The emotional aspect of epic performance is made clear in another passage in Plato. In Plato's day and well into the Roman period, the Homeric poems were recited by professionals known as rhapsodes or later as Homeristai. Ion was a famous Homeric rhapsode in Plato's day, and Plato wrote a dialogue known as the *Ion*, describing a conversation between Socrates and Ion in which the two discuss the rhapsode's art. The Greeks held contests between rhapsodes and other oral performers in many festivals. Ion declares that he knows he will not receive the prize in a competition if he does not see his audience weeping, casting terrible glances, and stricken with amazement.[7] Such an understanding of Homer is found in writings contemporary with the New Testament as well. In the first century C.E., the orator and philosopher Dio Chrysostom says of Homer, "He was able to implant in the soul any emotion he wished." The context of the remark makes it clear that the sound of the Homeric poems was an essential part of this effect.[8] Horace says much the same of dramatic poets: "That poet is able to walk a tight rope, who with airy nothings wrings my heart, inflames, soothes, fills it with vain alarms like a magician, and sets me down now at Thebes, now at Athens."[9]

The nonverbal acting of pantomimes also focused on the expression of emotion. The second century C.E. essayist Lucian of Samosata says of the pantomime dancer, "It is his profession to show forth human character and passion in all their variety; to depict love and anger, frenzy and grief, each in its due measure. Wondrous art!—on the same day, he is mad Athamas and shrinking Ino; he is Atreus, and again he is Thyestes, and next Aegisthus or Aërope; all one man's work."[10]

Roman declamation, in which orators showed off their skill in mock debates, tended to be very emotional. As speakers aimed more at entertaining than persuading their audiences in these debates, emotional appeal was freed from the constraints that persuasive rhetoric placed on it. In orations in a real court, one had to match the emotional appeal carefully to the character of the judges and avoid the appearance of using emotion to obscure the issues. In declamation as in drama, however, the expression of emotion became valued for its own sake.[11]

"Longinus" on Emotion

For the postclassical period, the most extensive treatment of emotion in the verbal arts is found in the essay *On the Sublime* attributed to Longinus. The attribution to Longinus is doubted by most scholars, and the work is generally dated to the early first century C.E. For the author of this essay, all verbal art should reach for sublimity, and sublimity was closely bound to emotions. The author lists five sources of the sublime: robust ideas, the inspiration of vehement emotion, the proper construction of figures of thought and speech, nobility of phrase (including choice of words, metaphor, and elaborated diction), and the general effect of dignity and grandeur. Emotion is more important an ingredient than the list itself suggests since it may be an element in producing the other factors.

The three sources of sublimity of ideas, for example, are nobility of mind, imitation of great writers of the past, and imagination. Imagination is closely linked with emotional description. Imagination, the author states, "has now come to be used predominantly of passages where, inspired by strong emotion, you seem to see what you describe and bring it vividly before the eyes of your audience."[12] Emotion is the aim of both poetry and prose. "The object of poetry is to enthral, of prose writing to present things vividly, though both indeed aim at this latter and at excited feeling."[13]

Similarly, figures of thought and speech are often related to emotion. For example, Demosthenes' oath, "No, by those who bore the brunt at Marathon!" is said to transform his argument into a passage of sublimity and emotion.[14] On the figure of question and answer, the author says, "this way of questioning and answering one's self counterfeits spontaneous emotion," and emotion is always more effective when it is perceived as spontaneous.[15] He warns that figures can antagonize a judge if they do not produce an effect of sublimity and emotion that makes them seem natural rather than artificial.[16] On Demosthenes' use of asyndetons (the absence of the connecting words that begin most Greek sentences) and repetition he states, "For monotony expresses quiet, while emotion, being a violent upheaval of the soul, demands disorder," and, "Emotion resents being hampered by connecting particles."[17] It was common in Greek to change the expected word order, and such inversion of word order is said to bear the stamp of vehement emotion. It resembled, the author says, the way those moved by strong emotion

> turn aside, and when they have taken one thing as their subject, often leap to another, foisting in the midst some irrelevant matter, and then again wheel round to their original theme, and driven by their vehemence, as by a veering wind, now this way now that with rapid changes, transform their expressions, their thoughts, the order suggested by a natural sequence, into numberless variations of every kind.[18]

Other figures, which the writer refers to as accumulation, variation, and climax, produce a sublime and emotional effect.[19] A sudden outbreak of emotion is suggested by the figure in which a writer, while speaking of one of his characters, suddenly speaks in the voice of the character.[20] A quick play of emotion is suggested when Demosthenes shifts in midsentence from addressing the jury to his opponent in a case.[21] In summing up his discussion of figures, the author says, "Our conclusion is that they all serve to lend emotion and excitement to the style. But emotion is as much an element in the sublime, as is the study of character in agreeable writing."[22]

Nobility of phrase is also linked to emotion. In his discussion of metaphor, the writer says that the right time for the use of metaphor is when emotion sweeps on like a flood and carries the multitude of metaphors along with it:[23]

> The proper antidote for a multitude of daring metaphors is strong and timely emotion and genuine sublimity. These by their nature sweep everything along in the forward surge of their current, or rather they positively demand bold imagery as essential to their effect, and do not give the hearer time to examine how many metaphors there are, because he shares the excitement of the speaker.[24]

Similarly, "the best hyperbole is the one which conceals the very fact of its being a hyperbole. And this happens when it is uttered under stress of emotion to suit the circumstances of a great crisis."[25]

When the writer discusses the final source of sublimity, the general effect of dignity and grandeur, he defines it in terms of arrangement of words and has in mind particularly aural effects such as rhythm and tone. "Men find in melody," he says, "not only a natural instrument of persuasion and pleasure, but also a marvelous instrument of grandeur and emotion."[26]

Sublimity and emotion, nevertheless, are not the same thing. There are mean-spirited emotions that are not sublime, such as pity, grief, and fear. There are many sublime passages that do not express emotion. Nevertheless, he states, "nothing produces loftiness more than noble emotion in the right place. It inspires the words as it were with a certain frenzy and fills them with a divine spirit."[27] Emotion invests a subject with grandeur, as does metaphor, amplification, and sublimity.[28] Demosthenes' sublimity, he says, comes in his intensity and violent emotion.[29]

The sublime itself, while not emotion, certainly has an emotional aspect in its effect on listeners:

> The Sublime consists in a consummate excellence and distinction of language. . . . For the effect of genius is not to persuade the audience but rather to transport them out of themselves. Invariably what inspires wonder casts a spell upon us and is

always superior to what is merely convincing and pleasing. For our convictions are usually under our own control, while such passages exercise an irresistible power of mastery and get the upper hand with each one of those listening.[30]

The author's discussion of a passage from Sappho shows clearly his appreciation of the connection of emotion and body that makes the voice and delivery such an importance part of the experience of verbal art for the ancients:

> One writer for instance attracts the reader by the selection of ideas, another by the soldering of these selected. Sappho, for instance, never fails to take the emotions incident to the passion of love from the symptoms which accompany it in real life. And wherein does she show her excellence? In the skill with which she selects and combines the most striking and intense of those symptoms.
>
> > I think him God's peer that sits near thee face to face, and listens to thy sweet speech and lovely laughter.
> > 'Tis this that makes my heart flutter in my breast. If I see thee but for a little, my voice comes no more and my tongue is broken.
> > At once a delicate flame runs through my limbs; my eyes are blinded and my ears thunder.
> > The sweat pours down: shivers hunt me all over. I am grown paler than grass, and very near to death I feel.
>
> Is it not wonderful how she summons at the same time, soul, body, hearing, tongue, sight, colour, all as though they had wandered off apart from herself? She feels contradictory sensations, freezes, burns, raves, reasons—for one that is at the point of death is clearly beside herself. She wants to display not a single emotion, but a whole congress of emotions. Lovers all show such symptoms as these, but what gives supreme merit to her art is, as I said, the skill with which she chooses the most striking and combines them into a single whole.[31]

The importance of emotion in literature could easily lead to its misuse. "Longinus" warns against misplaced and overdone emotion that fails to bring the listeners along.

[There] is a third kind of fault peculiar to emotional passages, what Theodorus used to call "Parenthyrson."[32] This is emotion misplaced and pointless where none is needed, or unrestrained where restraint is required. For writers often behave as if they were drunk and give way to outbursts of emotion which the subject no longer warrants. Such emotion is purely subjective and consequently tedious, so that to listeners who feel none of it their behaviour looks unseemly. And naturally so, for while they are in ecstasy, the listeners are not.[33]

"Longinus" does not separate the faults of misplaced emotion in writing and misplaced emotion in performance since he is primarily concerned with the performances of writers themselves, where overwriting and overacting would be part of the same performance. Such overacting could just as well be done by someone reading the work of another.

Emotion in Rhetoric

The writers on rhetoric also stressed the importance of emotions and recognized that emotion was superior to rational argument in convincing an audience.[34] According to Quintilian, a first-century teacher of rhetoric, there were three functions of rhetoric: to inform the intellect, to move the emotions, and to delight the artistic sense.[35] The philosopher Aristotle, who was one of the first to write on the art of rhetoric, would prefer that rhetoric dealt only with facts.[36] Actors, he complains, are getting more important than poets, and the same will soon be true in the assembly and the courts.[37] Nevertheless, he includes a long section in his *Rhetoric* on the importance of emotions in persuasion.[38] Emotional delivery is very persuasive because "the listener always shares the emotions of the person who speaks with emotion even if what is said is nothing."[39] Aristotle was not alone in his distrust of emotional appeals. There is some evidence that appeals to emotion were outlawed in Athens, at least in cases tried before the Areopagus.[40] According to Athenaeus, advocates in fourth century B.C.E. Athens were barred from lamentation as a result of the speech of Hypereides in which he bared the breasts of his lover Phryne and indulged in such piteous lamentation that he succeeded in gaining her acquittal.[41]

By the first century C.E. ambivalence about the role of emotional appeal in rhetoric had largely disappeared. The great Roman orator

and statesman Cicero wrote several works on the art of rhetoric. He
has Brutus state in the dialogue of that name, "Of all the resources of
an orator, far the greatest is his ability to inflame the minds of his
hearers and to turn them in whatever direction the case demands."[42]
In another dialogue, Cicero has Antonius state:

> Now nothing in oratory . . . is more important than to win for
> the orator the favour of his hearer, and to have the latter so
> affected as to be swayed by something resembling a mental
> impulse or emotion, rather than by judgement or deliberation.
> For men decide far more problems by hate, or love, or lust, or
> rage, or sorrow, or joy, or hope, or fear, or illusion, or some
> other inward emotion, than by reality, or authority, or any legal
> standard, or judicial precedent, or statute.[43]

In the same work Cicero has Antonius state, "The whole theory of
speaking is dependent on three sources of persuasion: that we prove
our case to be true; that we win over those who are listening; that we
call their hearts to what emotion the case demands."[44]

"Longinus," as we might expect from his treatment of other verbal
arts, makes a connection between imagination, vigor, and emotion in
rhetoric. "What then is the use of imagination in rhetoric? It may be
said generally to introduce a great deal of vigor and emotion into one's
speeches, but when combined with argumentative treatment, it not
only convinces the audience, it positively masters them."[45] In describing the genius of Demosthenes, "Longinus" gives emotion and intensity pride of place: "You could sooner open your eyes to the descent of
a thunderbolt," he says, "than face unwinking his repeated outbursts
of emotion."[46] Pliny's observations on oratory emphasize the importance of emotion just as much:

> The orator ought in fact to be roused and heated, sometimes
> even to boiling-point, and to let his feelings carry him on till he
> treads the edge of a precipice; for a path along the heights and
> peaks often skirts the sheer drop below. It may be safer to keep
> to the plain, but the road lies too low to be interesting.[47]

Different writers had different assessments of the types of speeches
in which emotional appeal should be made. Generally, speeches were
divided into three types by the ancient handbooks of rhetoric. Forensic

speeches were arguments presented in lawcourts. Deliberative speeches were designed to move a political body to vote for or against a certain measure. Epideictic referred to a variety of speeches of praise or blame, generally presented at ceremonial occasions. "Longinus" associates emotional appeal with forensic and deliberative oratory. Eulogies, panegyric, and epideictic speeches, he says, usually lack emotion.[48] The historian Polybius, on the other hand, has an opposite view of the use of emotion in funeral orations. In describing the effect of funeral orations on an audience, he says, "As a consequence, the multitude, and not only those who had a part in these achievements, but those also who had none, when the facts are recalled to their minds and brought before their eyes, are moved to such sympathy that the loss seems to be not confined to the mourners, but a public one affecting the whole people."[49]

Cicero indicates two areas of rhetoric designed to work the emotions of the audience, each designated by terms borrowed from Greek theorists. The first, *ēthikon*, relates to men's characters and habits. When the speaker creates a courteous and agreeable persona in his speech, he is able to secure the goodwill of his listeners. The other area, *pathētikon*, arouses and excites the emotions. It is in this area, Cicero says, that rhetoric reigns supreme. The rush of emotion delivered by an orator is irresistible to an audience.[50]

Quintilian, who often follows the opinions of Cicero, has a similar view: "The power of eloquence is greatest in emotional appeals."[51] "For it is in its power over the emotions that the life and soul of oratory is to be found."[52] He observes that when a speaker is moved by warmth of feeling, he may improvise a speech that is more successful than one that was carefully prepared.[53] Even the uneducated, he says, have no trouble expressing their meaning when they are stirred by some strong emotion.[54] He devotes a long section of his work to describing emotional appeals that are appropriate in the peroration, the concluding part of a speech,[55] as well as emotional appeals used throughout the speech.[56] There are some cases where the whole speech should be colored by emotion, as when a father has to speak of his son's death, a person pleads for the right to commit suicide, or if family members take each other to court.[57] Quintilian criticizes those who crowd their speeches with logical proofs. That is suitable for dialectical controversies among learned men but not for the lawcourts, where the judges are frequently ill educated. In order to vindicate truth in that circumstance, we must rely on the charm and force of our discourse and appeals to emotion.[58]

He sees the ability of the orator to stir emotions as being central to success, precisely because it allows him to win sympathy for a weak case:

> For as a rule arguments arise out of the case itself, and the bet-
> ter cause has always the larger number to support it. . . . But the
> peculiar task of the orator arises when the minds of the judges
> require force to move them, and their thoughts have actually to
> be led away from the contemplation of the truth. . . . Proofs, it
> is true, may induce the judges to regard our case as superior to
> that of our opponent, but the appeal to the emotions will do
> more, for it will make them wish our case to be the better. And
> what they wish, they will also believe. . . . So the judge, when
> overcome by his emotions, abandons all attempt to enquire into
> the truth of the arguments, is swept along by the tide of passion,
> and yields himself unquestioning to the rent. Thus the verdict
> of the court shows how much weight has been carried by the
> arguments and the evidence; but when the judge has been really
> moved by the orator, he reveals his feelings while he is still sit-
> ting and listening to the case. When those tears, which are the
> aim of most perorations, well forth from his eyes, is he not giv-
> ing his verdict for all to see?[59]

In another passage Quintilian is even more candid about the value of emotion in weak cases: "At times we must not merely avoid distinguishing between the various questions, but must omit them altogether, while our audience must be distracted by appeals to the emotion and their attention diverted."[60] On the other hand, judges might see through such a ploy, especially as one might expect one's opponent to point it out.[61]

The Christian theologian and rhetorician Augustine also regarded emotional appeal as an important component of eloquence. In *De doctrina Christiana*, which includes a discussion of Christian rhetoric, he lists as important parts of the rhetoricians' art the ability to make their listeners benevolent, attentive, or docile (the standard purposes for an exordium, a beginning section of a speech) as well as their ability to terrify, sadden, and exhilarate their audience.[62] He urges Christians to learn these abilities so that they may successfully argue against error.

Emotional Appeals in Philosophical Discourse

How philosophers make use of emotion is particularly relevant to our understanding of Gospel performances, since moral philosophers aimed at transforming the lives of their listeners, much the same way that a Christian missionary might. The writings of Paul have many similarities to the moral philosophers.[63] Some philosophers were generally opposed to emotional appeal in rhetoric.[64] The Stoics especially are mentioned in this regard. According to Cicero, the Stoics believed that emotions were mere fancies and frivolous opinions, and the wise man should be free from emotion.[65] As a result the philosopher could only appeal to his listener's intellect, an approach that Cicero found lacking. "Their meagre little syllogisms are mere pinpricks; they may convince the intellect, but they cannot convert the heart, and the hearer goes away no better than he came."[66] The complaint makes it clear that in Cicero's mind, appeals to the emotions were the most effective part of philosophical speech in producing change in conduct. He much preferred the rhetoric of the Peripatetics, who made appropriate use of more ornate diction.[67]

Nevertheless, even Stoic moral philosophers found appeals to the emotions just as important as did the rhetors, though the types of emotions they sought to tap were different.[68] Epictetus, a first-century Stoic philosopher, says the philosopher should aim at convincing his listeners that they are wretched and miserable, ignorant of good and evil. His teacher Musonius Rufus was so effective at this, he tells us, and so skillful at vividly setting before each man's eyes his own weaknesses that each of his students felt someone had told him of his faults. The effect of philosophical discourse, he says, should be to produce pain rather than pleasure.[69] The listeners should feel greatly disturbed about themselves, realize the miserable state they are in, and resolve to change.[70] Musonius himself says much the same:

> Whoever the listener [to a philosopher's exhortation] may be, unless he is wholly lost, during the course of the philosopher's address he must necessarily shudder and feel secret shame and repentance, or rejoice or wonder, and even show changes of countenance and betray varying emotions, according as the philosopher's discourse had affected him and his consciousness of the different tendencies of his mind, whether noble or base.[71]

Plutarch also indicates that philosophers often aimed at causing pain and shame with their reproof, "in words that penetrate like a biting drug."[72]

The speech of the popular Cynic street preachers was apparently quite emotional, judging from the Lucian's unflattering depiction of them. At the conclusion of *The Runaways*, one of the slaves who has been, in Lucian's view, a Cynic imposter, comes out with a number of emotional exclamations—"Alas my evil luck! Woe is me! Oh! Oh! Oh! Oh!"—and is upbraided by his master for bringing in material from tragic discourses.[73] Their speech is also characterized as quick-tempered, harsh-sounding, abusive, and exceedingly foul.[74] Similarly, in Lucian's *Passing of Peregrinus* a Cynic preacher is characterized as shouting in a loud, harsh voice and abusing everyone without exception.[75] One follower of Peregrinus is described as dripping in sweat through his speech on the impending death of his teacher, ending with tears and tearing his hair, "taking care not to pull very hard." His companions lead him off as the climax to the emotional presentation.[76] Lucian is not much more restrained in his own theatricality. He opens his own speech in rebuttal of the Cynic's presentation of Peregrinus by simply laughing for an extended time.[77] The emotional tenor of Peregrinus's own speeches is indicated by Lucian's characterization of him as a playwright whose spectacular performances outdid Sophocles and Aeschylus.

Explicit Emotions in the Text of Mark

The comparative emotionalism of the Markan Jesus is well-known. He is said to be angry (3:5) and filled with compassion (1:41). He snorts like a horse (1:43). He is troubled and distressed (14:33). Apart from the specific mention of emotions, Jesus' speech often implies emotion, as anyone who has read the Gospel expressively knows. Jesus is repeatedly irritated, annoyed, angry, or sarcastic.

In many passages Mark practically provides stage directions concerning voice or gesture.[78] Often the voice descriptions are quite emotional. In the garden of Gethsemane, Jesus is said to be "distressed and agitated" (14:33). The speeches and prayers that follow show him troubled and distressed: "I am deeply grieved, even to death. . . . "Abba! Father, for you all things are possible! Remove this cup from me! Yet not what I want, but what you want" (14:34–36). Jesus rebukes the demon in the synagogue: "Be silent, and come out of him!" (1:25). The people are amazed: "What is this?" (1:27). In healing the leper,

Jesus is moved to "pity": "I do choose. Be made clean!" (1:41). Then he warns him "sternly," "See that you say nothing to anyone! But go! Show yourself to the priest!" (1:43–44). After the healing of the paralytic, the crowd is "amazed": "We have never seen anything like this!" (2:12). After the stilling of the storm, the disciples are "filled with great awe" and say, "Who then is this?" (4:41). Demons plead with Jesus: "Send us into the swine! Let us enter them!" (5:12). The ruler of the synagogue pleads earnestly with Jesus, "My daughter is at the point of death! Come and lay your hands on her, so that she may be made well, and live!" (5:23). The people in Jesus' hometown are "astounded" and "took offense" at Jesus: "Where did this man get all this? . . . Is not this the carpenter, the son of Mary and brother of James and Joses and Judas and Simon?" (6:2–3). The crowd at the healing of the deaf man is "astounded beyond measure" and say, "He has done everything well! He even makes the deaf to hear and the mute to speak!" (7:37). The disciples "spoke sternly" to those bringing little children to Jesus (10:13). In response, Jesus is "indignant" and replies, "Let the little children come to me!" (10:14).

Once one begins reading of the Gospel with emotion, one quickly recognizes how Mark juxtaposes sharply divergent emotional tones. "To you has been given the secret of the kingdom of God. . . . Do you not understand this parable? Then how can you understand all the parables?" (4:11–13). "[Herod's soldier] brought [John's] head on a platter, and gave it to the girl. The girl gave it to her mother. When his disciples heard about it, they came and took his body, and laid it in a tomb. The apostles gathered around Jesus, and told him all that they had done and taught" (6:28–30). "'You are the Messiah!' And he sternly ordered them not to tell anyone about him. Then he began to teach them that the Son of Man must undergo great suffering. . . . Peter took him aside and began to rebuke him. But turning and looking at his disciples, he rebuked Peter and said, 'Get behind me, Satan!'" (8:29–33). It is hard to imagine anyone writing a narrative so full of emotional twists and not intending them to be emphasized through an emotional reading.

Hints from the Handbooks on the Interpretation of Specific Passages

In a list of emotions that might be excited in the judges, Quintilian says that the judges' anger will be aroused by the disrespectful attitude of the accused toward the court, if, for example, he appears arrogant or studiously indifferent.[79] Jesus' attitude toward both the Sanhedrin (14:60–62) and Pilate (15:2–5) might be described as indifference, and his reply to the Sanhedrin would certainly be understood as arrogance by that court. The performer of the Gospel would likely express the anger that would be aroused by Jesus when speaking the words of the high priest. On the other hand, since the performer would regard that anger as ill-founded, he would most likely attempt to present the high priest as arrogant in the same passage. For a Christian audience, there is an ironic role reversal in the scene, since Jesus is the real judge, who will be sitting on the right hand of God, and it is the Sanhedrin and the high priest who are expressing contempt. Thus the Gospel audience will be stirred to anger by the action of the high priest.

The audience's anger will similarly be aroused by the arrogance of those mocking Jesus during the crucifixion (15:16–39). That arrogance is underlined by the ironic nature of their outbursts. Their mocking statements of truth underline their ignorance and the fact that their own high opinion of themselves is misplaced. Even the others being crucified with Jesus join in the mocking. What an absurd act of arrogance for condemned criminals being subjected to the most humiliating and degrading form of torture to mock the Son of God! The performer of the Gospel would surely emphasize the arrogance of the ridicule in speaking all the mocking lines in order to stir up the anger of the audience. That anger in turn emphasizes the injustice of Jesus' death. The more anger the audience feels, the more deeply they are convinced that Jesus is innocent. It is much more difficult to arouse a modern audience to anger over the crucifixion of Jesus, since modern listeners have no concept of the horrors of crucifixion and tend to think of the cross chiefly as a theological symbol. We have sung about "the old rugged cross" too often for it to be a real event. We seldom run into people ridiculing the crucified Jesus, but for first-century Christians, the mocking of Jesus would hit close to home, since they likely have heard similar mocking themselves.

The effectiveness of Mark's crucifixion scene results in no small part from the interplay of the two emotions felt by the audience. The suffering of Jesus evokes pity. The arrogance of the mockers evokes anger. The rapid interplay between the suffering of Jesus and the ignorance of those mocking creates a surreal scene that brings to a climax the split between the apparent (the judgment of people) and the real (the judgment of God), which is emphasized throughout the Gospel.[80]

Peculiarly Christian Uses of Emotion

One striking thing about the Gospel of Mark is the type of emotions attributed to Jesus. One might well expect that the emotions of the Son of God would be restricted to those that "Longinus" would associate with the sublime. Yet that is not at all the case. Consider, for example, the prayer in Gethsemane (14:32–42). Jesus is described as distressed, agitated, and deeply grieved in the face of his impending death. In his prayer he asks to be spared from death before asserting his willingness to abide by the will of his Father. At least some manuscripts of Luke assert that in his anguish Jesus' sweat became like great drops of blood (Luke 22:43–44).

This contrasts starkly with the prayer of Ajax from the *Iliad*, which "Longinus" quotes as an example of the sublime:

> Zeus Father, rescue from out of the mist the sons of Achaia,
> Brighten the heaven with sunshine, grant us the sight of our
> eyes. So it be but in daylight, destroy us.[81]

"Longinus" makes the following comment on the noble emotion of Ajax:

> These are the true feelings of an Ajax. He does not plead for his life: such a prayer would demean the hero: but since the ineffectual darkness robbed his courage of all noble use, therefore, distressed to be idle in battle, he prays for light on the instant, hoping thus at the worst to find a burial worthy of his courage, even though Zeus be ranged against him.[82]

Ajax conquers death by spitting in its eye, by overcoming the fear that people ordinarily feel when faced with the loss of their lives. Homer's hero is sublime because he overcomes the baser emotions. In a way, he lifts himself up to the position of a god, who, being immortal, does not have to fear death. For Mark, on the other hand, the overcoming of death involves an encounter with the instinctual fears associated with death as well as with the actual physical experience. Mark is likely composing for an audience that may be facing persecution and even the possibility of death; thus, the sanctification of fear through the narrated experience of Jesus may in some way have carried the audience through their own fear. Weakness itself becomes sublime because of the sublimity of the one experiencing it. Mark's hero is a hero not because he knows no fear but because he knows fear and still acts obediently.

Adapting to the Emotional Predisposition of the Audience

It is much better for a case, Cicero states in *De oratore*, if the judges already have some emotion about the case or the people involved that is in harmony with what the advocate desires. In that case it is easier to fan the emotion already existing. Antonius, who is speaking at this point in the dialogue, states that he always investigates the judges in an important case and carefully considers how they think and feel about the case so that he can tailor his appeals to those already existing ideas and feelings. Nevertheless, he claims, eloquence is powerful enough to carry an audience even when they do not have a favorable disposition with which the orator can work.[83]

If Mark worked the same way in the composition and delivery of the Gospel, we would expect him to pitch the narrative according to his perception of the existing thoughts and feelings of the audience. If so, we can gain some inkling of the existing mind-set of the audience by analyzing what emotions Mark works on. We can consider whether the approach he takes in various parts of the Gospel would be effective without a predisposition of the audience in the direction to which he seeks to move them.

For example, if we examine the various attacks on Jesus' opponents, it is clear that Mark would like for the audience to feel animosity toward these groups. How successful would Mark be if the audience did not share a certain animosity to begin with? My own experience with Jewish students in my classes suggests that someone with a positive image of the Pharisees is not likely to change that opinion by reading or hearing Jesus' dispute with the Pharisees in Mark 7:1–23. Such a person is much more likely to be offended than convinced. Is someone committed to keeping the food laws of the Torah likely to be convinced by Mark having Jesus declare that all foods are clean? From my own experience, the answer is absolutely not.

The limitations of the power of persuasion should be kept in mind in assessing reconstructions of Mark's purpose that posit Mark making a radical attack on existing community beliefs. Certainly a well-crafted piece of rhetoric can influence opinion drastically. It is much harder to completely reform existing opinion. Care should be taken in assessing whether Mark's story has enough persuasive effect to accomplish the goals suggested by these reconstructions.

On the other hand, it will help our imaginative reconstruction of the experience of hearing the Gospel in its first-century setting to imagine the performer working with the existing passions of the audience. Another aspect of this interaction will be considered in chapters 8–10, where the audience's reactions to the Gospel will be considered, along with ways in which the Gospel writer and performer would work on eliciting those responses.

Notes

1. On emotion in rhetoric, see Ernest Alfred Lussky, "The Appeal to the Emotions in the Judicial Speeches of Cicero as Compared with the Theories Set Forth on the Subject in the De Oratore" (Ph.D. diss., University of Minnesota, Minneapolis, 1928); Harry J. Leon, "The Technique of Emotional Appeal in Cicero's Judicial Speeches," *ClWeek* 39 (1935): 33–37; Friedrich Solmsen, "Aristotle and Cicero on the Orator's Playing upon the Feelings," *CP* 33 (1938): 390–404; Thomas Schick, "Cicero and the Pathetical Appeal in Oratory," *ClBul* 42 (1965): 17–18. On emotion in tragedy, see W. B. Stanford, *Greek Tragedy and the Emotions: An Introductory Study* (London: Routledge & Kegan Paul, 1983). On emotional appeals in Paul, see Thomas H. Olbricht and Jerry L. Sumney, eds., *Paul and Pathos* (SBLSymS 16; Atlanta: Society of Biblical Literature, 2001).

The importance of emotional appeals in the Gospel of Mark is also recognized in a recent dissertation by Brian J. Incigneri, "My God, My God, Why Have You Abandoned Me? The Setting and Rhetoric of Mark's Gospel" (Ph.D. diss., Australian Catholic University, Fitzroy, Victoria, Australia, 2001), esp. 37–41. See also the analysis of Morris A. Inch, *Exhortations of Jesus according to Matthew; and Up from the Depths: Mark as Tragedy* (Lanham, Md.: University Press of America, 1997), 139–60.

2. For an analysis of Q in its oral environment, see Richard A. Horsley with Jonathan A. Draper, *Whoever Hears You Hears Me: Prophets, Performance, and Tradition in Q* (Harrisburg: Trinity Press International, 2000).

3. On the central role of emotionalism in Greek performance art, see W. B. Stanford, *Greek Tragedy and the Emotions: An Introductory Study* (London: Routledge & Kegan Paul, 1983), 1–10.

4. Aristotle, *Poet.* 6.2; cf. 13.2.

5. At 3.175. Cited by Richard C. Beacham, *The Roman Theatre and Its Audience* (Cambridge, Mass.: Harvard University Press, 1992), 238, n. 36.

6. Plato, *Resp.* 605c–606b.

7. Plato, *Ion* 535e.

8. Dio Chrysostom, *Or.* 12.69 (Cohoon, LCL).

9. Horace, *Ep.* 2.1.211–13 (Fairclough, LCL).

10. Lucian, *Salt.* 67 (Fowler and Fowler).

11. On the relationship between declamation and drama, see Ruth Scodel, "Drama and Rhetoric," in *Handbook of Classical Rhetoric in the Hellenistic Period 330 B.C.–A.D. 400* (ed. S. E. Porter; Leiden: Brill, 1997), 501.

12. Longinus, *[Subl.]* 15.1–2 (Fyfe, LCL).

13. Longinus, *[Subl.]* 15.2 (Fyfe, LCL).

14. Longinus, *[Subl.]* 16.2.

15. Longinus, *[Subl.]* 18.2.

16. Longinus, *[Subl.]* 17.1–3.

17. Longinus, *[Subl.]* 20.2; 21.2 (Fyfe, LCL).

18. Longinus, *[Subl.]* 22.1–2 (Fyfe, LCL).

19. Longinus, *[Subl.]* 23.1.

20. Longinus, *[Subl.]* 27.1.

21. Longinus, *[Subl.]* 27.3.

22. Longinus, *[Subl.]* 29.2 (Fyfe, LCL).

23. Longinus, *[Subl.]* 32.1.

24. Longinus, *[Subl.]* 32.4 (Fyfe, LCL).

25. Longinus, *[Subl.]* 38.3 (Fyfe, LCL).

26. Longinus, *[Subl.]* 39.1 (Fyfe, LCL).

27. Longinus, *[Subl.]* 8.1–4 (adapted from Fyfe, LCL).

28. Longinus, *[Subl.]* 12.1.

29. Longinus, *[Subl.]* 12.5

30. Longinus, *[Subl.]* 1.3–4 (adapted from Fyfe, LCL).

31. Longinus, *[Subl.]* 10.1–3 (adapted from Fyfe, LCL).

32. W. Hamilton Fyfe explains *parenthyrson* as "the poking in of the *thyrsus* [thyrsos, Bacchic wand wreathed in ivy] at the wrong time, i.e., the affectation of Bacchanalian fury where no fury need be" ("'Longinus' On the Sublime," in *Aristotle, The Poetics, "Longinus," On the Sublime, Demetrius, On Style* [LCL 199; Cambridge: Harvard University, 1987], 131, note c).

33. Longinus, *[Subl.]* 3.5 (adapted from Fyfe, LCL).

34. In addition to the works listed in note 1, see chapters in *Paul and Pathos* (ed. Olbricht and Sumney): Thomas H. Olbricht, "Pathos as Proof in Greco-Roman Rhetoric," 7–22; Carol Poster, "The Affections of the Soul: Pathos, Protreptic, and Preaching in Hellenistic Thought," 23–37; Steven J. Kraftchick, "Πάθη in Paul: The Emotional Logic of 'Original Argument,'" 39–68.

35. Quintilian, *Inst.* 3.5.2.

36. Aristotle, *Rhet.* 3.1.5, 1404a.

37. Aristotle, *Rhet.* 3.1.4, 1403b.

38. Aristotle, *Rhet.* 2.1.8–2.11.7, 1378a–1388b.

39. Aristotle, *Rhet.* 3.7.4, 1408a (adapted from David Wiles, *The Masks of Menander: Sign and Meaning in Greek and Roman Performance* [Cambridge: Cambridge University Press, 1991], 13).

40. Aristotle, *Rhet.* 1.1.5; Quintilian, *Inst.* 6.1.7. H. E. Butler, in *The Institutio Oratoria of Quintilian* (trans. H. E. Butler; 4 vols.; LCL; Cambridge: Harvard University Press, 1933-68), 2:386, n. 1, points out that appeals to pity are common in the speeches of fourth-century Athens, when the ban was supposed to be in place.

41. Athenaeus, *Deipn.* 13.6, 590e.

42. Cicero, *Brut.* 80.279 (Hendrickson, LCL).

43. Cicero, *De or.* 2.42.178 (Sutton and Rackham, LCL).

44. Cicero, *De or.* 2.27.115 (trans. George A. Kennedy, *A New History of Classical Rhetoric* [Princeton: Princeton University Press, 1994], 100). Cicero makes frequent references to the importance of emotional appeal. For a collection of references from *De oratore*, see Lussky, "Appeal to the Emotions," 14–17.

45. Longinus, *[Subl.]* 15.9 (Fyfe, LCL).

46. Longinus, *[Subl.]* 34.4.

47. Pliny, *Ep.* 9.26.1 (Radice, LCL).

48. Longinus, *[Subl.]* 8.3; cf., 12.5, where history, epideictic, and curiously even perorations are said not to need intensity of emotion.

49. Polybius, *Hist.* 6.53.3 (Paton, LCL).

50. Cicero, *Or. But.* 37.128.

51. Quintilian, *Inst.* 4.5.6, cf. 6.2.2.

52. Quintilian, *Inst.* 6.2.7.

53. Quintilian, *Inst.* 10.7.13.

54. Quintilian, *Inst.* 10.7.15.

55. Quintilian, *Inst.* 6.1.9–55.

56. Quintilian, *Inst.* 6.2.1–36.

57. Quintilian, *Inst.* 11.1.53, 56, 58–59.

58. Quintilian, *Inst.* 5.14.27–29.

59. Quintilian, *Inst.* 6.2.4–7 (Butler, LCL).

60. Quintilian, *Inst.* 4.5.6.

61. Quintilian, *Inst.* 6.1.4.

62. Augustine, *Doctr. chr.* 4.2.3.

63. Among others, see A. D. Nock, *Conversion: The Old and the New in Religion from Alexander the Great to Augustine of Hippo* (London: Oxford University Press, 1933); E. A. Judge, "The Early Christians as a Scholastic Community," *JRH* 1 (1960-61): 4–15, 125–37; Abraham J. Malherbe, *Paul and the Thessalonians: The Philosophic Tradition of Pastoral Care* (Philadelphia: Fortress, 1987); idem, *Paul and the Popular Philosophers* (Minneapolis: Fortress, 1989); Stanley K. Stowers, *The Diatribe and Paul's Letter to the Romans* (SBLDS 57; Chico, Ca.: Scholars Press, 1981); Wayne A. Meeks, *The Origins of Christian Morality: The First Two Centuries* (New Haven: Yale University Press, 1993); Poster, "Affections of the Soul," 23–37; Hubert Cancik, "Lucian on Conversion: Remarks on Lucian's Dialogue *Nigrinos*," in *Ancient and Modern Perspectives on the Bible and Culture: Essays in Honor of Hans Dieter Betz* (ed. A. Y. Collins; SPHS 22; Atlanta, Ga.: Scholars Press, 1998), 26–48; Troels Engberg-Pedersen, *Paul and the Stoics* (Louisville: Westminster John Knox, 2000).

64. Quintilian, *Inst.* 6.1.7.

65. Cicero, *Fin.* 3.10.35.

66. Cicero, *Fin.* 4.3.7 (Rackham, LCL). For Stoics and emotion, see Friedrich Solmsen, "The Aristotelian Tradition in Ancient Rhetoric," *AJP* 62 (1941): 178.

67. Cicero, *Fin.* 4.3.6.

68. Nock, *Conversion*, 177–86; Malherbe, *Paul and the Thessalonians*, 21–28.

69. Epictetus, *Diatr.* 3.23.28–30.

70. Epictetus, *Diatr.* 3.23.37.

71. Quoted by Aulus Gellius, *Noct. att.* 5.1.3–4 (adapted from Rolfe, LCL).

72. Plutarch, *Rect. rat. aud.* 46f–47d (Babbitt, LCL).

73. Lucian, *Fug.* 33.

74. Lucian, *Fug.* 7, 13, 27, 29.

75. Lucian, *Peregr.* 3.

76. Lucian, *Peregr.* 6.

77. Lucian, *Peregr.* 7.

78. As observed by David Rhoads, "Performing the Gospel of Mark," in *Body and Bible: Interpreting and Experiencing Biblical Narratives* (ed. B. Krondorfer; Philadelphia: Trinity Press International, 1992), 105.

79. Quintilian, *Inst.* 6.1.14.

80. On this issue, see especially Joel Marcus, "Mark 4:10–12 and Marcan Epistemology," *JBL* 103 (1984): 557–74.

81. Homer, *Il.* 17.645.

82. Longinus, *[Subl.]* 9.10 (Fyfe, LCL, for translations of this passage and the preceding passage from Homer).

83. Cicero, *De or.* 2.44.185–87.

CHAPTER FOUR
Delivery

There is a story about Demosthenes, the greatest of the Athenian orators, that underlines the importance that was accorded to delivery in
the ancient world.[1] When Demosthenes was asked, "What is the most
important thing in speaking?" he replied that the first most important
thing is delivery, also the second most important, also the third.[2] A
variation of the saying has Demosthenes equating delivery and
rhetoric.[3] The importance of delivery was widely stressed in antiquity.
Athanasius states that Theophrastus, who succeeded Aristotle as the
head of his philosophical school, considered delivery to be the greatest
factor in an orator's ability to persuade.[4] Theophrastus' own delivery
was quite spirited. He is said to have made use of every kind of motion
and gesture in presenting his discourses.[5] The philosopher Philodemus also maintains that delivery is the most important part of
rhetoric. Good delivery, he says, "lends dignity to the speaker, secures
the attention of the audience, and sways their emotions."[6] Cicero held
to the same position, and in his dialogue, *De oratore*, he has Crassus,
who generally represents his own views, state, "Delivery, I assert, is
the dominant factor in oratory; without delivery the best speaker cannot be of any account at all, and a moderate speaker with a trained
delivery can often outdo the best of them."[7] In the *Orator* Cicero
states, describing the importance of gestures and facial expression:
"Many poor speakers have often reaped the rewards of eloquence
because of a dignified delivery, and many eloquent men have been
considered poor speakers because of awkward delivery."[8] Quintilian
makes much the same point, noting that the power of good delivery
can be seen in the theater, where even worthless authors can be transformed into an interesting performance.[9] Without appropriate
expression, he states, words are wasted.[10]

One of the most eloquent statements of the importance of delivery
is ironically found in an oration of Isocrates, the first "orator" who

composed written speeches that he himself did not deliver. That he was
well aware of the disadvantage at which this placed him is evident from
a written "oration" that he sent to be read to Philip of Macedonia:

> And yet I do not fail to realize what a great difference there is in
> persuasiveness between discourses which are spoken and those
> which are to be read. . . . For when a discourse is robbed of the
> prestige of the speaker, the tones of his voice, the variations
> which are made in the delivery, . . . and when someone reads it
> aloud without persuasiveness and without putting any personal
> feeling into it, but as though he were repeating a table of fig-
> ures,—in these circumstances it is natural, I think, that it should
> make an indifferent impression upon its hearers. And these are
> the very circumstances which may detract most seriously also
> from the discourse which is now presented to you and cause it
> to impress you as a very indifferent performance; the more so
> since I have not adorned it with the rhythmic flow and manifold
> graces of style which I myself employed when I was younger
> and taught by example to others as a means by which they
> might make their oratory more pleasing and at the same time
> more convincing.[11]

Although the importance of delivery was recognized as early as Aristotle,[12] the writer of the handbook *Rhetorica ad Herennium* could claim in
the first century B.C.E. that no one had written carefully on rhetoric
before. In this, he is mistaken, since Theophrastus wrote a work on
delivery in the early third century B.C.E.[13] But the consideration of
delivery did not become a matter of course in the rhetorical handbooks before *Ad Herennium*. The reason for this lack of attention,
according to this author, was not the lack of recognizing its importance but the difficulty of the undertaking: "All have thought it
scarcely possible to describe clearly in writing things pertaining to
voice, countenance, and gesture."[14]

If the Gospels were recited aloud, it would be fair to say that the
impact they made on their audiences would be just as tied to the manner in which they were delivered. Nevertheless, delivery has received
relatively little attention in studies of the Gospels. Rhetoric and
recitations are communal activities. The meaning of any oral performance is found only in that communal context as it is presented by the

performer and as it is received by the audience. Delivery is the art of filling the lifeless words on a scroll with fire and life and emotion. Orations may later be studied privately as models of style, but the written oration is a museum piece, deprived of the breath that gives it life and the situation that gives it meaning.[15] The same is true of most literature in the Hellenistic world. It was published orally. It was read communally. It was inherently a community affair. As Cicero says when referring his readers to his written speeches, books lack the breath of life, and most passages of a speech are more impressive when spoken than when read.[16]

We cannot be entirely sure of the way in which the Gospel would have been delivered. It is possible, however, to make some informed conjectures by examining what we know about the expected approach to various related categories of oral presentation.

Emotion and the Voice

The importance of delivery was directly tied to the importance placed on emotion in ancient rhetoric and verbal art. The rhetorical hand-books generally divide delivery into two topics, the use of the voice and movement of the body or gesture.[17] This division goes back as far as Theophrastus, one of the first to write on the subject of delivery.[18] According to Plutarch, Theophrastus called hearing the most emotional of all the senses. "For nothing," Plutarch explains, "which can be seen or tasted or touched brings on such distractions, confusions, and excitements, as take possession of the soul when certain crashing, clashing, and roaring noises assail the hearing".[19] Plutarch himself takes issue with this position, arguing that hearing is more rational than emotional, since it is only through hearing that one can receive instruction.[20] It is significant that Plutarch does not consider sight a possible vehicle for instruction. Reading to oneself is not considered a way of receiving instruction, even in Plutarch's highly literate circle. Instruction comes through speech. Quintilian, recognizing the importance of gesture in delivery, presents a statement similar to that of Theophrastus, but includes sight as well as sound as a means of emotional expression. "All delivery . . . is concerned with two different things, namely, voice and gesture, of which the one appeals to the eye and the other to the ear, the two senses by which all emotion reaches the soul."[21]

The voice was considered the perfect instrument for moving the emotions. According to Cicero, this is the result of the close connection between the tone of voice and the emotions:

> There are as many variations in the tones of the voice as there are in feelings, which are especially aroused by the voice. Accordingly the perfect orator . . . will use certain tones according as he wishes to seem himself to be moved and to sway the minds of his audience.[22]

Rhythm and words have an ability to rouse excitement, smooth and calm us, to create mirth or sorrow.[23] Cicero compares the orator's use of his voice and gesture to the strings of a lyre:

> For nature has assigned to every emotion a particular look and tone of voice and bearing of its own; and the whole of a person's frame and every look on his face and utterance of his voice are like the strings of a harp, and sound according as they are struck by each successive emotion.[24]

The author of *On the Sublime* also makes use of a musical metaphor when describing the power of the voice to move people. He finds the power of the voice in the combination of the feeling induced by the sound itself with the meaning conveyed by the words.

> Does not the flute, for instance, induce certain emotions in those who hear it? Does it not seem to carry them away and fill them with divine frenzy? It sets a particular rhythmic movement and forces them to move in rhythm. The hearer has to conform to the tune, though he may be utterly unmusical. Why, the very tones of the harp, themselves meaningless, by the variety of their sounds and by their mutual pulsation and harmonious blending often exercise, as you know, a marvelous spell. Yet these are only a bastard counterfeit of persuasion, not, as I said above, a genuine activity of human nature. We hold, then, that composition, which is a kind of melody in words—words which are part of man's nature and reach not his ears only but his very soul-stirring as it does myriad ideas of words, thoughts, things, beauty, musical charm, all of which are born and bred in us; while, moreover, by the blending of its own manifold tones

it brings into the hearts of the bystanders the speaker's actual emotion so that all who hear him share in it, and by piling phrase on phrase builds up on majestic whole—we hold, I say, that by these very means it casts a spell on us and always turns **our** thoughts towards what is majestic and dignified and sublime and all else that it embraces, winning a complete mastery over our minds.[25]

Delivery and Emotion

Even before Aristotle, delivery was associated with emotion. One of the earliest works on rhetorical delivery is the lost work of Thrasymachus, *Appeals to Pity*.[26] Aristotle himself defines delivery as a matter of the voice and how it should be used in the expression of each emotion.[27] Concerning the expression of suffering, he says:

Since sufferings are pitiable when they appear close at hand . . . , it follows that those who contribute to the effect by gestures, voice, dress, and delivery generally, are more pitiable; for they make the evil appear close at hand, setting it before our eyes as either future or past.[28]

Delivery is effective because through it the speaker re-creates the pitiable situation. It is the reality of the re-creation that produces the emotion.

Longinus defines delivery, or *hypokrisis*, as "the representation of the true character and emotions of each person and the disposition of the body and the tone of voice which is suited to the matters set before one."[29] Philodemus also mentions the ability to sway the emotions as one of reasons why delivery is important.[30] "Much of delivery," he states, "is the natural and unconscious bodily expression of the emotions."[31] Cicero agreed as well:

Clever ideas frequently outfly the understanding of people who are not clever, whereas delivery, which gives the emotion of the mind expression, influences everybody, for the same emotions are felt by all people and they both recognize them in others and manifest them in themselves by the same marks.[32]

The main point of delivery in Cicero's presentation of the subject in the *De oratore* is the expression of emotion.[33] The whole of a speaker's body and voice are employed in the expression of emotion. He mentions a speech given by Gracchus that he delivered "with such effective glances and tone of voice and gestures that even his enemies could not restrain their tears."[34] The passionate style that Cicero says is most effective in swaying an audience needs a diction that is rich, diversified, and full, and an animated delivery to match it. Concise or quiet speakers may inform a judge but not excite him.[35] Quintilian also emphasized that the emotional force of a speech depends more on delivery as composition: "All emotional appeals will inevitably fall flat, unless they are given the fire that voice, look, and the whole carriage of the body can give them."[36]

The connection between believable emotion and delivery is emphasized in a story told of Demosthenes:

> A story is told of a man coming to him and begging his services as advocate, and telling him at great length how he had been assaulted and beaten by some one. "But certainly," said Demosthenes, "you got none of the hurts which you describe." Then the man raised his voice and shouted: "I, Demosthenes, no hurts?" "Now, indeed," said Demosthenes, "I hear the voice of one who is wronged." So important in winning credence did he consider the tone and action of the speaker.[37]

Cicero even recounts a case in which he used a speaker's lack of emotional delivery as an argument against his case. Marcus Calidius had charged Quintus Gallius with plotting to poison him. There was a great deal of evidence against Gallius, which Calidius laid out in a clear, logical manner. Apparently sensing that emotional appeal was better than discussion of facts, Cicero attacked Calidius for his delivery:

> Come now, Marcus Calidius, would you present your case in that way if it were not all a figment of your imagination? And that eloquence of yours, which you have always used so vigorously for the defense of others, is it credible that you should fail to invoke it for your own? What trace of anger, of that burning indignation, which stirs even men quite incapable of eloquence to loud outbursts of complaint against wrongs? But no hint of agitation in you, neither of mind nor of body. Did you smite

your brow, slap your thigh, or at least stamp your foot? No. In fact, so far from touching my feelings, I could scarcely refrain from going to sleep then and there.[38]

Both stories indicate the connection between emotional appeal and credibility in the ancient world. Certainly there were variations in how much speakers appealed to the emotions, and Cicero was an emotional speaker. Still, his argument is effective because it addresses a cultural value. A speaker was not believable if he was not emotional. For the Gospels to be credible, then, the performer would have to present them in an emotional manner. Otherwise, they could be dismissed as quaint stories.

Reading, Speaking, and Acting

The dividing line between acting, oratory, and recitation was not clear. The same Greek word, *hypokrisis*, was used for acting on a stage, the delivery of an oration, and expressive reading.[39] The English words "hypocrite" and "hypocrisy" are derived from this source. When Jesus denounces his opponents as hypocrites, the Greek word is a form of the same root. Literally, Jesus is calling his opponents "actors."

According to Suetonius, Virgil's poems known as the *Eclogues* were frequently performed on stage by actors.[40] Servius says that the famous actress Cytheris performed one of the *Eclogues* and impressed Cicero with her rendition.[41] Suetonius describes Virgil's own delivery as follows:

His own delivery, however, was sweet and wonderfully effective. In fact, Seneca has said that the poet Julius Montanus used to declare that he would have purloined some of Virgil's work, if he could also have stolen his voice, expression, and delivery *[hypokrisin]*; for the same verses sounded well when Virgil read them, which on another's lips were flat and toneless.[42]

Demosthenes, the greatest of the Athenian orators, had studied with a famous actor.[43] According to Plutarch, the young Cicero also attended the theater to study the delivery of the most famous actors of his time, Aesopus and Roscius.[44] Valerius Maximus describes how the same two actors attended speeches of the orator Hortensius in order to study his gestures for their own use on stage.[45] Quintilian brought comic actors to his school to train his students in the delivery of narrative so they might learn how to express such things as "the authoritative tone that should be given to advice, the excitement which should mark the rise of anger, and the change of tone that is characteristic of pathos."[46] Nevertheless, he makes it clear in another place that oratory should be more restrained in tone than the comic theater.[47] The concern with distinguishing oratory from acting was probably due at least in part to class distinctions. Most orators came from the aristocratic classes, and aristocrats were supposed to be moderate and self-controlled in character.[48] The comic theater, on the other hand, often depicted exaggerated behavior, especially when portraying lower-class characters. The close connection between reading and acting styles is indicated by Quintilian's warning that the speeches of characters in narrative are not to be read "in the manner of comic actors," as some teachers instruct.[49] Thus, while Quintilian advocates a more restrained reading style, with some modulation of the voice, many students were likely to have learned to read in a fully dramatic style. Quintilian also had his students read histories to train them in emotional inflection.[50]

Philodemus stresses the connection between rhetorical delivery and delivery of other forms of literature. Both rhetoric and drama, he says, have a type of delivery proper to their own sphere. Poets and writers of prose also possess a theory of delivery even if they have not committed it to writing, as have the teachers of rhetoric.[51] In another place he states, "Each profession has its own peculiar delivery."[52] In fact, he argues, delivery is important in all branches of literature, and it is ridiculous to claim it is more important for rhetoric than for any other form of prose.[53] Actors, Philodemus says, consider delivery to be everything in their art.[54] In teaching delivery, the rhetors have not invented anything new. They have simply made plain what orators had always done.[55] He also reports that even the greatest orators had problems with their delivery. Demosthenes was criticized by Aeschines for his shrill voice and overly loud delivery, and by Demetrius of Phalerum for being overly theatrical rather than simple and noble in his delivery.[56]

Lucian also indicates a close connection between acting and oratory. Both relied heavily on the ability to portray character:

The pantomime is above all an actor: that is his first aim, in the pursuit of which (as I have observed) he resembles the orator, and especially the composer of "declamations," whose success, as the pantomime knows, depends like his own upon verisimilitude, upon the adaptation of language to character: prince or tyrannicide, pauper or farmer, each must be shown with the peculiarities that belong to him.[57]

As Lucian indicates, in declamation the distinction between actor and orator was especially blurred since the declaimer often spoke as if he were the person involved in the case. Declaimers were praised for their success in representing the character of the person successfully.[58] Quintilian says that even comic actors do not have to play as many roles as do orators in their declamations.[59] In Lucian's own career the distinction between acting and oratorical delivery was especially blurred. Lucian began as an orator and later took up the presentation of satirical dialogues. In a dialogue the narration is presented only through the speech of the characters, and the performer is always in character rather than speaking in his own voice.[60]

Delivery in School

There is general agreement among ancient writers that students should be taught to read and recite with expression.[61] Quintilian says teachers should give instruction on proper delivery, including where to breathe, where to pause, how to divide sense, when to raise or lower the voice, the modulation given to each phrase, when to increase or slacken speed, and when to speak with greater or less energy.[62] It was understood that there was a direct relationship between the delivery learned in the earlier stages of education and oratorical delivery. Theon, an author of a book of exercises used in the intermediate level of education, indicates the connection this way: "For one who has recited narrative and fable correctly and in a variety of ways will also narrate well history and that which is called the narrative proper in a legal speech. For a history is nothing other than a composite narrative."[63] The style of delivery practiced in the rhetorical school is simply a continuation of the style of delivery learned in the earlier stages of education. For this reason Quintilian recommends that practice in reading history and oratory be continued in the early stages of training in the rhetorical school.[64]

There were a number of different styles of reading poetry, the material with which students began (usually Homer or Virgil). Quintilian criticizes, on the one hand, reading poetry in a singsong voice or "the effeminate modulations now in vogue" and, on the other, expressing character too strongly in speeches, "as it is by the comic actor." In contrast, he prefers reading with dignity and charm, indicating by some modulation of the voice the difference between speeches and passages where the poet speaks as narrator.[65]

As soon as they were able, students of rhetoric were made to memorize passages of speeches and deliver them "standing in the manner which actual pleading would require."[66] At least in the Latin system of education, *grammatice*, the teachers of literature included instruction in declamation in character and deliberative themes.[67] Quintilian says that in the Greek system such instruction was reserved for the teacher of rhetoric.[68] This is not the case, however, since the surviving Greek *progymnasmata*, the books that provided a series of elementary rhetorical exercises for use in schools at this level, include speeches in character and simple deliberative exercises. Theon, the author of one such book, mentions the importance of learning delivery at this level of education. Concluding a passage in which he encourages teachers to develop each student's natural abilities, he says, "Finally, one must attempt to learn thoroughly the delivery proper to each kind of discourse."[69] He gives no directions for the teaching of delivery, but one presumes the teacher would correct the students' delivery of each of the exercises included in the book.

Exercises in speaking in character, termed *prosōpopoiia*, are found in several of the *progymnasmata*.[70] Theon, writing in the first century C.E., defines *prosōpopoiia* as the representation of a person speaking words suitable to himself and to the suggested circumstances. He gives as typical examples a husband speaking to his wife before departing on a journey and a general speaking to his troops before a battle.[71] By the time of Aphthonius, writing in the late fourth or early fifth century C.E., the exercise of speech in character had developed a number of subdivisions, one set of which was divided in terms of the emphasis on emotion or on character (a variation known as *ēthopoiia*). The model of characterization that Aphthonius includes in his *Progymnasmata* is quite melodramatic; though it is considerably later than the time of the writing of the Gospels, it is not unlikely that the same emphasis on the emotional characterization would be found in the first century as well. The assignment is to present words appropriate for Niobe after the murder of her children. The first portion of the example is as follows:

Childless now, who seemed blest with many children before, what kind of fortune am I exchanging for others? And the great number has become a want and I have become the mother of not a single child, I who appeared to be the foremost of many in this regard, so that it was better to have lacked the power to give birth than to give birth for tears! Those robbed [of children] are more unfortunate than those not giving birth, for through the rivalry [with Leto] I have come to a grievous loss.[72]

Such a speech could hardly have been presented without extremely emotional inflection and a great deal of histrionic gesturing.

Popular Style

There were a number of competing approaches to rhetoric in the first century. Quintilian was a conservative when it came to oratorical style. He complains often about the contemporary style, which he sometimes calls popular. In his mind, this style played too much to the uneducated tastes of the people. "Others," he says, "revel in the voluptuous and affected style of today, in which everything is designed to charm the ears of the uneducated majority."[73] This may be taken as disparagement of a style that the rhetor opposed—for a man of Quintilian's upper-class tastes, appeal to the uneducated was to be despised. But he is probably correct in assuming that the more florid style of contemporary orators had a more popular following in the first century.

It is doubtful that the rhetorical taste of Mark and his audience was as refined as that of Quintilian, let alone as conservative. We are much more likely to find indications of their taste in Quintilian's admonitions against common failings that he tells his students to avoid. The refined style of Quintilian is emotional and theatrical by contemporary American standards, but the popular style was even more so. Quintilian suggests that many people, especially among the lower classes, preferred extreme vigor in rhetorical delivery. He characterizes the approach of such orators as follows:

They shout on all and every occasion and bellow their every utterance "with uplifted hand," to use their own phrase, dashing this way and that, panting, gesticulating wildly and wagging their heads with all the frenzy of a lunatic. Smite your hands together, stamp the ground, slap your thigh, your breast, your forehead, and you will go straight to the heart of the dingier members of your audience.[74]

Some of Quintilian's other complaints also suggest that orators often presented their material with extreme vehemence. He criticizes those who begin deliberative themes in a wild and exclamatory manner, beginning with a shriek and keeping their presentation at one high level of violence.[75] In another place he criticizes those who "feel that they have fallen short of eloquence, if they do not make everything echo with noise and clamour."[76] In particular, they are cited for "affected modulations of the voice, throwing back their heads, thumping their sides, and indulging in every kind of extravagance of statement, language, and style."[77] Quintilian also criticizes orators who perform too much like actors, with affected delivery having annoyingly restless gestures and too frequent changes in vocal tone.[78]

In another place, Quintilian records a jest made at the expense of a pleader who kept rushing back and forth, waving his hands, and letting his toga fall and replacing it.[79] He cautions against mere violence and noise when debating and such forms of pleasantry that appeal to the uneducated.[80] The popular style also included frequent pronouncements of quivering and passionate epigrams.[81]

The bombastic style of much oratory is mentioned, generally critically, by many writers. According to Plutarch, Cicero complained of orators who resorted to much loud shouting, jesting that they were led by their weakness to resort to clamor as cripples were to mount upon a horse.[82] Tacitus, complaining about the rhetoricians' schools, says, "Then, in addition to the subject-matter that is so remote from real life, there is the bombastic style in which it is presented."[83] Quintilian also criticizes the type of eloquence, resulting from the practice of making declamations for show, that regarded the pleasure given by a delicate and polished style to be more important than the persuasiveness of the speech and for that reason avoided harsh and forcible argumentation when such was necessary.[84] Quintilian repeatedly makes the point that the most important part of the orator's art is to make sure that his art is not detected and that his speech sounds natural rather than artificial.[85] The frequent repetition of the rule suggests that it was frequently broken and that the popular style delighted in artificial extravagance.

The Delivery of Mark

We shall consider in much greater detail the use of gestures in the delivery of Mark in the later chapters devoted to those subjects. In the present chapter, we will only make some comments on the general style of delivery. In recreating a Markan performance, one must first decide on the general tone of the narration. The rhetorical handbooks traditionally introduced three styles of speech: the plain style, the grand or forcible, and the intermediate. The plain was the simplest, both in terms of wording and delivery, while the grand or forcible is the most extravagant in its figures of speech and delivery, which Quintilian compares to a great torrent, carving its own banks through the rocks. Quintilian suggests that the plain style is more suited to instruction, while the forcible is more suited to moving the emotions.[86] One's reconstruction of the Markan performance hinges first of all on a determination of whether the Markan narrative is intended primarily as instruction or as drama, as addressing the intellect or the emotions. Mark's Greek is certainly too rough to qualify as the grand or forcible style when judged by the likes of Quintilian. Since Mark was probably not capable of writing anything Quintilian would regard as grand, a text in which figures of speech are generally restricted to the utterances of Jesus does not mean that the mode of delivery would have matched the plain style. In fact, it is hard to imagine a more grand subject matter in the minds of early Christians, and we have seen that the narration is full of forceful emotion. My own reconstruction sees emotion as a primary determinate of the meaning of the Gospel in its original setting.

Quintilian does not provide much practical information about how the forceful style is delivered. Instead, he provides a flood of metaphors:

> But he whose eloquence is like to some great torrent that rolls down rocks and "disdains a bridge" and carves out its own banks for itself, will sweep the judge from his feet, struggle as he may, and force him to go whither he bears him. . . . This is he that will inspire anger or pity, and while he speaks the judge will call upon the gods and weep, following him wherever he sweeps him from one emotion to another. . . . When [Homer] seeks to express the supreme gift of eloquence possessed by Ulysses, he gives a mighty voice and a vehemence of oratory equal to the

snows of winter in the abundance and vigour of its words. . . . It
is this force and impetuosity that Eupolis admires in Pericles,
this that Aristophanes compares to the thunderbolt, this that is
the power of true eloquence.[87]

It is unlikely that any performer of Mark had the oratorical power of a
Pericles, but not many of Quintilian's students did either. It is more of
an ideal that speakers strive for and only approximate to the best of
their ability.

Stereotyped Characters

We can understand something of the presentation of characters in the
Gospels from the presentation of characters in comic drama. This is
the form of drama that rhetoricians found closest to the style of oratory. That would also make it the closest to storytelling or a narrative
recitation. Characters in comic dramas were quite stereotyped. Most
forms of drama, including tragedy, comedy, and pantomime, were
performed by masked actors. The masks had a fixed, often exaggerated, emotional expression. In comedy, fathers sometimes wore masks
that had one eyebrow raised, indicating excitement, and one eyebrow
normal, for calmer scenes. The placement of the actors on the stage
was designed so that the father would have the appropriate side of the
mask facing the audience.[88] Pantomime masks were relatively realistic,
while comic and tragic masks were not.[89] There were a limited number of mask types, and one could recognize the nature of the character
from the mask. For example, there are masks for slaves, young men,
fathers, pimps, parasites, mothers, courtesans, and virgins. A virgin,
for example, has hair smoothed down with a part, straight and dark
brows, and a pale, slightly ochre complexion. A pseudovirgin, on the
other hand, had a paler complexion, binds her hair around the top of
her head, and looks like a newlywed. A mature courtesan is redder
than the pseudovirgin and has curls around the ears.[90] This system of
masks helps the audience to recognize characters immediately. While
it may take the characters most of the play to figure out that the virgin
is not really as she seems, the audience knows from the mask. In art
there are frequent representations of actors or playwrights contem-
plating masks.[91] Both actors and playwrights would likely assimilate
their own emotions to the emotion of the mask so that their characters would be in keeping with the mask type.

The stereotyped masks can be seen in the comic scene shown in figure 1. The figure on the far right wears the mask of a slave, while the figure next to him wears that of a young man. Generally in comedy, the slave takes the part of the young man against his master, the young man's father. In this scene the son is obviously upset with the slave. The two figures on the left wear masks of older men. The one on the far left is restraining the one closer to the son and the slave. In conventional plots this likely represents the father being restrained by a friend. Since the two character groups are not interacting, they may not be aware of each other's presence. In addition to the conventional masks, some characters had stereotyped costumes and ways of walking or carrying their bodies. This is most apparent in the slave. Slaves characteristically wore a short tunic. The slave is shown in a servile posture of cringing before the son. He is also shown with his feet wide apart, which was considered undignified. The son has his feet closer together, indicating greater dignity. Both older men have their feet

Roman bas-relief of a comedy scene. Copyright Scala/Art Resource, NY. Museo Archeologico Nazionale, Naples, Italy.

apart as well. In the case of the father, it indicates that he is beginning to move in the direction of the figures on the right, but the wide stance of both figures suggest lack of dignity, and it is likely that they are making fools of themselves. Slaves are typically shown as moving more quickly than free persons.[92] Dignified people could afford to move slowly. Slaves had to hurry to fulfill their masters' orders. The short cloak, besides being undignified, allowed the slave to run with less restraint. The boy playing the aulos, or flute, in the center is not masked and may be providing accompaniment rather than being a character in the play. None of the characters is paying attention to him, nor are any of them dancing.

The stereotyped mask, costume, and expression of characters in comic drama meant that characters were restricted to rather narrow ranges of expression. There were a limited number of character types with fixed ways of speaking, moving, and expressing themselves. Such an approach to character corresponds well with the characters found in the Gospels, most of whom play roles and have few if any individual characteristics. We would expect them to be presented in stereotyped ways, just as characters on the comic stage.

Voices and Dialogue

From all the evidence of delivery styles taught in schools and practiced by both actors and orators, we would expect the dialogue in Mark to be spoken as if the various characters themselves were speaking, at least to the extent that emotional inflection would reflect the character's meaning and emotional state. Actual voices may have been imitated as well, at least to suggest men and women, and perhaps giving different degrees of dignity to various voices. When speakers are not specifically named, it would only be by the inflection of the voice that the audience could determine transition from narrative to quotation. Thus the inflection of characters' speeches would be of great importance to the audience, so that they might distinguish dialogue from narrative and who is speaking within dialogue.[93] We do not have much material to indicate the particular types of voices that would be considered appropriate to different characters. Quintilian suggests that an actor playing a woman spoke shrilly; one playing an old man affected a trembling voice.[94] There is a suggestion of the proper tone for a demon in Philostratus' *Life of Apollonius*, where he describes a boy possessed by the ghost of a soldier. The boy speaks not in his own voice but with a deep and hollow voice like a man.[95] Another demon-possessed youth laughs and weeps for no reason and sings to himself. His laughter is loud enough to drown out Apollonius's voice. When Apollonius stares at him, he begins "to utter cries of fear and rage, such as one hears from people who are being branded or racked."[96] This suggests that demons speak in voices like humans, but are often loud, and their cries as they are expelled should reflect extremes of pain and terror.

Variation in Delivery

What Aristotle says about the variation necessary in the delivery in speeches of repetitious material or of sentences without the normal connecting words used in Greek gives us some insight into the approach to delivery appropriate to passages that present many events in rapid succession, such as Mark 1:29–45.[97] Because repetitious phrases can be delivered with various tones, he says, they do not sound the same when spoken. Similarly, a varied delivery would give variety to the repeated healings in this section of the Gospel. Aristotle says that sentences without the normal connecting words make one thing seem to be many, and if there may be many things to say, they impress hearers as being more important. This makes the material more memorable, but it is ineffective without the help of varied delivery to give the sense of a variety of distinct things. Mark may be taking a similar approach in this passage. Many short healing stories are more impressive and memorable than one extended episode, and the performer would rely on varied delivery to create in performance the impression of plurality.

Narrative Speed

The rhetorical handbooks say the pace of the narration should match the pace of the events. This means, for example, that the beginning of the Gospel of Mark, with the frequent repetitions of "and immediately" both within and between episodes, would probably have been narrated at an accelerated pace to create the impression of many events happening within a short time. In the first chapter Mark has been sparing in his use of detail in order to create that effect. The baptism of Jesus is narrated in three verses (with one *euthus* "immediately," 1:10), the temptation in two (with one "immediately," 1:12), the preaching of Jesus in two (1:14–15). The call of Simon and

Andrew comprises three verses (with one "immediately," 1:18); the call of James and John in two (one "immediately," 1:20). The healing of Simon's mother-in-law consists of three verses with two repetitions of "immediately" (in the Greek, 1:29–31), and many people are healed in the next three verses. The ensuing discussion between Simon and Jesus happens quite early, while it is still night, as immediately as possibly allowing for a night's sleep, and is compressed into two verses (1:37–38). All of this suggests that the performer would relate these events quickly but not rush the delivery so much that the clarity of the narration would be lost.

In the midst of this rush of narrated events, there is the more extended account of the preaching of Jesus at Capernaum, which consists of eight verses (1:21–28). There is still much happening in a short period of time, and there are three repetitions of "immediately" in those verses to present a rapid pace. Nevertheless, there are a number of features of the episode that slow down the delivery. The first is the comparative length of the episode. A narrator can get through two or three verses with a minimum of pause, so that the whole episode may be heard as a single event. A longer episode requires more time to breathe. The greater detail also requires more shifts in tone as the narrator adapts his voice to each occurrence. The second aspect of the episode that slows narration is the use of a great deal of direct address. Direct address is presented with the inflection appropriate to the speaker. Narration of direct address requires that the speaker pause before each quotation, both for the sake of clarity, so that the audience perceives what is the speech of a narrative character, and so that he can adjust his tone for the voice of each speaker. The demon-possessed man has one voice; Jesus has another; the wondering crowd has a third. This is by far the most complex presentation of direct address in the first forty verses of the Gospel. Many of the other events have no direct address at all (the temptation, the second call story, the healing of Simon's mother-in-law, the healing of many in the evening), and this is one of the factors that allows for the rapid unfolding of events. The nature of the direct address in this episode also slows delivery. The speech of both the demoniac and the crowd consists of a number of short statements or questions. Since the narrator must pause at the end of each statement or question, it takes a relatively long time to get through a small number of words. The third factor that slows down the delivery of the passage is the number of shifts in emotional tone. Each shift in emotional tone requires a shift in voice inflection. The narrator has to readjust his voice and likely makes a brief pause between each section to provide some clarity for the audience. This shift in narrative speed in the episode at the synagogue tends to set the episode apart from the rest of the events and provide it with special significance in the experience of the audience.

Another way that Mark emphasizes this episode is through the emotional intonation in the direct address. Because direct address is given the voice and intonation appropriate to the narrative speaker, it necessarily stands out from the flow of the narration and draws attention to itself. The interchange between the demon-possessed man and Jesus further stands out because it is loud and forceful. The demoniac cries out; Jesus rebukes the demon. As the scene is presented, the demoniac suddenly bursts into the consciousness of the synagogue audience that has been absorbed in their evaluation of Jesus. According to the rules of narrative presented in the rhetorical handbooks, the surprising effect of the demoniac's outburst should be reproduced by the narrator. The effect is to startle the audience hearing the Gospel. Anyone whose thoughts are wandering is brought back to the narrative.

Everything Mark has done to provide narrative emphasis for the episode tends to emphasize the content as well. The audience hears clearly the demon's shouted identification of Jesus as the Holy One of God. They also hear the comments about Jesus' authority and the questions about his identity. These are the primary themes of the first chapters. The second extended episode, the healing of the paralytic (2:1–11), emphasizes the same themes, the authority and identity of Jesus. Mark uses the shifts in narrative speed to emphasize the material that provides the audience with an understanding of the meaning of the narrative.

Imitative Sound Effects

We have seen that in Plato's day rhapsodes included a great deal of imitative sound effects into their performances. The rhetorical handbooks do not refer to such effects, which would be considered out of place in oratory. I expect one would be more likely to find sound effects in storytelling. It is possible that such sound effects were used in a performance of Mark. Certainly the storm scenes (4:35–41; 6:45–52) lend themselves to such effects. Jesus' command to the storm, "Hush! Be silent!" (4:39, author) is quite effective, with plenty of storm noise preceding it. Notice that the commands are related to the noise of the storm rather than the power of the wind itself. The verb *epitimaō* generally translated "rebuke," is repeatedly used by Mark to indicate silencing someone (silencing demons, 3:12; silencing the storm, 4:39; silencing Bartimeaus, 10:48; preventing the disciples from speaking, 8:30; silencing Peter, 8:33; after Peter may have tried to prevent Jesus from speaking more about the crucifixion, 8:32). Both details suggest that the audience would be experiencing the storm aurally.

I have tried presenting the stilling of the storm scene with sound effects and some rocking and cringing to indicate the storm and the disciples' fear. It creates a much stronger contrast between the disciples' fear and Jesus calmly asleep on his pillow, which I indicate by lack of noise and leaning my head peacefully on my folded hands. The storm noise also allows one to indicate clearly the storm's obedience to Jesus by the cessation of the rocking and storm sounds. I usually allow the storm a few halfhearted puffs before it quiets completely. I have found that such a presentation tends to create a comic effect because the contrast between the disciples' fear and Jesus' calm control becomes so stark. It also speeds up the audience's recognition that the disciples are not understanding all that well. Use of storm sounds in both storm scenes helps to tie the scenes much more closely together. While an audience may miss the connection between the scenes from the verbal clues alone, the repetition of the distinctive sound effects tends to create an expectation: "Here we go again."

I believe that the comic effect of the first storm scene may in fact be intended. It is easy to play the disciples for comic effect from chapter 4 through the recognition scene in chapter 8. The repetitive nature of the two feeding stories (6:33–44; 8:1–10) makes the disciples' response in the second scene, "How can one feed these people with bread here in the desert?" sound quite ludicrous, especially if it is presented with great perplexity. The ludicrous nature of the situation is underlined by the use of nearly identical lines for Jesus' response to their confused questioning in both scenes, followed by a great deal of verbal repetition of the first scene in the remainder of the second.[98] Repetition is much more apparent in oral performance because one tends to use the same gestures and the same inflection of the voice for similar lines. Thus the audience has both visual and auditory clues that indicate repetition.[99]

Once the audience has decided that the disciples are comic, the other scenes of misunderstanding tend to be perceived that way as well. If an audience has perceived the disciples' question about bread in the second feeding story as comic, it follows that in the third boat scene (8:14–21) their confusion about having no bread will be seen as comic as well. That makes the seriousness of the scene including the disciples' recognition of Jesus, the first passion prediction, Jesus' rebuke of Peter, and the speech about discipleship (8:27–9:1), stand out much more strongly by contrast. Modern audiences certainly vary greatly in the extent to which they are ready to see comedy in the Gospel. I expect that first-century audiences, who had not yet developed such an awe of the Gospel, would be somewhat more ready to see comic effects.

Another place I have tried sound effects in the narrative is in the scene of Herod's birthday banquet (6:21–28). Recently I have provided Herod's daughter with a little dancing music as well as a mock belly dance. "There's a Place in France," sounding like a cartoon snake charmer's flute, works quite well and completely deflates Herodian pomposity. Judging by the type of dancing that was the norm for dinner parties, a lascivious dance is to be imagined here whether it is performed or not. One would not expect a father to applaud a sexually suggestive dance by his daughter, but the whole scene is designed to show Herod's household as horrifically degenerate. The mother's suggestion to her daughter to ask for the head of John the Baptist certainly marks her as an unnatural mother. The daughter's idea of having the head served on a platter is grotesque even by first-century standards and flies in the face of the expected behavior of young maidens. I am unsure that a first-century Christian performer would indulge in my pseudolasciviousness, but most people enjoy being horrified by behavior of which they disapprove. The situation is similar to Republicans being horrified at Clinton's cigar or Democrats being horrified at Clarence Thomas's sexual innuendoes. In spite of their horror, both groups made sure each detail was presented to the nation as graphically as possible. An imitation of a more restrained female dance with some mock piping would probably create the same comic effect.

A comic dance sets the proper tone for Herod's party, since the king's brash offer to give his daughter anything she wants is clearly a ridiculous, though sick, response to her dancing. The ridiculous nature of the response is underlined by Herod's repetition of the offer in an even more extreme form. I have found it natural to present Herod as extremely boastful and considerably more than half drunk. The comic rendition of Herod's degenerate party increases the horror of John's beheading since it stresses the frivolous way in which it came about. The cold demand for John's head contrasts forcefully with the earlier silly tone; it allows the audience to experience some of the shock that Herod felt at the demand. That in turn makes Herod's weakness all the more apparent.

Notes

1. For delivery in ancient rhetoric, see Robert P. Sonkowsky, "An Aspect of Delivery in Ancient Rhetorical Theory," *TAPA* 90 (1959): 256–74; Ray Nadeau, "Delivery in Ancient Times: Homer to Quintilian," *QJS* 50 (1964): 53–60; Elaine Fantham, "Quintilian on Performance: Traditional and Personal Elements in *Institutio* 11.3," *Phoenix* 36 (1982): 243–63; Andrea G. Katsouris [Andreas G. Katsourēs], Ῥητορικὴ Ὑποκρίση [Oratorical delivery] (Iōannina, Greece: Panepist mio I annin n, 1989); Georg Wöhrle, "*Actio:* Das fünfte *officium* des antiken Redners," *Gym* 97 (1990): 31–46; Thomas H. Olbricht, "Delivery and Memory," in *Handbook of Classical Rhetoric in the Hellenistic Period, 330 B.C.–A.D. 400* (ed. S. E. Porter; Leiden: E. J. Brill, 1997), 159–67. For interpretive reading, Eugene Bahn, "Interpretive Reading in Ancient Greece," *QJS* 18 (1932): 432-40; Eugene Bahn and Margaret L. Bahn, *A History of Oral Interpretation* (Minneapolis: Burgess, 1970), 1–46.

On the delivery of the Gospel in modern times, see Thomas E. Boomershine, *Story Journey: An Invitation to the Gospel as Storytelling* (two audiocassettes; Nashville: Abingdon, 1988; available at NOBS Business Office, Becky Schram, Office Manager, 1810 Harvard Blvd., Dayton OH 45406); David Rhoads, "Performing the Gospel of Mark," in *Body and Bible: Interpreting and Experiencing Biblical Narratives* (ed. B. Krondorfer; Philadelphia: Trinity Press International, 1992); Elizabeth Struthers Malbon, *Hearing Mark: A Listener's Guide* (Harrisburg, Penn.: Trinity Press International, 2002).

2. Repeated in Cicero, *De or.* 3.56.213; *Or. Brut.* 17.56; *Brut.* 142; Plutarch, *[Vit. X orat.]* 845B; Philodemus, *Rhet.* 1.196.3 XVa; Valerius Maximus *Fact. dict.* 8.10.3; Quintilian, *Inst.* 11.3.6.

3. Theon, *Prog.* 3.256–258 (Butts ed.).

4. Athanasius, *Prolegonemon* 552 (Rabe, 177; Walz, 6:35–36); cited by George Kennedy, *The Art of Persuasion in Greece* (Princeton: Princeton University Press, 1963), 283.

5. Athenaeus, *Deipn.* 1.a–b.

6. Philodemus, *Rhet.* 1.193, XIa.

7. Cicero, *De or.* 3.54.213 (Sutton/Rackham, LCL).

8. Cicero, *Or. Brut.* 17.56.

9. Quintilian, *Inst.* 11.3.4.

10. Quintilian, *Inst.* 11.3.152.

11. Isocrates, *Or.* 5.25–27 (Norlin, LCL).

12. Aristotle, *Rhet.* 3.1.3–7.

13. Diogenes Laertius, *De vita* 5.48.

14. *Rhet. Her.* 3.11.19.

15. For scepticism about the written word in general, see Loveday Alexander, "The Living Voice: Scepticism towards the Written Word in Early Christian and in Graeco-Roman Texts," in *The Bible in Three Dimensions: Essays in Celebration of Forty Years of Biblical Studies in the University of Sheffield* (ed. D. J. A. Clines, S. E. Fowl, and S. E. Porter; JSOTSup 87; Sheffield: Sheffield Academic Press, 1990), 221–47.

16. Cicero, *Or. Brut.* 37.130.

17. Cicero, *Or. Brut.* 17.55; *Rhet. Her.* 3.11.19; Quintilian, *Inst.* 11.3.14.

18. Kennedy, *Art of Persuasion*, 283.

19. Plutarch, *Rect. rat. aud.* 2; 38a (Babbitt, LCL).

20. Plutarch, *Rect. rat. aud.* 2; 38a–d.

21. Quintilian, *Inst.* 11.3.14 (Butler, LCL).

22. Cicero, *Or. Brut.* 17.55.

23. Cicero, *De or.* 3.51.197.

24. Cicero, *De or.* 3.57.216.

25. Longinus, *[Subl.]* 39.2–3 (Fyfe, LCL).

26. Aristotle, *Rhet.* 3.1.7; 1404a.

27. Aristotle, *Rhet.* 2.1.4; 1403b.

28. Aristotle, *Rhet.* 2.8.14; 1386a (adapted from LCL).

29. Longinus, *Rhet.* (Walz 9.567 = Spengel-Hammer 1.2.194). Citation from William G. Rutherford, *A Chapter in the History of Annotation*, vol. 2 of *Scholia Aristophanica* (New York: Macmillan, 1905), 128, n. 7.

30. Philodemus, *Rhet.* 1.193, XIa.

31. Philodemus, *Rhet.* 1.195, XIVa (Hubbell).

32. Cicero, *De or.* 3.59.223 (Sutton/Rackham, LCL).

33. Cicero, *De or.* 3.57.215–3.58.219; cf. *De or.* 3.59.221: "Delivery is wholly the concern of the feelings."

34. Cicero, *De or.* 3.57.214 (Sutton/Rackham, LCL).

35. Cicero, *De or.* 2.53.214–215.

36. Quintilian, *Inst.* 11.3.2–9.

37. Plutarch, *Dem.* 11.2 (Perrin, LCL).

38. Cicero, *Brut.* 80.278 (Hendrickson, LCL).

39. Dionysius Thrax, *Ars gram.* 2, uses *hypokrisis* for inflection when reading. Dio Chrysostom uses *hypokrinasthai* for reading expressively (*Or.* 18.6). The use of that term for rhetorical delivery will be familiar to all readers of the Greek rhetorical handbooks. See also LSJ, ad loc.; Nadeau, "Delivery," 53.

40. Suetonius, *Poet.: Vita Verg.* 26.

41. Servius on Virgil, *Eclogues* 6.11. Citation from Kenneth Quinn, "The Poet and His Audience in the Augustan Age," *ANRW* 30.1:152–53.

42. Suetonius, *Poet.: Vita Verg.* 28–29 (adapted from Rolfe, LCL).

43. Quintilian, *Inst.* 11.3.7; Cicero, *De or.* 3.56.213; Plutarch, *Dem.* 7.1–2; *[Vit. X orat.]* 845a–b.

44. Plutarch, *Cic.* 5.3.

45. Valerius Maximus, *Fact. dict.* 8.10.2.

46. Quintilian, *Inst.* 1.11.12 (Butler, LCL).

47. Quintilian, *Inst.* 11.3.182. For a good discussion of Quintilian's ambivalence about gestures borrowed from the stage, see Gregory S. Aldrete, *Gestures and Accla-*

mations in Ancient Rome (Baltimore: The Johns Hopkins University Press, 1999), 68-71.

48. Fritz Graf, "Gestures and Conventions: The Gestures of Roman Actors and Orators," in *A Cultural History of Gesture* (ed. J. Bremmer and H. Roodenburg; Ithaca: Cornell University Press, 1986), 36-58, citation on 47.

49. Quintilian, *Inst.* 1.8.3.

50. Quintilian, *Inst.* 2.4.1–6.

51. Philodemus, *Rhet.* 1.194, XIIIa.

52. Philodemus, *Rhet.* 1.200, XVIIIa (Hubbell).

53. Philodemus, *Rhet.* 1.195, XVa.

54. Philodemus, *Rhet.* 1.195, XVa.

55. Philodemus, *Rhet.* 1.200, XVIIIa.

56. Philodemus, *Rhet.* 1.195, XVa.

57. Lucian, *Salt.* 65 (Fowler and Fowler).

58. Seneca the Elder, *Controversiae* 2.4.8; Quintilian, *Inst.* 3.8.51; 4.1.47. S. F. Bonner, *Roman Declamation in the Late Republic and Early Empire* (Liverpool: University Press of Liverpool, 1949), 53.

59. Quintilian, *Inst.* 3.8.51.

60. H. Tarrant suggests that Lucian may have had an assistant to play some of the small parts in the frame dialogue in order to add more realism to the performance (Harold Tarrant, "Dialogue and Orality in a Post-Platonic Age," in *Signs of Orality: The Oral Tradition and Its Influence in the Greek and Roman World* [ed. E. A. Mackay; MnemSup 188; Leiden: Brill, 1999], 181–97, esp. 193–94).

61. For reading in schools, see H. I. Marrou, *Education in Antiquity* (trans. G. Lamb; New York: The New American Library of World Literature, 1964), 230–31, 375; Stanley F. Bonner, *Education in Ancient Rome: From the Elder Cato to the Younger Pliny* (Berkeley: University of California Press, 1977), 223–26; M. L. Clarke, *Higher Education in the Ancient World* (Albuquerque: University of New Mexico Press, 1971), 22-23.

62. Quintilian, *Inst.* 1.8.1.

63. Theon, *Prog.* 1.26–30 (Butts ed.).

64. Quintilian, *Inst.* 2.4.1–6.

65. Quintilian, *Inst.* 1.8.2–3.

66. Quintilian, *Inst.* 1.11.14.

67. Quintilian, *Inst.* 2.1.2–4.

68. Quintilian, *Inst.* 2.1.13.

69. Theon, *Prog* 2.196-197 (Butts ed.).

70. On *prosōpopoiia* (προσωποποιία), see Stanley K. Stowers, "Romans 7.7–25 as a Speech-in-Character (προσωποποιία)," in *Paul and His Hellenistic Context* (ed. T. Engberg-Pedersen; Minneapolis: Fortress, 1995), 180–202.

71. *Theon, Prog.* 115.12–16.

72. Aphthonius, *Pros.* (Rabe, 35, line 17–36, line 2). Translation from Ray Nadeau, "The Progymnasmata of Aphthonius in Translation," *SpMon* 19 (1952): 278.

73. Quintilian, *Inst.* 10.1.43 (Butler, LCL).

74. Quintilian, *Inst.* 2.12.9–10 (Butler, LCL); cf. Quintilian's summary of the popular style in *Inst.* 12.10.73.

75. Quintilian, *Inst.* 3.8.59–60.

76. Quintilian, *Inst.* 4.2.37 (Butler, LCL).

77. Quintilian, *Inst.* 4.2.39 (Butler, LCL).

78. Quintilian, *Inst.* 11.3.183.

79. Quintilian, *Inst.* 6.3.54.

80. Quintilian, *Inst.* 6.4.15.

81. Quintilian, *Inst.* 12.9.3.

82. Plutarch, *Cic.* 5.6.

83. Tacitus, *Dial.* 35.4 (Peterson and Winterbottom, LCL).

84. Quintilian, *Inst.* 5.12.17–22.

85. Quintilian, *Inst.* 4.1.9; 5.14.32; 6.3.30, 33; 12.9.5–6; and frequently; cf. 8.Preface 22–28.

86. Quintilian, *Inst.* 12.10.58–65.

87. Quintilian, *Inst.* 12.10.61–65 (Butler, LCL).

88. Quintilian, *Inst.* 11.3.73–74.

89. E. J. Jory, "The Drama of the Dance: Prolegomena to an Iconography of Imperial Pantomime," in *Roman Theater and Society: E. Togo Salmon Papers I* (ed. W. J. Slater; Ann Arbor: University of Michigan Press, 1996), 18–20.

90. A catalogue of mask types is found in Julius Pollux, *Onom.* 4.143–154. Illustrations of a large number of masks and other artifacts related to ancient drama are presented in three titles by Thomas Bertram Lonsdale Webster: *Monuments Illustrating New Comedy*, 2 vols. (3d ed.; rev. and enlarged by J. R. Green and A. Seeberg; [London]: Institute of Classical Studies, University of London School of Advanced Study, 1995); *Monuments Illustrating Tragedy and Satyr Play* (2d ed.; London: Institute of Classical Studies, 1967); *Monuments Illustrating Old and Middle Comedy* (3d ed.; rev. and enlarged by J. R. Green; London: Institute of Classical Studies, 1978). For a discussion of dramatic masks, see David Wiles, *The Masks of Menander: Sign and Meaning in Greek and Roman Performance* (Cambridge: Cambridge University Press, 1991), 68–187; a list of Pollux's mask types is found on 75–77.

91. For example, "The Tragic Actor," a wall painting from Herculaneum; see Theodor Kraus and Leonard von Matt, *Pompeii and Herculaneum: The Living Cities of the Dead* (trans. R. E. Wolf; New York: Harry N. Abrams, 1975), 43; Gisela M. A. Richter, *The Portraits of the Greeks*, (3 vols.; London: Phaidon, 1965), vol. 2: figs. 1524, 1526–27 (Menander).

92. Quintilian, *Inst.* 11.3.112.

93. The same point is made in regard to the performance of Lucian's dialogues by Alfred Raymond Bellinger, *Lucian's Dramatic Technique* (YCS 1; [New Haven, 1928]), 24.

94. Quintilian, *Inst.* 1.11.1.

95. Philostratus, *Vit. Apoll.* 3.38.

96. Philostratus, *Vit. Apoll.* 4.20 (Conybeare, LCL).

97. Aristotle, *Rhet.* 3.12.1–4, 1413b–1414a.

98. For a detailed analysis of the repetitions in the two scenes, see Robert M. Fowler, *Loaves and Fishes: The Function of the Feeding Stories in the Gospel of Mark* (Chico, Calif.: Scholars Press, 1981), 43–90.

99. This understanding of the feeding scenes is at odds with my earlier arguments in *Follow Me! Disciples in Markan Rhetoric* (SBLDS 145; Atlanta: Scholars Press, 1995). "A foolish consistency is the hobgoblin of little minds" (Ralph Waldo Emerson).

CHAPTER FIVE
Memorization

Before going on to examine in detail the use of voice and gesture in delivery, we shall examine a question that has great importance for the delivery of the Gospel. Would the Gospel be read from a scroll or codex, or would it have been memorized? The question is essential for understanding the type of delivery that was possible, since reading from a scroll would occupy both hands of the reader and thus make expressive gesturing impossible. If the Gospel was presented from memory, on the other hand, the performer would be able to present a much more dramatic rendition.

Expressive reading was facilitated by a great deal of preparation, including quite often the memorization of texts.[1] There are two factors that made preparation and memorization important. First, as mentioned earlier, ancient texts were hard to read because of the absence of punctuation and divisions between words. Second, it was considered quite important to read or perform expressively. The primary written medium in the first century was the scroll, which is extremely cumbersome when compared to the codex, the form of book with which we are familiar. It takes two hands to manipulate a scroll, leaving no hand free for gesturing. That is why teachers interpreting texts spoke from a chair.[2] Scrolls were too cumbersome to be handled while standing. To read from a scroll meant to perform in a straitjacket, deprived of mobility and gesture.[3]

There were certainly some people who could read fluently at sight, but since it was a skill addressed only in the secondary level of education, which only a few received, it would not be common. Even the ability to read the words off the scroll still fell short of what was considered an adequate reading. In *The Ignorant Book-Collector*, Lucian describes a pseudointellectual who can read quickly from a scroll, keeping his eyes in front of his lips.[4] That is best understood as looking ahead on the roll to have some sense of the meaning before articulating the words aloud. Yet the same man is ridiculed for his reading because he barbarizes the language, spoils its beauty, and warps its meaning.[5] Proper reading for Lucian means conveying orally the beauty of the language and expressing its meaning. In the same work, he recounts an anecdote about Demetrius the Cynic, who was so incensed at a bad reading of the Bacchae of Euripides that he grabbed the book from the reader and tore it up, saying it was better for Pentheus to be torn up once and for all than to suffer being repeatedly torn up by the man's reading.[6] One might remember also Isocrates's complaint about readers who read "without persuasiveness and without putting any personal feeling into it, but as though he were repeating a table of figures."[7]

Would the Gospel of Mark have been memorized for performance? Once again we cannot be sure about any actual historical performances. Nevertheless, we can say that for a performance that approached the cultural ideal for oral delivery, the Gospel would have been memorized at least in outline, if not word for word, and would have been presented without the performer actually reading from a scroll or codex. Actual historical performances of the Gospel most probably included both types of presentation, depending on the performer's ability and how familiar he was with the material.[8] The author himself would likely have been familiar enough with his material to present it without a text.

Memory Ability in Mediterranean Cultures

Because our culture does not emphasize memorization, we tend to underestimate the ability to memorize found in other cultures. In the traditional Islamic form of education in Turkey, young students were expected to memorize the entire Koran. A tale singer studied by İlhan Başgöz had completed this task by the age of seven.[9] There is no indication in the account that this was an extraordinary achievement, and that suggests that the capacity for memorization we find described in ancient Mediterranean sources would not have been a rare talent, limited to a few unusual individuals.

Perhaps because the culture was much more oral than our own, there was generally a greater capacity for memory in the ancient Mediterranean world. The ability to remember was cultivated, and memory was highly valued. The discussion of writing in Plato's *Phaedrus*, while much earlier than the first century, suggests a different approach to the written word than that found in our culture. According to the myth told by Socrates, writing was invented by the Egyptian god Theuth and presented to the king of Egypt. Theuth praises his invention as a recipe for memory. The king in turn criticized writing as weakening the memory. Reliance on writing makes the memory sloppy. Writing can only remind one of what one already knows.[10] On both sides of the discussion the characters assume that writing is an intermediary step to memory. It is clear that the same attitude continued into the first century. The point of reading is not to hear the material only once. The educated man knows the material. He can quote the material. He has made the material part of his life.

There are many stories that display an ability to remember vast amounts of material. For example, Simonides, who is reputed to have discovered the memory system that assigns images to places in a memorized space, is said to have been able to remember the exact seating at a large banquet in a hall that collapsed, killing all of those in attendance.[11] The elder Seneca claims to have been able to remember two thousand names in order and to recite in reverse two hundred lines of verse chosen by his fellow students.[12] He also gives examples of orators with prodigious memories. Latro was able to memorize his work as he wrote it. Seneca finds this wondrous only because Latro wrote so quickly. Those who debate with themselves about every word they write, he says, naturally end up remembering it. Latro had developed a memory technique that allowed him to remember every declamation he had ever spoken. He was also able to describe the accomplishments of any general in history that anyone would name. Cineas, who was sent as an ambassador to Rome by Pyrrhus, remembered on the second day the name of every one of the senators as well as the crowd of townspeople around the senate. At the end of a day-long auction, Hortensius could remember in the right order all the articles sold, their prices, and who purchased them. An unnamed man, after hearing a poem recited once, claimed it was his own and recited it from memory.[13] Charmandas was reputed to be able to recite the contents of whole libraries of books.[14]

These feats may strike us only as curious parlor games. The man with the prodigious memory peddling his system on television may not strike us as particularly admirable. In the ancient world, however, a man's memory ability was a common object of praise. For example, Philostratus includes it in his description of Apollonius of Tyana, which looks suspiciously like a standard catalog of qualities included in a speech of praise. Apollonius is said to have had a better memory than Simonides and to have chanted a hymn from memory, in which memory was said to make time immortal.[15] Philostratus in another work praises his own teacher, the sophist Proclus of Naucratis, with the same phrase, that he had a better memory than Simonides.[16] Similarly, Suetonius says of the grammarian Quintus Remmius Palaemon that men were attracted to him because of his remarkable memory, in spite of his bad character.[17]

At least among the educated elite, memory contests were common. For example, Lucian reports that when those listening to a sophist present a speech tacked together from the earlier speeches of others, he and his companions competed with each other to name the sources from which various portions of the speech had been taken.[18] Athenaeus's *Deipnosophists* contain long passages with dinner guests, citing places where various words are found in ancient authors.

Rhapsodes recited the works of Homer by heart. Solon instituted the practice of having Homer recited sequentially in competitions. Thus the second performer had to take up the poem where the first left off.[19] This meant that rhapsodes had to be able to perform the entire poem effectively and could not win the competition by having learned well a particularly moving part. Much written material was committed to memory either for love of the material or so that it might be used later in one's own oral presentations. Quintilian recommends learning the speeches of Demosthenes by heart and apparently assumes that the point of reading is to commit material to memory for later use in oral performances.[20] In Cicero's *De oratore*, Crassus recommends memorizing as many Greek and Latin pieces as possible.[21] Examples of memorized material are frequently found. Diogenes could quote back the next line in the *Iliad* when Alexander used the poem to criticize his late sleeping.[22] According to Lucian, the philosopher Demonax knew most of the poets by heart.[23] In another place he describes a properly educated man as having all the works of antiquity at the tip of his tongue.[24] Augustine expects Christian speakers to have memorized significant portions of Scripture.[25] Pliny claims that his wife read his works over and over and even committed them to memory. Some of his poems she set to music and performed, accompanying herself with a lyre.[26]

Audiences of oral performances also committed to memory notable parts of what they heard. In a figure in which he compares a lecture hall to an audience, Lucian describes the echoes of a lecture hall as "committing to memory all that one says, like an appreciative hearer, and applauding the speaker and gracefully repeating his phrases."[27] Aper, the defender of the modern style in Tacitus' *Dialogue on Orators*, indicates that young men when listening to speeches sought to bring home from a speech something remarkable and worthy of recollection that they might pass on among themselves or write to their friends.[28] The principal speaker in Lucian's *Wisdom of Nigrinus* describes how he revels in calling to mind the words he has heard from the philosopher and repeats them to himself two or three times a day.[29] Ovid describes common people camping by the Tiber River for a religious festival, singing songs they had learned from the theater, which suggests that untrained people could learn a song from a few repetitions.[30]

Many dialogues are presented as the report of an earlier conversation that one character in the dialogue is able to reproduce from memory. For example, Plutarch's *Dialogue on Love* opens with a reference to the memorization of the discussion that forms the body of the dialogue:

> Was it on Helicon, Autobulus, that the discussion about love took place, which you either wrote out or committed to memory by repeatedly asking your father about it, and which you are now going to relate to us at our request?[31]

The purpose of writing down a discussion was to facilitate memorization. In Lucian's dialogue *The Carousal*, one character expects the other to be able to give an accurate report of the symposium he attended the night before, including a recitation of the speeches given.[32] Certainly the repetition of past discussions had become a stock literary strategy, but it may reflect as well the nature of contemporary discussions among intellectuals.[33]

We might expect, then, not only for the performer of the Gospel to have memorized the work, but for many in the audience to be able to recite large portions of it after repeated performances, just as some people today can recite the dialogue of their favorite movies. Certainly the example of Nigrinus's student suggests that Christians would frequently repeat to themselves words of Jesus that provided them with guidance or comfort. These people would then be able to perform the Gospel themselves if called upon to do so. It is quite possible, and even likely, that many Gospel performers were themselves illiterate.

Memorization Technique

There are three major sources for our understanding of the techniques of memorization practiced by rhetoricians, the *Rhetorica ad
Herennium*, Cicero's *De oratore*, and Quintilian's *Institutes*. Though
they differ somewhat in their attitudes toward memorization and
memorization technique, they give a rather consistent overall view of
the practice in the ancient world. The rhetorical handbooks indicate
two approaches to the memorization of speeches. Some speakers
learned their speeches verbatim while others were content to memorize the order and essence of their speeches. Quintilian prefers the
former method,[34] although he suggest that those with weak memories
adopt the latter.[35]

There was a well-known system of memorization in which one
imagined images associated with either the material to be covered or
the actual words to be used.[36] The system was so well-known that
Cicero feels he can simply allude to it and be understood,[37] and none
of the extant handbooks give a complete description of it. The images
were placed in one's imagination at set points in a building or landscape that one had memorized earlier for this purpose. Since one
could move in one's imagination through the building or landscape in
a set order, one could then remember one's material in the proper
order. One could pick up the series at any point. One could even move
backward through the landscape and present the material in the
reverse order. This was presumably the way people were able to perform the more spectacular feats of memory, such as the recall of thousands of names or the backward recitation of Virgil. The practice was
based on the observation that memories associated with places are
particularly strongly imprinted on one's mind. This fact was strongly
associated with the story of Simonides, who had remembered the
position of all those diners at the ill-fated banquet during which the
roof of the house collapsed, killing the diners and disfiguring them
beyond recognition.[38]

The landscape for one's notebook of the mind had to be chosen
with care. Quintilian indicates that it should be a place of the largest
possible extent and a great variety of features. A large house with
many rooms is appropriate, but one might use public buildings, a long
journey, or the ramparts of a city. One might even use the pictures of
artists or simply imagine a place. Metrodorus is said to have developed
360 locations within the signs of the zodiac.[39] These backgrounds

have to be memorized quite vividly and with the greatest care. The *Ad Herennium* advises that every fifth background be visually marked with a sign to indicate its position. For example, the fifth might have a hand above it. We might imagine in the tenth a friend of ours named Decimus (Tenth, a common Roman name for a tenth child).[40]

Even though Quintilian describes the landscape and image memory technique,[41] he indicates that the only effective method is repeated reading, or hearing, if another reads the speech to the orator.[42] Ease of memorization is greatly facilitated by clear division and artistic structure, which explains many of the organizing devices used by Mark, such as chiasmus and the use of threefold repetitions to structure sections of the Gospel.[43] Since a good memory was of the utmost importance to a speaker, daily practice of memorization is suggested.[44]

Markan Attitude toward Oral Performance

There is not a great deal of evidence in Mark about the types of oral performance that would be expected in the Markan community. We have seen, however, that within the culture, there is a high valuation placed on spontaneous speaking, and the ideal of performance was to reproduce in prepared material the impression of spontaneous speech. Jesus in Mark is presented as always speaking spontaneously. To the extent that Jesus' example was taken as a model for later Christian speakers, we might expect that spontaneous speech was taken as the norm. The instructions given to Christians in Mark 13:11 direct those forced to appear in courts or before governors and kings not to prepare a speech beforehand.[45] Instead, they are to rely on the inspiration of the Holy Spirit, who will tell them what to say. This, of course, is contrary to the method of the rhetorical tradition, which stressed careful preparation that would present the appearance of spontaneity. Nevertheless, the contrast is not absolute. Plato could describe the performance of Ion as inspired by a god,[46] and the poet's invocation of the muses may have been more than mere formality even in the first century.[47] In the *Life of Aesop*, the hero is given his ability to speak well by the goddess Isis and the muses.[48] Quintilian reports that old orators, such as Cicero, used to say that a god had inspired a speaker when he was carried away by warmth of feeling and inspiration to present an improvised speech successfully.[49] The shouting of the phrases "Divine!" and "Inspired by a god!" as a form of applause shows that the idea of divine inspiration of speech was still current in the first century, as also reflected in Acts 12:22.[50]

Other evidence of early Christian speaking styles suggests that spontaneity was the norm for Christian speakers. In Acts, there is no suggestion of preparation in any of the speeches. On the contrary, the speeches usually take as their point of departure some happening in the narrative. Peter's first sermon (Acts 2:14–42) brings spectacular results and immediately follows the coming of the Holy Spirit at Pentecost (Acts 2:1–13), thus suggesting that a connection between the Spirit and Christian speech is to be understood. In the early second century Hippolytus indicates that church teachers were inspired by the Holy Spirit:

> [When you gather at the assembly,] indeed it shall be given to him who speaks to utter things which are profitable to all, and you will hear things which you do not think [to hear] and you will be profited by the things which the Holy Spirit will give to you by him who instructs.[51]

The inspiration of the Spirit happens at the time of the assembly, implying spontaneous speech rather than inspiration in a previous period of planning and composition.

The argument from silence is never a strong one, but the lack of written material from Paul other than the letters suggests that he spoke spontaneously as well, or at least that he spoke without a text. Some passages in Paul suggest premeditation in speaking, but it is clear from Quintilian's discussion of extempore speaking that the ability to speak well on the spur of the moment required a great deal of preparation.[52] If so many of his letters were carefully preserved, likely any other available written material from Paul would be preserved as well. In fact, the complaint of his opponents in Corinth that Paul's letters are strong, but his speech in person is weak (2 Cor 10:10), suggests that Paul was at his best in the written medium, when he had time to consider his words more carefully. The distinction, however, may be due more to Paul's faulty delivery than to his abilities in composition.

There is limited evidence about why early Christians preferred the spontaneous speech of the Holy Spirit. Jesus' saying about relying on the inspiration of the Spirit in lawcourts (Mark 13:11) suggests that the reason may be the value placed on one's reliance on God. Sayings of Paul such as "It is no longer I who live, but it is Christ who lives in me" (Gal 2:20) suggest that part of the reason may be a suspicion of ego-controlled activity. The careful planning involved in preparing a speech beforehand suggests, or at least allows for, reliance on oneself, something about which one could boast. Part of the attraction may simply be the possibility of claiming that spontaneous speech is Spirit inspired.

Some modern-day groups that stress being led by the Spirit likewise count spontaneous speech as being important. In the groups with which I am familiar, spontaneous speech is understood to allow the Spirit to speak directly to the situation of the people present. The Spirit knows the inner situation of the listeners. The Spirit can understand what they can understand and what they need to hear. No prepared speech can do that.

Within fully oral environments, performances of extended narratives have a great deal of flexibility.[53] Although performers may claim to present the same narrative word for word, in reality they compose the narrative anew for each performance from an outline of the plot and a collection of typical scenes and useful verbal formulas. It has been suggested that Mark's Gospel was intended as an attack on the spontaneous speech of Spirit-led prophets, which was composed in a similar manner.[54] Yet in that case Mark likely would not perpetuate instructions that emphasize spontaneous Spirit-directed speech. It is more likely that Mark's Gospel was intended to have a place alongside Spirit-directed speech. There are a number of ways the written text could work in an environment that valued Spirit-directed speech. The Gospel may have functioned much as a letter. Through a written Gospel, Mark could share his narrative with those with whom he could not be present because of either distance or impending death. In that case, it would be understood as one instance of a Spirit-inspired narrative. It may also have served as an aid for others in their presentations of the Gospel narrative. It is quite likely, given the general attitude toward texts at the time, that the author expected the text to be modified in performance. In that case, the Spirit could still operate to inspire the individual performances. If Plato can credit a rhapsode's performance of the fixed text of Homer to divine inspiration, even the performance of a fixed text might be understood as Spirit inspired. In any case, the value placed on spontaneous speech in early Christianity suggests that the Gospel would be best received if its performance approximated as closely as possible Spirit-led spontaneity. That would mean either the simulation of spontaneity through memorization or the limited spontaneity of Spirit-directed modification of the narrative in performance.

The loose connection between performance and text operated in both directions. As mentioned above, Cicero is said to have prepared only notes for large portions of his orations. When he later wrote out versions of his orations for "publication," he often made substantial changes from the spoken version. It is quite possible that Mark did the same thing. A narrative like Mark could easily be organized, either in written form or in the performer's mind, as a series of episodes. The presenter, already familiar with the separate episodes, could fill in the details as he went. If our Gospel is a "published" version of an existing semistandardized performance in the same way that the written Ciceronian speeches were adapted versions of the actual orations, it is quite possible that our text corresponds to no actual performance in antiquity. Mark may have "improved" the Gospel for "publication." Subsequent performers may have only memorized the progression of episodes and filled in details themselves. Such a relationship between text and performance would be fairly typical for the rhetorical culture of the first century.

Memorization of Mark

Would the Gospel of Mark have been memorized? We cannot know for sure, but a number of factors suggest that was the case. First, there is the fact that the cultural ideal for the oral delivery was in most cases performance without a text. Second, we see within Mark itself a bias in favor of spontaneous, Spirit-inspired speech. It is likely that if Mark presents such speech as the ideal, those performing the Gospel would attempt to approximate that ideal. Memorization would allow for much greater spontaneity in performance. The performer could move and gesture freely. He could modify the text without losing his place in the scroll.

Of the two types of memorization described by Quintilian, word-for-word memorization and memorization of content, the latter would be more conducive to a semispontaneous Spirit-inspired performance.[55] If the performer was free to develop the details of the episodes, then the Spirit could inspire the performer to develop the episodes according to the needs of the listeners. The treatment of Markan episodes in Matthew and Luke suggests that such free development of the material was the norm. If audiences were used to hearing variations in the telling of the episodes, the Matthean and Lukan retellings would not have been considered out of the ordinary. In fully oral contexts, the audience plays a great role in maintaining the continuity of traditional material. The audience knows the stories. Listeners may suggest what they want included, and may object if material is presented not in accord with the norm.[56] In the semioral context of early Christianity, we might expect much the same dynamic. To be successful, a retelling of the Gospel would have to fit within the norms of audience expectation. If audiences are used to fixed versions of the Gospel episodes, that fixed form would rather quickly achieve semicanonical status and would be hard to change. On the other hand, if audiences expected a certain flexibility in the performance of the episodes, Matthew and Luke would feel no constraint in their own retelling of familiar material.

Flexibility in the performance of individual episodes would also be consistent with cultural norms expressed in the early levels of rhetorical education. Students were taught how to expand narratives of various types and how to present them in more concise form.[57] This reflects the value the culture placed on the ability to tailor traditional material to fit a specific social or rhetorical situation. This ability was valued for its own sake. We find, for example, in the *Life of Aesop* the one-line *chreia* ("what is useful/needed," a saying or anecdote cited to make a point) attributed by Plutarch to Bias expanded into a narrative of considerable length.[58]

Even for those like Quintilian, who advocates word-for-word memorization, the ability to depart from the text was valued. If some brilliant improvisation should occur to us while speaking, he says, we should not cling to our premeditated scheme. The best form of preparation allows us to depart from our prepared speech and to return to it at will. Our words should flow from the subject on which we are speaking rather than our memory. Preparation and memory are tools for allowing us to speak better.[59] The crowning achievement in the study of rhetoric, he says, is the ability to improvise. This is necessarily so for most speakers since in the lawcourts and other public forums, we are not able to script our opponents' speech and may find our prepared words irrelevant.[60]

Another analogy for flexibility of performance can be found in the Hellenistic schools. There was a preference for oral over written teaching in the schools, and schoolbooks, such as Galen's medical texts, were often versions of material presented in lectures. Galen says his notes should only be read with the help of a teacher.[61] Teachers were expected to explain the material in the books and to add their own material to what was written.[62] The need for a teacher to explain the content of books is implied by Plato in the *Phaedrus*, where one of King Thamus's complaints about the invention of writing is that students will read many things without instruction and will therefore think they know many things while remaining ignorant.[63]

Memorization Structure

If the general arrangement of the narrative of Mark was memorized, the structure of the Gospel is well designed to facilitate that task.[64] The Gospel, while maintaining a narrative continuity, is divided up into relatively short sections on the basis of a series of triplet episodes. The material between these triplets consists of a relatively small number of individual episodes that generally form a clear development of the narrative. To memorize the Gospel structure, then, one only has to remember the structure of triplets and the development of episodes associated with each triplet episode. For anyone trained in the method of associating material with an architectural image, keeping the small number of episodes between the triplet markers in order would not require great effort. There are also four sections standing outside the triplet structure, the prologue, two relatively long discourses, and the passion narrative, which has an easily remembered narrative line. Since the material in each section generally forms a clear narrative development or allows for a clear contrast between reactions to Jesus, the structure would facilitate delivery since the performer could develop a particular narrative effect for each section. If memory sections and performance sections coincide, then it is easier to match delivery and content, because one can work on a particular effect for each section. Movement from one memory section to another is a cue for the performer to shift the focus of the performance as well.

A number of triplet sections have chiastic structures, named after the Greek letter chi, of the form ABA, ABCBA, ABCDCBA, and so on.[65] The purpose of chiastic structures is more likely to be to help the memory of the performer than to guide the audience.[66] In spite of arguments that ancient audiences would be used to following chiasms, my observation is that chiasms are generally quite hard to follow in a conscious manner. Chiastic structures help to balance the narrative and give it a pleasing shape even if the audience is not aware of them. For the performer trying to remember all the episodes that make up the narrative, however, chiasms are very helpful in providing a structure on which to hang the episodes.

Such a memory structure is well suited for flexibility of performance. If the performer improvises by adding or embellishing material in the course of the performance, the sectioned structure makes it easy to find a place to resume the memorized narrative with a minimum of effort or disjunction. The use of an architectural image would also facilitate such flexibility, since the speaker can keep in mind the place in the image where the narrative left off. The architectural image also facilitates leaving out material for whatever reason the speaker may decide to do so. The performer may fast-forward by skipping over architectural features or by beginning the image over with the material from the next section.

The memory structure of the Gospel will be most clear if we look first at the overall structure of triplets and discourses and then look at the structuring of the individual sections. I understand the overall structure as presented below. Some episodes are transitional and might be placed in either adjoining section.[67]

    I. Preface (1:1–13 or 15)
   II. First Triplet: Calling and Commissioning the Disciples
      A. Call one (1:16–20), marking beginning of section one (1:16–2:12)
      B. Call two (2:13–14), marking beginning of section two (2:13–3:12)
      C. Commissioning (3:13–19), marking beginning of section three (3:13–35)
  III. Major Discourse One: The Parables (4:1–34)
  IV. Second Triplet: Boat Stories
      A. Stilling of the storm (4:35–41), marking transition to section one (4:35–44)
      B. Walking on the water (6:45–52), marking transition to section two (6:45–8:26)
      C. Discussion in the boat (8:14–21), marking end of section two
   V. Third Triplet: Passion Predictions
     Preface: Peter's confession (8:22–30)

      A. First passion prediction (8:31), marking beginning of
         section one (8:31–9:29)
      B. Second passion prediction (9:30–32), marking beginning
         of section two (9:30–10:31)
      C. Third passion prediction (10:32–34), marking beginning
         of section three (10:32–52)
  VI. Fourth Triplet: Entries into Jerusalem
      A. The triumphal entry (11:1–10), marking beginning of the
         first section (11:1–11)
      B. Second entry, cursing the fig tree part one (11:12–15a),
         marking beginning of section two (11:12–18)
      C. Third entry, cursing the fig tree part two (11:20–27a),
         marking beginning of section three (11:20–12:44)
 VII. Second Major Discourse (13:1–36)
VIII. Passion Narrative (14:1–16:8)

If one takes this as the structure of the Gospel, it is a simple matter
to memorize it. There are two major discourses, one after the first
major block of material, the second preceding the last major block.
There are four sets of triplet episodes, which structure most of the
material, and the types of episodes form a clear narrative progression:
calling and commissioning the disciples, boat episodes involving the
disciples' misunderstanding, passion predictions with associated disciple misunderstandings, and entries into Jerusalem. Only the passion
narrative is not divided into a triplet structure, but it has a clear narrative development, and one can easily remember the development of
the episodes, especially with the help of an architectural memory aide.

The triplet structure is not applied with slavish consistency, and
one might understand it in slightly different ways. For example, one
might see the three boat scenes as marking the end of three sections,
with the parable discourse being the first of the three sections. There
are overlapping structures at some points. One common method of
indicating structure in antiquity was the use of similar words or
episodes at the beginning and end of a section, a technique termed
inclusio, literally "a confinement" in Latin. This provides an artistic
rounding off of the narrative. One might take the healing of the blind
man at Bethsaida (8:22–26) as forming an *inclusio* with the healing of
blind Bartimaeus (10:46–52) and thus attached to the passion prediction triplet. On the other hand, the same episode forms an *inclusio*
with the healing of the deaf-and-dumb man (7:31–37) and might be

considered part of the boat triplet section. Such interlinkings are confusing in a linear outline but help facilitate memory in performance.
The end of one section is the beginning of another.[68]

The triplet structure is abandoned in the passion narrative where
the narrative development is more clear and one does not have to rely
on such structuring aides. The second set of triplets, at least as I have
outlined the structure, marks two rather than three sections. The
episodes in these sections are generally much longer than in other
parts of the Gospel, and Mark has modified the structure accordingly.
Three sections of episodes of that length would retard the flow of the
Gospel and unbalance the structure. As it is, Mark provides a pleasing
variation in the length of episodes. The entry-into-Jerusalem triplet
is also given a different treatment. Instead of maintaining a structure
of sections with approximately the same narrative duration, the
length of the sections in this case differs greatly. In the first section,
there is almost no narrative other than the entry into Jerusalem. The
second section is also short, consisting of a single episode in addition
to the entry. The third section, in contrast, is more extensive and
progresses through a number of debates between Jesus and his opponents.

The variation in the structure creates a more pleasing narrative.
The rhetoricians often state that the best art is invisible to the audience.[69] The variations in using the triplet structure allow the performer to keep a clear structure in his mind without giving the
narrative an artificial feel. The audience will be aware of repetitions
within the narrative. It creates the effect that Joanna Dewey has
likened to an interwoven tapestry.[70] This is an important part of oral
artistry and has a valuable didactic function as well. The repetitions
stress important material that the audience is more likely to remember
because they have heard it more than once.

Memory Structure of Individual Sections

If we examine the individual sections of this memory structure, we
generally find a fairly clear structure that often reflects a narrative
development or contrast, allowing ease of memorization of the order
of episodes as well as facilitating the delivery of the narrative with the
proper emotional tone. An examination of the preface and the first
triplet section will give a suggestion of the interaction between structure and meaning.

The Preface. The preface exhibits a clear and natural development of the narrative. First, there is a formal introduction to the Gospel with a composite quotation from Scripture (1:1–3). The quotation from Scripture leads into the introduction of John, which connects through the catchphrase "in the wilderness." The section on John consists of a general statement (1:4), a description of the crowds he attracted (1:5), a description of his clothing and food (1:6), and finally his proclamation relating to Jesus (1:7–8). The section on Jesus naturally follows that proclamation and is connected by catchwords "baptize" and "Spirit." It progresses through the baptism (1:9–11), the temptation (1:12–13), and a summary of Jesus' proclamation (1:14–15). The last segment might be seen as the beginning of the next section, but the density of words that echo verses 1:1 and 1:4 suggest that it would also be heard as bringing the preceding section to a close. Again we hear repetitions of "John," "Jesus," "preaching," "gospel," "of God," "repentance," and "gospel."[71] The density of verbal repetition in those two passages suggests that for the author those were relatively fixed pieces. The intervening material might be treated more flexibly. I might, for example, give a longer or shorter quotation of Scripture. I might drop out the description of John's clothing and dining habits. I might add a few more sayings of John, particularly if my audience is interested in teaching material. I might give a fuller version of John's prophecy concerning Jesus if I am familiar with it. I might provide a little dialogue explaining why Jesus is getting baptized if my audience is concerned about that issue. I might, that is to say, present on occasion Matthew's or Luke's version of the passage. That amount of variation would be quite consistent with separate performances, even by the same performer.[72]

Section I: 1:16–3:35. This section is split into three subsections by the triplet of call and commissioning stories.[73] If we think of those three stories as primarily structuring devices, the rest of the section has a quite clear narrative development: Jesus heals, he is opposed by the authorities, and the section ends with a discussion between Jesus and the authorities on the nature of his healing activities. The call and commissioning stories establish a secondary theme. Because they occur at regular intervals through the section, they create the impression of another ongoing activity, which through repetition impresses the listeners as important.

The first subsection begins with the call of Simon and Andrew and James and John (1:16–20). That is easy to remember because they are the four major disciples in Mark. The two stories are in fact variations of the same story. There are five episodes that follow. One can easily keep five episodes in mind even without special memory training. The first episode is the preaching at Capernaum (1:21–28). This episode allows a transition between the preaching with which the preface ended to the healing with which this section is concerned. It has two parts. In the first Jesus preaches and is favorably received. In the second, Jesus casts out the unclean spirit, and his action provokes wonder. Each of the first three major triplet-defined sections begins with an episode concerned with a question about Jesus' identity. The boat-scene section begins with the stilling of the storm, in which the disciples ask, "Who then is this?" (4:41), a question closely reminiscent of the "What is this?" in the Capernaum synagogue scene (1:27). The passion-prediction section opens with Jesus' questions to the disciples about his identity (8:27, 29). The repetition of similar material in each of these opening scenes gives the performer another way of remembering the material. From the point of view of the audience, it provides for the repetition of an important theme, the question about the identity of Jesus.

The Capernaum synagogue scene (1:21–28) is followed by a healing related to the disciples, a general healing, a discussion between Peter and Jesus contrasting healing and preaching, the healing of the leper, and the forgiving and healing of the paralytic. The repetition of many healing stories establishes Jesus as an effective healer. The discussion about healing and preaching is a digression, but it establishes an important point. It is important not be too emphatic about one's own accomplishments so as not to arouse feelings of envy. In a culture in which honor is understood as a scarce commodity, the accomplishments of one person are seen as a threat to the status of others. To avoid that problem, Mark presents Jesus as a somewhat reluctant healer. He did not intend to heal in Capernaum, but was forced into it by the unclean spirit, who would have made him known prematurely. Then his disciples and the crowd request healings. The discussion between Peter and Jesus emphasizes that Jesus is not seeking notoriety for his healings. Everyone is seeking him in Capernaum, presumably for healing, but Jesus indicates that he came to preach (1:38). Thus the apparent digression is an important part of the presentation of Jesus as a healer. The healing of the leper (1:40–45) makes similar points about Jesus not being a threat to the honor of others. He orders the healed leper not to make his healing known, showing Jesus is not seeking fame for his healing; he also tells the leper to go to the temple to make the customary sacrifices, indicating that he is not, at least initially, attacking the position and honor of the authorities.

The final episode in the first subsection provides a fitting climax to the narrative and provides a transition to the next section. In the healing of the paralytic (2:1–12), a healing is combined with a controversy between Jesus and the Jewish authorities. For the first time, we hear a negative reaction to Jesus. The reaction of the authorities is in stark contrast to the enthusiasm of the crowds and sets the emotional tone for the audience's reaction to Jesus' opponents. The contrast is emphasized by waiting until the middle of the episode to introduce Jesus' opponents. The first five verses of the episode are focused on the enthusiasm of the crowd and the faith of the friends of the paralytic. The grumbling of the scribes intrudes upon the otherwise exultant narrative and portrays them as mean-spirited. The episode also introduces the theme of the passion, since the complaint of the scribes, "He is speaking blasphemy," foreshadows the charge at the trial of Jesus. If the Markan audience is familiar with the trial material, they will recognize the allusion to Jesus' passion imbedded in this episode. The second subsection also ends with an allusion to the death of Jesus (3:6). So we can see again the technique of beginning or ending sections with similar material, both for emphasis and to enable ease of memory. We also find a return to the opening theme to close the subsection. The synagogue scene provoked questions about the identity of Jesus and comments about his authority. The healing of the paralytic specifically links the healings of Jesus with his authority to forgive sins. The opening contrast between the authoritative teaching of Jesus and the scribes' lack of authority (1:22) is developed into an open dispute between the scribes and Jesus about the nature of Jesus' authority (2:7, 10). The initial contrast helps to place the scribes' complaint in a bad light. The scribes, it implies, react negatively because they are jealous of Jesus' authority since they lack real authority of their own.

The first subsection, then, provides the performer with both an easy-to-remember structure and a clear narrative development. As a performer, I would want to demonstrate the marvelous nature of Jesus' healings, I want to show him to be a humble person not seeking fame in spite of his ability, I want to arouse odium against the scribes, and I want to stress the link between the healings and the identity of Jesus.

There is no way to tell what kind of structure, if any, was in the mind of the author of Mark. I simply offer this structure as an example of how the narrative may be structured for ease of memorization.

Memorization Structure and the Composition of Mark

We cannot know for certain whether the Gospel was written before it was performed or whether the written Gospel is a record of a preexisting oral narrative. It certainly is possible for an oral performer to develop a narrative with this level of structural complexity. Triple repetitions are certainly common in folktales. It is a typical way for an oral performer to elaborate or extend a narrative. We find triple repetitions in Mark within single episodes as well, as in the Gethsemane scene (14:32–42) or the scene of Peter's denial (14:66–72). We find three mistaken answers to the question about Jesus' identity (6:14–16; 8:28). Clearly, the use of triplets is an important part of Mark's narrative technique at all levels. Thus it is perfectly possible that the structure could be developed through repeated oral performances. For someone making use of an architectural image to assist his memory, it would be natural that one's narrative would develop a structure related to architectural rhythms, and the triplet structure is one way to do that.

I think it is much more likely that the Gospel of Mark developed through repeated oral performance. It has an unnecessarily complex structure for a written narrative, where we might expect a more simple linear development. The number of interconnections between parts of the narrative are quite extraordinary for an author without great literary skill to produce in a single setting. In the course of repeated performances, however, a good storyteller, even without literary sophistication, would be able to develop the connections between episodes and find ways to hold the narrative together. Once he had a basic narrative, he could figure out how to weave into that narrative other themes that he wanted to develop. Through a process of trial and error, he could develop a narrative that evoked the emotions he wanted his audience to feel. It is much easier to produce a narrative like the Gospel of Mark if one has twenty or thirty performances in which to test out different approaches.

Notes

1. The most through discussion of memorization is found in Frances A. Yates, *The Art of Memory* (Chicago: University of Chicago Press, 1966). See also Bromley Smith, "Hippias and a Lost Canon of Rhetoric," *QJSE* 12 (1926): 129–45; L. A. Post, "Ancient Memory Systems," *ClWeek* 15 (1932): 106–10; Donald E. Hargis, "Memory in Rhetoric," *SSCJ* 17 (1951): 114–24; W. W. Meissner, "A Historical Note on Retention," *JEGP* 59 (1958): 229–36; Wayne E. Hoogestraat, "Memory: The Lost Canon?" *QJS* 46 (1960): 141–47; G. B. Matthews, "Augustine on Speaking from Memory," *APQ* 2 (1965): 157–60; Thomas H. Olbricht, "Delivery and Memory;" in Heinrich Lausberg, *Handbook of Literary Rhetoric: A Foundation for Literary Study* (trans. M. T. Bliss, A. Jansen, and D. E. Orton; Leiden: Brill, 1998), 478–80. On the relationship of written texts, memory, and performance in classical Greece, see Rosalind Thomas, *Literacy and Orality in Ancient Greece* (Cambridge: Cambridge University Press, 1992), 113–27.

2. E.g., Juvenal, *Sat.* 7.203; Martial, 1.76.14; Seneca, *Dial.* 10.10.1; Epictetus, *Diatr.* 3.23.31.

3. Cf. Tarrant on Lucian: "Unless he brandished a text before his eyes when giving oratorical entertainment, then his dialogues too would have been performed from memory. This is what the audience would have expected, and spontaneity will have assisted comic performance" (Harold Tarrant, "Dialogue and Orality in a Post-Platonic Age," in *Signs of Orality: The Oral Tradition and Its Influence in the Greek and Roman World* [ed. E. A. Mackay; MnemSup 188; Leiden: Brill, 1999], 181-97, quote from 194). Lucian, of course, is a professional performer and a very gifted one at that. A church audience may have had lower expectations.

4. Lucian, *Ind.* 2.

5. Lucian, *Ind.* 7.

6. Lucian, *Ind.* 19.

7. Isocrates, *Or.* 5.26 (Norlin, LCL).

8. See also Thomas E. Boomershine, "Peter's Denial as Polemic or Confession: The Implications of Media Criticism for Biblical Hermeneutics," *Semeia* 39 (1987): 61-62; 66, nn. 6–7.

9. İlhan Başgöz, "The Tale-Singer and His Audience," in *Folklore: Performance and Communication* (ApSem 40; ed. D. Ben-Amos and K. S. Goldstein; The Hague: Mouton, 1975), 156.

10. Plato, *Phaedr.* 274c–275e.

11. Cicero, *De or.* 2.86.352; Quintilian, *Inst.* 11.2.11–13.

12. Seneca, *Controversiae* 1.pr.2.

13. Seneca, *Controversiae* 1.pr.17–19; Cineas's memory also described in Cicero, *Tusc.* 1.59; Pliny, *Nat.* 7.26.88.

14. Pliny, *Nat.* 7.26.89.

15. Philostratus, *Vit. Apoll.* 1.14.

16. Philostratus, *Vit. soph.* 604.

17. Suetonius, *Gramm.* 23.

18. Lucian, *Pseudol.* 6.

19. Diogenes Laertius, *De vita* 1.57.

20. Quintilian, *Inst.* 10.1.105; 10.1.19.

21. Cicero, *De or.* 1.34.156.

22. Epictetus, *Diatr.* 3.22.92.

23. Lucian, *Demon.* 4.

24. Lucian, *Ind.* 30.

25. Augustine, *Doctr. chr.* 4.3.7–8.

26. Pliny, *Ep.* 4.19.

27. Lucian, *Dom.* 3.

28. Tacitus, *Dial.* 20.

29. Lucian, *Nigr.* 6.

30. Ovid, *Fast.* 3.523–536.

31. Plutarch, *Amat.* 1, 748e-f; cited by Tarrant, "Dialogue and Orality," 188, n. 19.

32. Lucian, *Symp.* 2.

33. Tarrant, "Dialogue and Orality," 182–92.

34. Quintilian, *Inst.* 11.2.44–45.

35. Quintilian, *Inst.* 11.2.48–49.

36. Cicero, *De or.* 2.86.351–2.88.360; *Rhet. Her.* 3.16–24; Quintilian, *Inst.* 11.2.11–31. The system is fully explained in Yates, *Art of Memory*, 1–26. Yates shows throughout her book how the system was developed throughout European history.

37. Cicero, *De or.* 1.34.157.

38. Quintilian, *Inst.* 11.2.11–17. Joanna Dewey, "Mark as Aural Narrative: Structures as Clues to Understanding," *STRev* 36 (1992): 50.

39. Quintilian, *Inst.* 11.2.18, 21–22. L. A. Post has plausibly suggested that Metrodorus visualized ten backgrounds under each of the three decan figures associated with each sign of the zodiac (10 x 3 x 12 = 360). Thus the zodiac would have been the beginning point for the development of the system ("Ancient Memory Systems," 109).

40. *Rhet. Her.* 3.17.31.

41. Quintilian, *Inst.* 11.2.11–31.

42. Quintilian, *Inst.* 11.2.32–35.

43. Quintilian, *Inst.* 11.2.36–39.

44. Quintilian, *Inst.* 11.2.40–44.

45. This passage, together with 1 Cor 1–2, plays a central role in Kennedy's contention that early Christians had a radically different approach to rhetoric than did those in the surrounding culture; see George A. Kennedy, *A New History of Classical Rhetoric* (Princeton: Princeton University Press, 1994), 125–33, especially 127 for the Markan passage. For a careful nuancing of Kennedy's thesis and supporting evidence from Jewish sources, see John R. Levison, "Did the Spirit Inspire Rhetoric? An Exploration of George Kennedy's Definition of Early Christian Rhetoric," in *Persuasive Artistry: Studies in New Testament Rhetoric in Honor of George A. Kennedy* (ed. D. F. Watson; JSNTSup 50; Sheffield: JSOT Press, 1991), 25–40.

46. Plato, *Ion* 535b–536d.

47. On the idea of inspiration by the Muses in classical Greece, see E. R. Dodds, *The Greeks and the Irrational* (Berkeley: University of California Press, 1951), 80–82.

48. *Vit. Aes.* 48.

49. Quintilian, *Inst.* 10.7.13–14.

50. Plutarch, *Rect. rat. aud.* 45f–46a.

51. Hippolytus, *Trad. ap.* 35.3 (Dix and Chadwick edition and translation, archaisms removed).

52. Levison, "Did the Spirit?" 36–39.

53. Albert Lord, *The Singer of Tales* (2d ed.; ed. S. Mitchell and G. Nagy; Cambridge: Harvard University Press, 2000). Also see Jan Brunvand, "An Indiana Storyteller Revisited," *MidFolk* 11 (1961): 5–14; Linda Dégh, *Folktales and Society* (Bloomington: Indiana University Press, 1969), 177–79; Daniel J. Crowley, *I Could Talk Old-Story Good: Creativity in Bahamian Folklore* (Berkeley: University of California Press, 1981), 108–13; Richard Bauman, *Story, Performance, and Event: Contextual Studies of Oral Narrative* (CSOLC 10; Cambridge: Cambridge University Press, 1986), 78–111; Werner H. Kelber, *Oral and Written Gospel: The Hermeneutics of Speaking and Writing in the Synoptic Tradition, Mark, Paul, and Q* (Philadelphia: Fortress, 1983), 30.

54. Kelber, *Oral and Written Gospel*.

55. Quintilian, *Inst.*11.2.44–49.

56. John Miles Foley, "The Traditional Oral Audience," *BalS* 18 (1977): 145–53.

57. Theon, *Prog.* 3.224–240 (Butts ed.); Burton L. Mack, "Elaboration of the Chreia in the Hellenistic School," in Burton L. Mack and Vernon K. Robbins, *Patterns of Persuasion in the Gospels* (FF; Sonoma, Cal.: Polebridge, 1989), 36–37.

58. Plutarch, *Rect. rat. aud.* 2; 38b; *Sept. sap. conv.* 146f; *Vit. Aes.* 51–55.

59. Quintilian, *Inst.* 10.6.5–7.

60. Quintilian, *Inst.* 10.7.1–3.

61. Galen, *De libr. propr.* 11 (Kühn 19.42 = Scripta Minora 2.118.22–24); citation from Loveday Alexander, "The Living Voice: Scepticism towards the Written Word in Early Christian and in Graeco-Roman Texts," in *The Bible in Three Dimensions: Essays in Celebration of Forty Years of Biblical Studies in the University of Sheffield* (ed. D. J. A. Clines, S. E. Fowl, and S. E. Porter; JSOTSup 87; Sheffield: Sheffield Academic Press, 1990), 230.

62. Alexander, "Living Voice," 230–42.

63. Plato, *Phaedr.* 275b.

64. Many suggestions have been made about the structure of Mark's Gospel. Most attempts at outlining the Gospel have been based on narrative devices such as summaries or on general perceptions of the development of the narrative. In addition, numerous suggestions have been made concerning the structuring of specific portions of the Gospel. My own suggestion is different in that it is based on a concern for memorization. It obviously overlaps with a number of other suggested outlines, as would be expected, and I owe a great deal to earlier suggestions about the nature of the Markan structure.

65. Nils Wilhelm Lund, *Chiasmus in the New Testament: A Study in Formgeschichte* (Chapel Hill: University of North Carolina Press, 1942); Joanna Dewey, *Markan Public Debate: Literary Technique, Concentric Structure, and Theology in Mark 2:1–3:6* (SBLDS 48; Chico, Cal.: Scholars Press, 1980); H. Van Dyke Parunak, "Oral Typesetting: Some Uses of Biblical Structure," *Biblica* 62 (1981): 153–68; John W. Welch, ed., *Chiasmus in Antiquity: Structures, Analyses, Exegesis* (Hildesheim: Gerstenberg, 1981); John Breck, *The Shape of Biblical Language: Chiasmus in and beyond the Scriptures* (Crestwood, N.Y.: St. Vladimir's Seminary Press, 1994).

66. Dewey sees chiasms as helping both listener and performer ("Mark as Aural Narrative," 50–52). For a fuller discussion, see Augustine Stock, "Chiastic Awareness and Education in Antiquity," *BTB* 14 (1984): 23–27.

67. The suggestion for understanding the structure of Mark that is closest to the following presentation is that of Bas van Iersel (*Reading Mark* [trans. W. H.

Bisscheroux; Collegeville, Minn.: Liturgical Press, 1988], 20–26), who divides Mark into the same major divisions.

68. For an excellent discussion of the difference between linear outlines and structure in oral performance, see Joanna Dewey, "Mark as Interwoven Tapestry: Forecasts and Echoes for a Listening Audience," *CBQ* 53 (1991): 221–36.

69. Quintilian, *Inst.* 4.1.9; 5.14.32; 6.3.30, 33; 12.9.5–6; and frequently; cf. 8.pr.22–28.

70. Dewey, "Mark as Interwoven Tapestry," 221–36. On repetitions, see also Elizabeth Struthers Malbon, "Echoes and Foreshadowings in Mark 4–8: Reading and Rereading," *JBL* 112 (1993): 211–30.

71. "Son of God" in Mark 1:1 is missing in many manuscripts, but I judge it to be the original reading.

72. Albert Bates Lord, who extensively studied epic poets in the Balkans, has argued that the Synoptic Gospels are variations of a single oral narrative ("The Gospels as Oral Traditional Literature," in *The Relationship among the Gospels: An Interdisciplinary Dialogue* [ed. W. O. Walker; San Antonio: Trinity University Press, 1978], 33–91). In my opinion, it is more likely that Matthew and Luke are dependent on a written version of Mark, but many of the ways they adapt Mark are consistent with variations among different oral performances of the same narrative.

73. I presented some of the material in this section as "Authority, Controversy, Displacement: The Structure of Mark 1.14–3.35" (paper given at the Chesapeake Bay Regional Society of Biblical Literature/Catholic Biblical Association Meeting, April 1986). Mary Ann Tolbert outlines 1:16–3:14 in a similar way but takes 3:7 as the beginning of an new major section that extends to 6:34; see her book *Sowing the Gospel: Mark's World in Literary-Historical Perspective* (Minneapolis: Fortress, 1989), 120, 132).

CHAPTER SIX
Gesture and Movement

Along with the voice, the use of gesture was considered essential for the expression of emotion.[1] Gesture was considered a natural part of oral communication. A statement made by Plato describes the connection between body and voice:

> And in general, when a man uses his voice to talk or sing, he finds it very difficult to keep his body still. This is the origin of the whole art of dancing: the gestures that express what one is saying. Some of us make gestures that are invariably in harmony with our words, but some of us fail.[2]

One of the reasons why the ancients considered the disembodied words of written books to be lacking was the understanding that communication involved the whole body. Words and gesture had not been divorced from each other as they are in print-oriented cultures. The connection between gesture and emotion is shown by Plato's observation earlier in the dialogue that gestures are more vigorous when pleasure is more intense, less vigorous when pleasure is less intense.[3]

The importance of gesture for communication may be seen also in stories of the early life of Apollonius of Tyana. Philostratus, his biographer, depicts Apollonius as a Pythagorean philosopher, and Pythagorean initiates were not allowed to speak for a period of several years. This discipline insured that they could keep secret the esoteric teachings of the sect. Philostratus indicates that during Apollonius's period of silence, he was still able to maintain a conversation by means of his hand gestures and facial expression, and several times he was able to end people's quarrels by the same means.[4] Throughout his biography, Philostratus portrays Apollonius as an ideal speaker. These stories are intended to point up his ability as a "speaker." Apollonius is such a good speaker that he can communicate persuasively even without words.

The importance of gesture in public performance was increased by the noise of the crowds with which speakers often had to contend. The first century B.C.E. historian Diodorus Siculus provides a memorable, though somewhat extreme, example of the near riot that met Phocion's attempt to defend himself against charges of treason brought against him.

> Those who were near him could hear the justice of his case, but those standing further off heard nothing because of the noise made by the people who were interrupting with shouts: they could only see the motions he was making with his body, motions that became passionate and varied because of the greatness of his danger.[5]

Speakers were not always drowned out by the crowd, but to communicate in spite of crowd noise, speakers needed to combine every possible means of expression. Hence, gestures naturally became exaggerated so that they would be clear to the largest possible part of the crowd. Both public speeches and theater productions were often given to crowds of thousands, and both rhetoric and acting developed methods to help performers communicate with such large groups. It is likely that exaggerated gesturing would become such an expected part of oral performance that it carried over into more intimate settings as well, where audience size and noise was not such a serious problem.

If the estimates of crowd sizes in the Gospels are at all correct, then Jesus' own speaking style must have included the kind of exaggerated gestures that were necessary to communicate to these crowds. In Mark's first feeding story, Jesus is said to teach a crowd of five thousand men, presumably accompanied by a considerable number of women and children (Mark 6:34–44). The second feeding story does not mention teaching, but presumably this crowd of four thousand people had also gathered to hear Jesus speak (Mark 8:1–9). In the parable discourse scene, Jesus teaches from a boat to a crowd on the shore (4:1–2). Since Jesus had earlier asked for a boat because he was fearful of being crushed by the crowd (3:9), Mark probably imagines a large crowd for this scene as well. When Jesus is depicted as speaking in the temple in Jerusalem, it is that crowds numbering in the thousands should be imagined. The vast dimension of the temple in

Jerusalem and the presence of large crowds for the Passover festival would make the use of a full-throated oratorical voice and expansive gestures necessary if Jesus hoped to gain any attention when he disrupted the buying and selling of sacrificial animals in the temple (11:15–18). The dispute between Jesus and the chief priests, scribes, and elders about the authority of Jesus (11:27–33) should also be understood as a public debate, with both sides speaking in loud voices, with expansive gestures in order to communicate with the surrounding crowd. If large numbers of people are not listening to the debate, Jesus' opponents would not have been afraid of the crowd. The other debates in the temple would be carried out in the same way. They are public debates in which Jesus and his opponents challenge each other's honor, and the crowd is the judge of the outcome.

In a first-century performance of the Gospels, Jesus would be portrayed much more as an orator than we usually think of him. Even when the scene specifies a large crowd, we often think of Jesus speaking as if he were in a rather intimate setting. Movie portrayals of Jesus also perpetuate this image, since even the most lavish spectacle movies do not hire and costume ten thousand extras for crowd scenes and the close-ups of Jesus speaking bring him close to the viewer. No movie Jesus could ever be heard in the crowds the Gospels report.

Gestures from the Terence Manuscripts

The most valuable sources for the study of gesture on the Roman stage are a number of manuscripts of the comedies of Terence that contain illustrations of scenes.[6] Although the extant manuscripts date from the ninth to twelfth centuries, they are copied quite carefully from a much older original, which can be dated from the styles of hair, clothing, and masks to the middle of the third century C.E.[7] There has been a great deal of debate whether these illustrations portray actual theatrical gestures from antiquity.[8] Since the illustrator was aware of conventions of masking and costuming, it is likely, however, that he was familiar with stage productions of the plays and that the gesturing would reflect the actual conventions of the Roman stage.[9] Some of the gestures correlate with oratorical gestures described by Quintilian in the first century C.E., and others correspond with descriptions of gestures found in the plays of Terence from the second century B.C.E. This shows that the conventions of stage gesture were fairly stable for a considerable period of time, and that the gestures would for the most part correspond to conventions of the first-century stage. Some of these are similar to gestures used in our culture, but others are quite unfamiliar.

Since the manuscripts give illustrations of nearly all the scenes, it is possible to correlate the gestures with emotions that are either expressed or implied in the plays.[10] Quintilian describes three of the gestures for use by orators, and their use in the miniatures corresponds fairly well to the meaning ascribed to them by the teacher of rhetoric. One is used for exhortation. This is done by cupping the hand slightly with the fingers spread and extending the hand and arm in front of one, above the level of the head. Sometimes, especially on the stage, the speaker made his hand quiver for emphasis.[11] This gesture is found in the second-century B.C.E. statue of Aulus Metullus. known as L'Arringatore or the Orator, which appears on the cover of this book.[12] This gesture of exhortation would be appropriate in several speeches of Jesus. For example, in Mark 8:34 Jesus says, "If any want to follow me, let them deny themselves and take up their cross and follow me!" (author). As we shall see, Quintilian expects that several gestures would be made in a single sentence. For this sentence, the performer might use the exhortation gesture for "If any of you want to follow me," the emphatic pointing-down gesture described below for "let them deny themselves," lift his open hands upward on "and take up their cross," and bring his hand to his chest for "and follow me!"

I suggest that you try out the gestures to see how they feel and how they correspond the emotions. Better yet, stand up and try it. And speak up! You want the folks in the back of the room to follow you!

The gesture would also be appropriate for many parts of Jesus' speech in chapter 13, such as, "Watch! Stay awake! for you do not know when the time will come" (13:33, author). Here I might suggest pointing at the audience for "Beware/watch!"; the exhortation gesture for "Stay awake!"; and pointing at a series of individuals in the audience, moving from right to left, in time with "For you," "do not know," "when," "the time," and "will come." The frequency of gestures corresponds to a retarded pace of delivery and emphasizes every group of words. I am fitting gestures to the English; the Greek word order is sometimes different and might require different movements.

The second of the gestures found both in Quintilian and the manuscripts is used for reproaching or refuting others in the plays. In addition to these two functions, orators used it for the beginning of

their speeches and for narrations of fact. This gesture is made by join-
ing the tips of the thumb and middle finger while leaving the other
fingers open. According to Quintilian, this position of the hand was
combined with left and right movement, a slow movement for the
beginning of a speech or for a narration of facts, more energetically
for reproaching someone or refuting something.[13] Because the gesture
is so adaptable, we would expect to find it used often in a performance
of Mark. Jesus frequently reproaches both the disciples, as in 4:13,
"Do you not understand this parable?" and his opponents, as in 7:6,
"Isaiah prophesied well about you play actors!" What Quintilian
means for the movement of reproach or refuting is not a smooth back-
and-forth movement, I imagine, but a more jerky reach. It is combined with a slight up-and-down movement and extension of the arm
so that the speaker is using the gesture to point the hand at the audience. I believe that when reproaching a single person, the back-and-
forth movement would cover only a short distance so that the arm is
always generally pointing at the person being reproached. For a larger
group, one might use a broader left-and-right sweep of the arm, with
several jerky movements as the hand reached in each direction. So one
might get a single left-to-right movement, with the hand stopping at
four different positions for "Do" "you not" "understand" "this parable?" Verse 7:6 might be delivered as "Isaiah" (gesture to the left)
"prophesied well" (gesture to the right) "about you" (gesture toward
the middle, with the hand slightly rotated toward the vertical to make
more of a pointing gesture) "play actors!" (gesture to the left).

The calmer version of the movement would be used for more neutral portions of the narration including the opening words of many
episodes. "And again he began to teach beside the sea" (4:1) may suit-
ably be one sweeping gesture left to right, or a left-right gesture followed by pointing in front to indicate the place of the sea. In 4:10,
"When he was alone" might be a smooth left-right gesture. One
might bring the arm so fully to the left for "those who were around
him" that the arm forms a surrounding gesture. The arm comes back
to the front for "with the twelve."

The third gesture is one of insistence. This consists of pointing
with the extended index finger toward the ground in front of one,
keeping the palm of the hand down.[14] This is a useful gesture, since
Jesus can be very insistent. I expect it is used for all acts of casting out
demons, as in 1:25, "Be silent and come out of him!" I would point
once for "Be silent!" and again for "and come out of him!" with slight

up-and-down movement of the arm between the two. It is also useful for rebuking the sea (4:39), "Quiet! Be silent!" again with two gestures, though more distinct than in the previous instance since the two commands are more distinctly separated here. It is excellent for rebuking a student or a disciple (8:33), "Get behind me, Satan!" with one emphatic gesture.

If you have been a good reader and have followed my instructions to try out the gestures yourself, you may notice that although these gestures are not ones with which we are familiar, they fit the emotions well. They may even help elicit the feelings from you as you use them to accompany the words. That is one reason why gestures were considered so important for speaking.

Other gestures in the Terence manuscripts are not found in Quintilian, but their meaning may be inferred from the scenes in with they appear. In general, all gestures are made by the right hand, as is the case with oratorical gestures as well. A gesture unique to the stage consists of holding the right arm at a right angle with the forearm pointing upward and hand's palm forward, with only the thumb and little finger extended. The hand position is much the same as that often used today to indicate talking on a telephone, but the tip of the thumb points toward the ear, and the little finger points away from the head, not at the mouth. This gesture is used to indicate that a character is eavesdropping but cannot be seen by the speaker. By extension, a performer might have used it for scenes such as the healing of the paralytic (2:1–12), in which Jesus "overhears" the thoughts of others.

An actor can express sorrow by inclining the head to the right and bringing the open right hand to the temple. When bad news comes from the house of Jairus, "Your daughter has died. Why bother the teacher any more?" (5:35), the gesture might be used. I find this gesture remarkably effective in eliciting a feeling of sorrow, almost of tears, in myself when I speak the words. Belligerence is shown by forming a fist and raising it to the level of the face. The demon probably makes the gesture in 1:24, "What have you to do with us, Jesus of Nazareth?" Stoop down a little and shake your fist slightly, and you should feel properly demonic.

To show restraint one extends the right arm moderately to the side, with the palm of the hand down or slightly forward, and all the fingers extended. In dispute episodes, one might use the gesture to begin Jesus' reply to his opponents. "Why does he eat with *tax collectors* and *sinners?*" (2:16). Jesus might well take offense at the attack, but he gives no sign of doing so. I would use the restraint gesture for the introductory "Hearing this, Jesus said to them . . . " (2:17). This saying of Jesus requires gestures that show contrast. Since one's hand is already slightly to the side and pointing downward, it is natural to make the first contrast with a down-and-up movement: "Those who are strong have no need of a doctor. . . ." Since my hand is already slightly downward, I extend it more fully down: " . . . but those who have problems." The natural contrast is to lift my hand upward. But up is usually better than down. The gesture indicates graphically the reversal of valuation. "I have come not to call the righteous . . . " I point toward the scribes, agreeing with their own view of themselves: " . . . but sinners." We need a contrasting gesture. My hand sweeps to the side, indicating and embracing the audience. The righteous are few, indicated by pointing. The sinners are many, indicated by the sweeping motion. But the sinners receive the more embracing gesture, the righteous a slightly accusing point. Once again, the shifted valuation can be indicated with gestures. The Syrophoenician woman might also use the restraint gesture in replying to Jesus' comment about throwing food to the dogs (7:28).

The gesture for compliance is made by extending the arm in front of one and bent into a right angle, the forearm pointing upward, palm toward one's face, with the index and middle fingers extended. This is good for the call of the disciples (1:18): "And immediately, leaving the nets . . . " One might indicate with one's hands the place where the nets are being left: " . . . they followed him." Here one uses the compliance gesture, indicating one's own identification with the obedient fishermen.

Dissent is shown by extending the arm to the side, palm down about waist high and with the fingers open. Notice how the use of this gesture clarifies Jesus reply to the disciples' question about Elijah (9:12–13). "Elijah is coming first and restores everything." In this part Jesus agrees with the scribes. Next Jesus raises an objection: "And how is it written of the Son of Man . . . ?" By using the dissent gesture at this point, I can communicate that I am raising an objection before I even speak the words.[15]

To show approval one extends the forearm in a more or less right angle in front of one, palm upward, with the thumb and index finger forming a circle and the other fingers extended. "Amen!" "I say" "to you" "that this" "poor widow" "dropped in" "more . . . " I give the approval gesture, adding a bounce to emphasize each group of words:

" . . . than all those others. . . ." The performer points to the side to show contrast. " . . . who dropped money in the treasury." Point to the front to indicate the treasury.

Puzzlement is shown by pointing to the face with the forefinger ("What is this?" in 1:27); and love by raising the open hand, palm down, above the head ("Jesus loved him and said . . . " in 10:21). Fear is shown by extending both open hands moderately to the side with the palm or palms forward, hands about shoulder height. This gesture is similar to the orans posture of prayer often found in early Christian art, and is good for disciples in storms—"Teacher! Do you not care if we die?" (4:38)—or women fleeing from the tomb (16:8). Supplication, a common attitude in the Gospel, is shown by moderately extending one or both arms, midtorso height, with fingers open and palms more or less upward. "My little daughter is about to die! Come, lay your hands on her, so that she may be saved and live!" (5:23). Surprise or amazement is shown by holding the arm to the side, elbow crooked, hand about shoulder height, with the fingers open and the palm more or less upward. "And all were amazed" (1:27). "All were astonished" (2:12). "And everyone was amazed" (5:20). "Pilate was amazed" (15:5, 44).

Pondering may be shown by bringing a half-closed fist to the side of one's jaw in a position somewhat similar to that of the statue known as the Thinker.[16] The Gospel is too fast paced for a great deal of pondering, but Pilate may ponder for a while in the middle of interrogating Jesus, and then ask, "Will you not answer at all?" (15:4). Jesus may ponder the temple for a while before saying, "Not one stone will be left here upon another" (13:2). Jesus may also ponder for a while after the request of James and John to sit on his right and his left in glory (10:37). I always indicate right and left here by extending my arms fully in a crucifix position. A moment of pondering before the reply of Jesus brings home even more the ridiculous nature of the request and the almost horrible contrast with the way of the cross.

In some cases the gestures from the Terence manuscripts are different from those used in art to express the same emotions. In Roman art, surprise was usually shown with a gesture of raising one or both hands with the palm outward. Perplexity was generally shown by bringing the hand toward the face or grasping the beard. This suggests that the gestures used in the theater may not always be the same as those used in everyday life.[17] We cannot determine with certainty the exact vocabulary of gestures that would be used in a narrative recitation. The performer may borrow from the stage, from rhetoric, or from everyday life. It is clear, though, that systems of gesturing were available to express a variety of emotions and attitudes, and a performer of oral narrative would surely use gestures much in the same way.

Implied Gestures in the Text of Mark

There are two main types of gestures that a performer of Mark might use. In one type are the rhetorical gestures that would accompany the speeches of different characters. The other type is imitative, in which the performer acts out the deeds of a character. The rhetorical handbooks make a point of distancing rhetorical gestures from those of actors. Quintilian cautions against imitating either the action or characterizing the voice of another whom the orator is describing.[18] Actors, on the other hand, imitated both action and voice. Storytelling, or the performance of narrative, falls somewhere between these two styles, more imitative than orators but with more restrained action than the comic stage or the dance. One possible analogy is Theophrastus' delivery of his *Characters*, which was rather imitative. He is said to have stuck out his tongue and licked his lips while portraying the character of the epicure.[19] The performer can bring the scene before the eyes of the audience either by describing the scene as happening in front of the audience, as if both the performer and the audience are watching, or the performer can step more into the action and partially act out the described behavior. Since the rhetorician's aversion to imitation is linked to class distinctions, Christian performers, who would not have come from the aristocratic class, may have been less wary of crossing the line into acting.

It is likely that reference to the gestures of characters would be incorporated into the performance if that can be done without disruption of the narrative flow of the story. In healing Simon's mother-in-law, for example, Jesus *approaches* her, *grasps* her hand, and *helps her up* (1:31). In healing of the leper, he *stretches out* his hand and *touches* him (1:41). When healing the man with the withered hand, he *looks around* at his opponents in anger (3:5). When his mother comes to seize him, Jesus *looks around* at those seated in the circle and says, "Here are my mother and my brothers!" (3:32–33). When touched by the woman with a hemorrhage, Jesus *turns around* in the crowd and asks, "Who has touched my clothes?" (5:31). He *looks around* to see who has done it (5:32). Healing the little girl, he *takes* her by the hand (5:41). Feeding the five thousand, Jesus *looks up* to heaven, says the blessing, and *breaks* the loaves (6:41). Healing the deaf man, he *puts his finger* into the man's ear, *spits*, *touches* his tongue, and *looks up* to heaven (7:33–34). Generally these are gestures of reaching, touching, or looking.

Some gestures of other characters are also reported. The woman with the hemorrhage *touches* his cloak (5:27). Many in the crowd *spread* their cloaks and leafy branches on the road in front of Jesus during his entry into Jerusalem and form a parade ahead and behind him (11:8–9). The high priest *tears his clothes* when Jesus states that he is the Messiah, the Son of the Blessed One (14:63). Some of the assembled priests, elders, and scribes *spit on* Jesus (14:65). The soldiers *salute* Jesus, *spit on* him, and *kneel down* in mock homage (15:18). Some actions may take the performer too far out of his or her role as narrator. For example, a number of suppliants either fall, bow, or kneel down at the feet of Jesus (5:6, 22; 7:25; 10:17), and the boy with an unclean spirit lies like a corpse after being delivered from its grip (9:26). Actions such as these may be indicated by hand gestures so that the performer can maintain an attitude of addressing the audience.

There are also places where Jesus employs rhetorical props to make a point. Twice Jesus makes use of children as rhetorical props. He answers the question, who is the greatest, by taking a child, putting it in the middle of the disciples, and then taking it in his arms to illustrate the meaning of serving all, even a little child (9:33–37). Jesus combines the saying about entering the kingdom of God as a little child with the gesture of taking the children in his arms, laying his hands on them, and blessing them (10:15–16).

Jesus' action in the temple is an extreme version of a rhetorical gesture (11:15–17). Turning over the tables and chairs of the moneychangers and merchants in the temple would have disrupted their commerce for a while, but it is unlikely to have any long-term effect. Presumably, they were back in business as soon as Jesus left. It is quite effective, though, in underlining Jesus' point, that God is unhappy with what is being done in the temple. The merchants, their tables and chairs, and their coins and merchandize are used as props to make a point. I have on occasion knocked over tables and chairs in performances, which effectively presents how forceful Jesus' action is, though it is sometimes perceived as comic because it is so unexpected. On one famous occasion, I flipped the wooden lectern off its table in a classroom, cracking it rather severely.

When asked whether it is lawful to pay taxes to the emperor, Jesus calls for a denarius coin. As he asks whose head and title is on the coin, he must be holding the coin up and pointing, though the specific gesture is not described (12:13–17). This is easy to work into a performance because it is a simple matter to have a coin along. I have found that using a coin to perform the scene tends to shift the meaning of the debate, since Jesus' statement, "Give to the emperor the things that are the emperor's," is no longer ambiguous when the performer is holding up the coin. Clearly, the coin belongs to the emperor, and when acted out with the coin, the statement denigrates money. I found it natural to flip the coin away disdainfully at the end of the saying, though I admit that I generally use a quarter rather than a coin worth a whole day's earnings. The gesture provoked great applause from one of my classes, but not because of agreement with the sentiment. The quarter had landed in the tray below the chalkboard behind me, and the applause was for the skill with which I had aimed it.

Jesus later uses another action with coins to make a different point. The poor widow contributing her two small coins to the treasury is used to teach about the relative value of different offerings (12:41–44). Roman orators often made use of statues and buildings in the environments in which they spoke to arouse patriotic or religious feeling or to make other points in their speeches, and on occasion they even set up props in the environment before a speech.[20] Jesus may have located himself near the treasury so that he could make observations about the people contributing, so the observation may not have been entirely spontaneous.

Gestures for Specific Scenes

Some of the gestures described by Quintilian and Cicero are appropriate for particular episodes in the Gospel. Cicero mentions striking the brow, stamping the foot, and slapping the thigh as expressions of anger, and Quintilian mentions with disapproval the additional gestures of clapping the hands and beating the breast.[21] Gestures such as these would likely be used for passages where Jesus expresses anger, such as the denunciation of the Pharisees and scribes (7:6–8), or Jesus' quotation from Isaiah as he drives the money changers and merchants out of the temple (11:17). It might also be used in the episode of the man with the withered hand, as Jesus looks around in anger (3:5). I find it more appropriate to stamp or slap one's thigh in that scene than to use the theatrical gesture of belligerence with the fist. Stamping portrays anger but is not threatening. Such gestures would also surely accompany the denunciation of scribes and Pharisees in Matthew (23:1–39). According to Herodotus, the Spartans struck their foreheads while lamenting the death of their king, so we might also find such a gesture in the scenes of the death of John the Baptist and the passion of Jesus.[22]

A pose that is frequently found in the depiction of women has been called the *pudicitia*, or modesty, gesture. This is made by bending the left arm across the waist with the palm held open and facing downward while the right elbow rests on the back of the left hand. The right arm is bent upward toward the face with the forefinger extended and the others curled inward. The forefinger typically ends up at the level of the chin or cheek and often lightly touches the face.[23] This gesture is generally understood to convey a woman's modesty. It would be quite appropriate for women seeking healing from Jesus. The woman with the issue of blood (5:24–34) wants to receive healing unnoticed by the crowd and is terrified when Jesus draws attention to her. It would be appropriate to emphasize her modesty with some variation of the gesture. One might hold the left hand toward the face with the forefinger extended while reaching out for Jesus' garment with the right hand, thus softening the boldness of action and showing the woman's effort to overcome her natural modesty. One might also assume the gesture when the woman, after her discovery, comes before Jesus in fear and trembling.

The same gesture might be used ironically in the scene of Herod's banquet. Herod's daughter might well assume the pose both when she asks her mother what she should request from the king and later while requesting the head of John the Baptist on a platter (6:24–25). The modesty of the gesture would emphasize the immodest nature of her demand and add to the somewhat surreal degeneracy of the scene. The Syrophoenician woman may assume the pose when replying to Jesus, "Lord, even the dogs under the table eat from the children's crumbs" (7:28). When combined with the restraint gesture from the theater, it would be quite effective. It matches the self-deprecation of the remark and at the same time softens her impertinence in talking back to Jesus.

In all three cases, the women are acting with a boldness that is at odds with the prevailing assumptions of the culture about the roles of men and women, at least as recorded by men. The modesty gesture would keep the "good" but bold women within the cultural norms while they in fact act with power. Since the gesture is the most common one for women in artistic representations, a male performer might assume the posture whenever he switches into a woman's role, to indicate a gender shift.

Connecting Passages through Gesture

In my own performances of Mark, I have noticed that I tend to use the same gestures for similar words or situations. This has a tendency to emphasize the similarities between scenes, especially when the gestures are in some way distinctive. In a previous chapter, I suggested that the repetition of the feeding episodes is emphasized by the use of similar inflections for repetitive dialogue as well as by similar gestures for similar actions. Since Jesus blesses the bread in both scenes (6:41; 8:6), it is natural to assume the same pose for each blessing. The first episode specifies that Jesus looks up to heaven. From catacomb paintings, we know that early Christians prayed with hands outstretched and palms lifted upward. Jesus might assume that position, or he might lift imaginary bread (or even real bread, if one imagines the Gospel presented after dinner or in conjunction with a Lord's Supper) in a gesture reminiscent of the ritual blessing of the bread. In each case the blessing is followed by a distribution to the disciples, which suggests some gesture of distribution. The combination of two distinctive gestures in both episodes draws the episodes together in the experience of the audience.

The same effect can even take place in widely separated episodes. The baptism of Jesus and the death scene both make use of the Greek word *schizō* meaning to spit, cleave, or tear, often in a violent manner (1:10; 15:38). In the baptismal scene, the heavens are torn open; in the crucifixion scene, the curtain of the temple is torn apart. The word does not appear anywhere else in Mark. The curtain of the temple was embroidered with stars to represent heaven, and God was understood to dwell both in heaven and in the temple; hence, Mark intends to make a connection between the two events[24] Since Paul assumes a general understanding of baptism as a participation in the death of Jesus (Rom 6:3–4), it is symbolically appropriate to connect the two scenes. Yet one is at the beginning of the Gospel and the other is at the end. How could anyone ever notice the repetition of a single word separated by nearly two hours of narration? With the addition of gestures, the connection between the scenes becomes clearer. I found that I naturally used the same gesture for splitting in both episodes, lifting my hands above my head, firmly seizing an imaginary cloth, and forcefully ripping it apart. In both cases the ripping gesture is followed by an up-to-down gesture, indicating the descent of the dove or the tearing of the curtain from top to bottom. In both cases, I raise my right hand high above my head and bring it straight down. The gestures are not identical, since I indicate the descent of the dove with an open hand, palm mostly upward, while the top-to-bottom sweep is more of a pointing gesture, but the hand movement is identical. Both of these gestures occur only in these places in the narrative. They are very distinctive and striking, and so it is much easier for the audience to make a connection. Since the inclusion of the detail that the curtain of the temple split from top to bottom is rather gratuitous, it may even have developed in order to mirror the descending gesture of the baptismal scene. In one performance, which took place in a glass-enclosed space, the gesture of tearing the heavens met with an unexpected roar of approval from the audience. I only discovered the reason at the conclusion of the performance. At the very instant that I had torn the heavens open, a great deluge of rain poured down from the clouds. I had been concentrating on the performance and the audience and had not even noticed. I am sure that gathering recognized the tearing gesture the second time around.

The use of repeated gestures also helps to point out details of the Gospel that may otherwise go unnoticed. For example, I had never observed how often a large crowd surrounds Jesus until I started using sweeping hand gestures to indicate the presence of the crowd. The word for crowd occurs thirty-eight times in the Gospel. I certainly do not use the sweeping-crowd gesture for all those occurrences, since the crowd is not always an important part of the narrative, but I find myself using it so often that the crowds become a major feature of the Gospel in performance. The crowds become almost ever present, and the apparent popularity of Jesus makes both the misunderstanding motif and the betrayal and death of Jesus even more poignant.

Notes

1. On gesture in various forms of oral delivery in the Greco-Roman world, see Karl Sittl, *Die Gebärden der Griechen und Romer* (Leipzig: B. G. Teubner, 1890); Barthélemy-A. Taladoire, *Commentaires sur la Mimique et l'Expression Corporelle du Comédien Romain* (CFLUM 1; Montpellier: Ch. Délian, 1951); Fritz Graf, "Gestures and Conventions: The Gestures of Roman Actors and Orators," in *A Cultural History of Gesture* (ed. J. Bremmer and H. Roodenburg; Ithaca: Cornell University Press, 1986), 36–58; Ursula Maier-Eichhorn, *Die Gestikulation in Quintilians Rhetorik* (EHKSL ser. 15, vol. 41; Frankfurt am Main: Peter Lang, 1989); James Anthony Fredal, "Beyond the Fifth Canon: Body Rhetoric in Ancient Greece" (Ph.D. diss., Ohio State University, Columbus, 1998); Alan L. Boegehold, *When a Gesture Was Expected: A Selection of Examples from Archaic and Classical Greek Literature* (Princeton: Princeton University Press, 1999); Gregory S. Aldrete, *Gestures and Acclamations in Ancient Rome* (Baltimore: The Johns Hopkins University Press, 1999), 3–84; C. R. Dodwell, *Anglo-Saxon Gestures and the Roman Stage* (prepared for publication by Timothy Graham; CSASE 28; Cambridge: Cambridge University Press, 2000); Andrea G. Katsouris [Andreas G. Katsourēs], Ῥητορικὴ Ὑποκρίση [Oratorical delivery] (Iōannina, Greece: Panepistēmio Iōanninōn, 1989), which includes over one hundred plates, mostly from Greek and Roman sources, illustrating gestures. For gesture in Greek and Roman art, see Richard Brilliant, *Gesture and Rank in Roman Art: The Use of Gestures to Denote Status in Roman Sculpture and Coinage* (CAASMem 14; New Haven: The Academy, 1963); Gerhard Neumann, *Gesten und Gebärden in der griechischen Kunst* (Berlin: de Gruyter, 1965).

2. Plato, *Leg.* 816a (Saunders); citation from Boegehold, *When a Gesture*, 13.

3. Plato, *Leg.* 815e.

4. Philostratus, *Vit. Apoll.* 1.14–15.

5. Diodorus Siculus, *Bib. hist.* 18.67; citation and translation from Boegehold, *When a Gesture*, 13.

6. For the complete set of miniatures, see L. W. Jones and C. R. Morey, *The Miniatures of the Manuscripts of Terence prior to the Thirteenth Century* (2 vols.; Princeton: 1930–31). An extensive selection is included in Dodwell, *Anglo-Saxon Gestures.*

7. I take the evidence presented by Dodwell as conclusive (*Anglo-Saxon Gestures*, 4–21).

8. K. E. Weston suggested that a number of these illustrations include hand gestures that correspond to the descriptions of Quintilian (Karl E. Weston, "The Illustrated Terence Manuscripts," *HSCP* 14 [1903]: 37–54, esp. 49–53). Jones and Morey, however, argued that Weston's comparisons were overdrawn and the gestures in the manuscripts have more similarity with the gestures recorded in medieval art (Miniatures of Terence). More recently, Aldrete has argued for a correlation with the gestures of Quintilian (Aldrete, *Gestures and Acclamations*, 55–58).

9. Dodwell, *Anglo-Saxon Gestures*, 22–33.

10. On the meaning of the gestures, I am following Dodwell, *Anglo-Saxon Gestures*, 22–96. See also Aldrete, *Gestures and Acclamations*, 54–67. From the manuscripts Dodwell includes illustrations of all the gestures for which he has determined a meaning.

11. Quintilian, *Inst.* 11.3.103.

12. Diana E. E. Kleiner, *Roman Sculpture* (New Haven: Yale University Press, 1992), 34.

13. Quintilian, *Inst.* 11.3.92.

14. Quintilian, *Inst.* 11.3.94.

15. For an excellent analysis of the form of the argument in this passage, see Joel Marcus, "Mark 9,11–13: As It Has Been Written," *ZNW* 80 (1989): 42–63.

16. All these are taken from Dodwell, *Anglo-Saxon Gestures,* 22–96. From the Terence miniatures he includes illustrations of all the gestures.

17. Dodwell, *Anglo-Saxon Gestures,* 86–88.

18. Quintilian, *Inst.* 11.3.89–91.

19. Athenaeus, *Deipn.* 1.21b.

20. For examples, see Aldrete, *Gestures and Acclamations,* 17–34.

21. Cicero, *Brut.* 80.278.

22. Herodotus, *Hist.* 6.58.1.

23. Aldrete, *Gestures and Acclamations,* 65.

24. Josephus, *B.J.* 5.5.4; 213.

CHAPTER SEVEN
The Audience

In oral performance, the performer is only one side of the equation. Oral performance also involves an audience, and a significant part of the experience is found in the reactions of the listeners.[1] Thus, if we are to understand the actual experience of hearing the Gospel as a communal event, we have to imagine audience response as part of that experience. If we are to recover the meaning of the Gospel as an aural event, we need to think about how the performer would try to move and involve the audience in and through the recitation of the Gospel. We have already observed some ways in which audiences affected delivery. Performers can tailor their material to fit specific audiences and situations. The size of the crowds had a great effect on performance styles. Crowd noise was often a problem, and a hostile crowd could drown out a performer. With a high degree of probability we can reconstruct the general norms for audience reaction in the first-century Mediterranean world.

Audiences at Philosophical Gatherings

The style of audience reaction varies with the type of performance and the social situation in which it is presented. Both church and synagogue assemblies had resemblances to philosophical schools, which the apologists of both religions exploited when attempting to explain their faiths to the outside world.[2] Thus the behavior of audiences at philosophical lectures may give us the clearest indication of how Christian audiences might react. Philosophers were expected to indulge in less of the vocal gymnastics and verbal ornamentation that earned the rhetors such hearty applause. It was, nevertheless, common for audiences at philosophical lectures to respond with applause, although some writers felt it was not appropriate to applaud such serious lectures as enthusiastically as rhetorical show speeches. The Stoic philosopher Musonius Rufus complained about inappropriate applause that greeted many philosophical lectures.

> When a philosopher, . . . [Musonius] says, is uttering words of encouragement, of warning, of persuasion, or of rebuke, or is discussing any other philosophical theme, then if his hearers utter trite and commonplace expressions of praise without reflection or restraint, if they shout too, if they gesticulate, if they are stirred and swayed and impassioned by the charm of his utterance, by the rhythm of his words, and by certain musical notes, as it were, then you may know that speaker and hearers are wasting their time, and that they are not hearing a philosopher's lecture, but a fluteplayer's recital.[3]

Another first-century philosopher, Epictetus, complains about those who present philosophical lectures for the sake of display and are discouraged when their listeners do not cry out their applause.[4] Such lecturers, in Epictetus's portrayal, fill their speeches with descriptions of Pan and the Nymphs, the death of Achilles, the exploits of Xerxes, and the battle of Thermopylae as well as literarily ornamented thoughts and phrases.[5] They read accounts of Socrates as if his words were the speeches of the orators Lysias or Isocrates, debating about fine points of style.[6] He contrasts this with the attitude of Musonius Rufus, "If you have nothing better to do than to praise me, then I am speaking to no purpose."[7]

Plutarch provides careful instructions on the proper way to applaud philosophical lectures in his talk entitled *On Listening to Lectures*. He warns listeners against losing their critical judgment as a result of the exuberant applause of others who shout and leap to their feet.[8] Plutarch admonishes listeners not to be overly concerned about matters of style, whether the speaker used pure Attic diction, or matters of phrasing and delivery.[9] Like Musonius, he faults extravagant applause more suited for the displays of sophists or the performances of flute-players, harpists, or dancers.[10] Philosophers often aimed at causing pain and shame with their reproof, "in words that penetrate like a biting drug," and it was inappropriate to applaud lines intended not to entertain but to move the soul to reform.[11] The proper response to a philosophical lecture is to continue thinking over the topic oneself after the lecture is over.[12] Such a response is described in Lucian's *Wisdom of Nigrinus*, where the narrator describes calling the philosopher's words to mind two or three times a day, just as lovers constantly call to mind the words and actions of their sweethearts.[13] Members of the audience also had the ability to guide the subject of a philosopher's talk. They frequently proposed problems, interjected questions, and advanced difficulties, often sidetracking the speaker's lecture.[14] When the listeners suggested questions for discussion, some would pose questions outside the speaker's area of expertise in order to show off their own profundity or show up the limitations of the speaker.[15]

Audiences at Religious Gatherings

Audiences in some religious gatherings were considerably more restrained than those that we have discussed so far. Among the Gentiles were a number of religious rites that go by the general name of "mysteries." The mystery religions involved initiations that generally took place at night and included performances of various types. We do not know the details about the initiations because the initiates were sworn to secrecy. It was well-known, however, that the initiates kept silent during at least part of the ritual. The silence of the mysteries was such a commonplace that it can be invoked as a simile to describe a dead silence.[16] Audiences were also silent during the sacrifices of animals. Music was played on the flute and the priest recited a prayer, but the audience remained silent. Then, when the death blow was struck, the women raised a shrill cry.[17]

The inscription of the Rule of the Iobacchoi (about 178 C.E.) contains rules of conduct at one Bacchic society and gives the following direction: "No one may either sing or shout or clap during the sacrifice, but each shall speak and act as his function requires quietly and in good order as directed by the priest or the archbacchos."[18] The silence during the sacrifice stands in contrast with behavior during the meal, during which the rules of no fighting, taking the seat of another, or use of abusive language apply.[19] The same inscription records acclamations from the audience that accompanied adoption of the rule, such as the following: "The priest has done well!" "We always observe these!" "Restore the statutes!" "It is fitting for you!" "Tranquility and good order to the Bacchic Society!" "Put the statutes on a stele!" "Put the question!" "Long life to the most excellent priest Herodes!" "Now you will prosper!" "Now we are the first of all Bacchic Societies!" "The vice-priest has done well!" "Let the stele be made!"[20] The acclamations of the Senate, the army, and the people were essential parts of the process of proclaiming an emperor, and the acclamations of the society may be included in the inscription for similar legitimating function.[21] It is clear from the inscription that different standards for audience behavior apply for different parts of these religious gatherings.

Although the synagogue scenes in the Gospels are only presented in schematic form, they indicate active audience interaction with speakers. Jesus' inaugural sermons in both Mark (1:21–28) and Luke (4:16–30) meet with vigorous responses. In Mark, the audience is amazed at the authority of Jesus' teaching. One man, possessed by a demon, yells out disruptively, causing Jesus to seriously modify his presentation. Audience members discuss with each other the meaning of Jesus and his teaching. In Luke, the audience bears witness to Jesus, which in this context implies some form of applause, and discuss their opinions of him while he is speaking. After Jesus changes his tone, suggesting that the gifts of God have come for the Gentiles, the audience becomes enraged, throws him out of town, and tries to kill him.

We can also gain some indication of audience interaction in Jewish and Christian contexts from the accounts of assemblies in the Acts. Acts depicts several speeches made by Christian leaders and often includes audience response in the descriptions. At Pentecost, the crowd attracted by the believers' speaking in tongues are amazed and debate the meaning of this occurrence among themselves. Some think they are drunk. Peter begins his address by refuting that charge (Acts 2:4–21). At the end of the speech, members of the audience ask a question, which leads to a continuation of the speech (Acts 2:37–40). Peter's speech at the temple also begins from the crowd's reaction, this time to a healing, but is cut short by the arrest of Peter and John before the crowd reacts to the speech itself (Acts 3:11–4:3). When Stephen speaks, members of the synagogue of the Freedmen stand up and argue with him (Acts 6:8–10). After his long speech in chapter 7, the audience is enraged, grind their teeth, cover their ears to show their disapproval, and shout. Then they rush at him, drag him out of the city, and stone him (Acts 7:54–58).

The first-century Jewish monastics described by Philo in the *Contemplative Life* also respond enthusiastically to their speakers, although in an unusual way. As might be expected, they clap at the end of the discourse of the president, but during the speech they applaud with nods and facial expressions and indicate difficulty by movements of the head and hand.[22] Philo describes their silent applause during the speech as if his audience would find it a curious anomaly. John Chrysostom compares synagogue gatherings to effeminate choruses and complains about the Jews, "They drag the whole theater and the practices of the stage into the synagogue. For there is no difference between the theater and the synagogue."[23] Raucous audience reaction was at some point incorporated into the ritual of synagogue readings of the book of Esther at Purim, where the stamping of feet, hissing, booing, and clamor of noisemakers accompanies every mention of the evil Haman. Christian audiences may have greeted mention of the Pharisees or high priests with the same passionate disapproval.

Audience Reaction in Early Christian Gatherings

There was certainly considerable audience participation in many Christian gatherings. The church in Corinth, founded by Paul, is the first-century group about which we know the most. Audience participation was definitely the norm at Corinth. "When you come together," Paul says, "*each one* has a hymn, a lesson, a revelation, a tongue, or an interpretation" (1 Cor 14:26b, emphasis added). Paul, in seeking to create more orderly gatherings, does not oppose the participation of many individuals. He seeks only to reduce the participation to one person at a time, so that each presentation is a communal act. He does not want the group to fragment into factions competing in spiritual gifts or into individuals pursuing their own experience with the Spirit without reference to the group. Paul's list of spiritual gifts presupposes interaction. One person speaks in tongues, another interprets (1 Cor 12:10; 14:5, 27). The one who discerns spirits presumably acts as a check on those exercising other spiritual gifts (1 Cor 12:9). Paul's argument assumes response from more passive members of the audience as well. How can an outsider respond with "Amen" to someone speaking in tongues, since the outsider cannot understand what is said (1 Cor 14:16)? If all speak in tongues, unbelievers who are present will respond with jeers and say, "You are out of your mind" (1 Cor 14:23). If a prophet discloses the secrets of an unbeliever's heart, the unbeliever responds with praise: "God is really among you!" (1 Cor 14:24–25).

It was also common for early Christian audiences to interrupt a speaker's exhortation with questions, just as audiences did at philosophical gatherings. Paul's injunction against women speaking in church presupposes such a situation. If women want to learn anything, Paul says, they should "ask their husbands at home" (1 Cor 14:34–35). They are not to interrupt the speaker. The result, Paul hopes, will be a more orderly meeting of the assembly. Interruptions of the speaker will be reduced, and discourse will be limited to male members of the assembly.[24] The Corinthian church may not be typical of all early Christian gatherings, and certainly Paul wants to correct some of their excesses, but the reliance on the Spirit in other Pauline churches (1 Thess 5:19–21) as well as non-Pauline churches (1 John 4:1–3) suggests that much the same kind of audience interactions would be found there as well.

Paul's complaints about the way the Corinthians practice the Lord's Supper suggests a great deal of informality (1 Cor 11:17–33). The supper is treated like an ordinary dinner gathering, where one would expect both conversation and entertainment presented by various diners. In the context of the church the entertainment may take on a religious tone, with the offering of hymns, teachings, or prophecies, as practiced when the church gathered without dinner. If church members are drinking enough to become drunk (1 Cor 11:21), that would surely increase the liveliness of the festivities, though probably not in the most beneficial manner. If analogous behavior at non-Christian dinners is any guide, the division into factions at dinner suggests division by seating. The factions would indulge in a certain amount of heckling and jeering when someone from another faction spoke or sang, as well as loudly applauding their own speakers. Since at least some factions identified themselves with different apostles (1 Cor 1:12), the mention of their apostle-patrons undoubtedly provoked an enthusiastic response. They might take the opportunity at dinner to argue for their own theological positions. Those who rejected a final bodily resurrection (1 Cor 15:12) might argue against those who believed in it; those who approved of the man living with his father's wife (1 Cor 5:1–6) might argue with those who rejected such behavior. One would expect the same sort of competitive interaction between the associates of the members who had brought litigation against each other (1 Cor 6:1–8).

Many of the Corinthians are impressed with the "superapostles" (2 Cor 11:5), who complain about Paul's contemptible ability as a speaker (2 Cor 10:10) and may well have been trained in rhetoric (2 Cor 11:6). Those Corinthians would certainly expect the same rhetorical display from their own leaders that they would find in many philosophical gatherings or in the show speeches of the rhetoricians. If so, they would be inclined to react in church just like the audiences attending those gatherings.

If I am correct about the level of audience response in Christian churches, the reading or recitation of Paul's letters must have been quite an exciting event, especially in situations like Corinth or the Galatian churches, where Paul seeks to correct beliefs and behavior common in a church. We would expect the different factions in the church to be loudly supporting their own point of view by cheering or jeering the words of Paul. In the Galatian churches, where Paul's position may not have much following, it would require a great deal of rhetorical skill for someone to present the letter to the church without being shouted down by Paul's opponents. Because of the importance of delivery for the way the letters would be received, one would expect Paul to send the letter with a trusted and rhetorically adept assistant, and to demonstrate to his representative the proper delivery. The assistant would likely spend much of his or her traveling time studying and memorizing the letter so that it could be properly delivered.[25]

Christian sermons of a later period also met with enthusiastic applause.[26] In the early fifth century C.E., Jerome complains about heretical preachers: "They persuade the people that what they invent is true; then, in a theatrical manner, they invite applause and shouting."[27] Augustine expects frequent and vigorous applause in reaction to Christian speakers and recounts how one of his own speeches was met with both applause and tears.[28] Hesychius praises Christians for continually applauding their speakers.[29] John Chrysostom, on the other hand, opposes loud applause, saying that Christians should practice stillness and orderliness, not the applause and handclapping that are found in the theater and at drinking parties.[30] Though Chrysostom opposed loud applause, many in his churches must have felt it was appropriate, or he would not have needed to make the argument.

Audience Response to Mark

It is clear that just as audiences of the first-century Mediterranean world preferred a much more vigorous and florid speaking style than is popular today, they applauded much more readily and vigorously than do most audiences today. I for one must admit that no one has ever mistaken one of my New Testament classes for a rock concert because of the loud cheers escaping the windows of my classroom. Thus, in thinking of the reaction of a Markan audience to the delivery of the Gospel, we should not be bound by contemporary expectations of what might provoke applause but must, as well as we can, place ourselves in the frame of mind of a first-century audience.

We have seen, however, that audience response in those gatherings varied from the silence of mystery initiations to raucous applause for philosophical and religious sermons. Thus, the reception for the Gospel depends in large part on how the event was understood. A performance of the Gospel in conjunction with a ritual such as baptism or the Lord's Supper might have received a more subdued response than a performance in a different context.

Given the standards of first-century recitations, we should expect a spirited performance of the Gospel. I have argued here that the audience response would be equally spirited. Although this cannot be shown from parallels in the culture, it is certainly possible that a Christian audience might have a spirited response in a quite literal way, with various charismatic reactions being provoked by the experience of the Gospel performance. There are certainly parallels to that found in audience responses to preaching in Spirit-filled churches today, where members of the audience may be "slain in the Spirit" or dance in the aisles during a sermon. A negative version of spirited response is reported by Tertullian, who records the case of a Christian woman who attended the theater, came back possessed by a demon, and had to undergo an exorcism.[31]

The fact that applause was understood to be a weapon to be used in competitive situations may have some bearing on the reception of the Gospel of Mark. A number of scholars have suggested that Mark was written within a context of factional fighting in the early church. If that was the case, a performance of the Gospel would be accompanied by loud cheering at appropriate points in the narrative from the pro-Markan forces within the audience. In response, the anti-Mark faction might heckle the performer when the Gospel expressed points of view with which they disagreed. With a Gospel performance, however, heckling might be reduced since the opposing points of view would generally be expressed by Jesus. The audience might find it uncomfortable to voice opposition to Jesus, even in the form of a narrative Jesus. It would certainly be possible, however, to attack the veracity of the performer. The audience might yell out things like "Liar!" or "Jesus never said that!" or the Greek equivalent of "What a crock!"

One could easily imagine a performance degenerating into a yelling match between factions in the audience. In fact, it might be impossible to perform the Gospel before a divided audience if the audience understood the Gospel to be the expression of a factional opinion.

To some extent one could test theories that see Mark as part of factional fighting within the church by examining the passages at which a pro-Markan audience ought to applaud if the Gospel is in fact addressing factional issues. As we will see in the next chapter, there may be stylistic indicators of intended applause points. Since any competent writer would design the narrative to elicit, or at least allow for, applause when he was making an important point, stylistic analysis of the Gospel for applause points should offer one more tool for the evaluation of such theories.

Notes

1. There has been little discussion of audience reaction in relationship to the Gospels. Richard A. Burridge has some insightful comments about audiences and audience reaction in "About People, by People, for People: Gospel Genre and Audiences," in *The Gospel for All Christians: Rethinking the Gospel Audiences* (ed. R. Bauckham; Grand Rapids: Eerdmans, 1998), 113–45. Much information on Roman theater audiences can be found in Richard C. Beacham, *The Roman Theatre and Its Audience* (Cambridge: Harvard University Press, 1992); Shadi Bartsch, *Actors in the Audience: Theatricality and Doublespeak from Nero to Hadrian* (Cambridge: Harvard University Press, 1994). For audiences in rhetoric, see William M. A. Grimaldi, "The Auditor's Role in Aristotelian Rhetoric," in *Oral and Written Communication: Historical Approaches* (ed. R. L. Enos; WCA 4; Newbury Park, Calif.: Sage, 1990), 65–81.

2. Comparisons between early Christian communities and philosophic schools have been made by E. A. Judge, "The Early Christians as a Scholastic Community," *JRH* 1 (1960-61), 4–15, 125–37; Abraham J. Malherbe, *Social Aspects of Early Christianity* (2d, enlarged ed.; Philadelphia: Fortress, 1983), 45–54; and with reservations, Wayne A. Meeks, *The First Urban Christians* (New Haven: Yale University Press, 1983), 81–84.

3. Quoted in Aulus Gellius, *Noct. att.* 5.1.1 (Rolfe, LCL); cf. Epictetus, *Diatr.* 3.23.29.

4. Epictetus, *Diatr.* 3.23.10.

5. Epictetus, *Diatr.* 3.23.11, 35, 38, 31–32.

6. Epictetus, *Diatr.* 3.23.20–21.

7. Epictetus, *Diatr.* 3.23.29.

8. Plutarch, *Rect. rat. aud.* 41c.

9. Plutarch, *Rect. rat. aud.* 42d–e.

10. Plutarch, *Rect. rat. aud.* 45f–46c.

11. Plutarch, Rect. rat. aud. 46f–47d (Babbitt, LCL).

12. Plutarch, *Rect. rat. aud.* 48c.

13. Lucian, *Nigr.* 6–7.

14. Plutarch, *Rect. rat. aud.* 42f, 47d–48b.

15. Plutarch, *Rect. rat. aud.* 43b–d.

16. Philostratus, *Vit. Apoll.* 1.15.

17. Walter Burkert, *Greek Religion* (trans. J. Raffan; Cambridge: Harvard University Press, 1985), 56.

18. Wilhelm Dittenberger, ed., *Sylloge Inscriptionum Graecarum* (3d ed.; 4 vols.; Hildesheim: Georg Olms, 1960), 3.267–75 (no. 1109), lines 62–66.

19. Ibid., lines 74–90.

20. Ibid., lines 14–29.

21. Gregory S. Aldrete, *Gestures and Acclamations in Ancient Rome* (Baltimore: The Johns Hopkins University Press, 1999), 147–54.

22. Philo, *Contempl.* 77, 79.

23. John Chrysostom, *Adv. Jud.* 1.2 (PG 48:846–47); citation from Dieter Georgi, *The Opponents of Paul in Second Corinthians* (Philadelphia: Fortress, 1986) 114, n. 246.

24. It has been suggested that this passage is an interpolation, conflicting with instructions in 1 Cor. 11.3–13 that women should have their hair covered when they pray or prophesy. Paul may, however, have a different standard for different types of speech. Women may be allowed ecstatic speech, under the influence of the Spirit, but be disbarred from disputing with a speaker. Certainly, Paul's direction to the Thessalonians not to quench the Spirit nor to despise prophetic utterance (1 Thess 5.19–20) logically leads to a position of allowing the Spirit to speak through women, even if they are barred from speaking in their own right.

25. See Pieter J. J. Botha, "The Verbal Art of the Pauline Letters: Rhetoric, Performance and Presence," in *Rhetoric and the New Testament: Essays from the 1992 Heidelberg Conference* (ed. S. E. Porter and T. H. Olbricht; JSNTSup 90; Sheffield: Sheffield Academic Press, 1993), 409–28.

26. Franz Joseph Dölger, "Klingeln, Tanz und Händeklatschen im Gottesdienst der christlichen Melitianer in Ägypten," in idem, *Antike und Christentum: Kultur- und religionsgeschichtliche Studien,* (4 vols.; Münster: Aschendorff, 1934), 4:254–55.

27. Jerome, *Comm. Ezech.* 11.412 (PL 25:331b); citation and translation from Georgi, *Opponents of Paul,* 113–14, n. 245.

28. Augustine, *Doctr. chr.* 4.24.53.

29. Hesychius, *Serm.* 6.5, in *Homilia ii de sancta Maria deipara* (PG 93:1456).

30. John Chrysostom, *Exp. Ps.,* on Ps 47 (PG 55:208). For evidence against clapping in Christian liturgical settings, see H. F. Stander, "The Clapping of Hands in the Early Church," delivered at the Eleventh International Conference on Patristic Studies, Oxford, 19–24 August 1991. Stander is concerned with handclapping as a part of worship more than with applause as such. Handclapping as a form of applause is especially associated with the theater, and the disapproval of handclapping is associated with the church's disapproval of the immorality of the theater. Most applause in the ancient world was verbal or took forms other than handclapping, but some of his observations apply to applause in a more general sense.

31. Tertullian, *Spect.* 26.

CHAPTER EIGHT
Applause Lines

If the meaning of the Gospel is found as much in the way it moves the emotions as in the facts that it presents, then applause, both as a marker of emotional reaction and as a factor inducing its own emotional response, is a significant part of a Gospel performance. We have seen that we should expect a great deal of audience reaction during a presentation of the Gospel, but can we go further and determine the sorts of things for which an audience would applaud? There are many comments in our sources indicating the types of things that usually induced applause. Once again, if we apply that norm with care, making allowances for peculiarly Christian approaches, we should be able to form a fairly accurate idea of the kinds of passages in the Gospel for which an audience would be most likely to applaud or to express disapproval.

It goes without saying that it is impossible to reconstruct how and when any particular audience would have reacted to a performance of the Gospel of Mark. Different audiences would react differently, and even the same group of listeners might react differently at different times. The first-century Mediterranean world contained a number of rhetorical subcultures, and from our scanty evidence it is impossible to know all the ways the responses of typical audiences might differ from one group to another. As with the rest of this investigation, we are dealing with probabilities rather than certainty.

The applause that the Gospel would elicit also depended on the composition of the audience. We can expect Christians to react much more enthusiastically than non-Christians. I follow the majority of Markan scholars in believing that the Gospel was intended for a Christian audience. I understand the Gospel to be a form of epideictic rhetoric, primarily designed not to convince the audience but to reinforce the existing values of the group. Writers on rhetoric considered both history and encomium, or speeches of praise, as forms of epideictic oratory, and the Gospel shares elements with both of those genres.[1] If the Gospel had a Christian audience that shares most of Mark's perspective, then we have some idea how one might work the audience emotionally to produce audience involvement and applause.

Reasons for Applause

Earlier we saw that audiences were ready to applaud on many occasions, not only for speeches or other oral performances. Here we will consider more carefully aspects of oratory that were greeted with applause. Our sources indicate that audiences applauded primarily for three different features of oratory: the substance of a speech, florid verbal style, and extravagant delivery.[2]

Applause for content needs little comment because we are all familiar with that phenomenon. One need only think of the tiresome applause of Congress during State of the Union addresses, as each party indicates by applause which proposals match its own agenda for the nation. Ancient audiences applauded for a wide range of substantive material. Lucian tells a story of a woman applauding a poet for flattering her.[3] Seneca indicates that audiences applauded for moral principles with which they agreed.

> Have you not noticed how the theatre re-echoes whenever any words are spoken whose truth we appreciate generally and confirm unanimously?

>> "The poor lack much: the greedy man lacks all.
>> "A greedy man does good to none: he does most evil to himself."

> At such verses as these, your meanest miser applauds and rejoices to hear his own sins reviled.[4]

Abusing one's opponent customarily provoked applause, and Quintilian advises advocates not to indulge in excessive abuse for the sake of the applause that usually follows.[5]

Sententiae

We are less likely today to think of interrupting a speech with applause for a speaker's verbal style, though we are more likely to applaud a point with which we agree if it is well phrased. For example, "Ask not what your country can do for you—ask what you can do for your country" (John F. Kennedy). First-century audiences, on the other hand, were quite aware of verbal art and willing to reward a well-turned phrase with applause. The audiences' concern for verbal art could work against performers as well. If an orator produced a sentence with an unpleasing rhythm or incorrectly lengthened a vowel, the audience would protest. Actors were driven off the stage for faulty pronunciation.[6] Cicero was a master of the well-turned period and says that such periods often induced applause. Audiences also applauded sentences constructed with a pleasing rhythm.[7] Not all orators thought that such ornamentation was appropriate. Cicero carried on a vigorous debate with the Atticists, orators whose imitation of classical Greek models led them to disapprove of Ciceronian periods.

In the first century of the common era there was a change in the popular style of rhetoric. Audiences and speakers alike turned away from Ciceronian rhythms and became enamored of pithy and memorable epigrams or *sententiae*.[8] The term *sententia* was originally used as an equivalent of the Greek *gnōmē*, a short statement expressing a general truth, but by the first century it came to mean any striking statement.[9] Quintilian adds that they occur primary at the end of a section of discourse. He also discusses various types.[10]

Many of the surviving sources complain about the overuse of epigrams in the new style. Plutarch mentions audiences being carried away by a speaker's evenly balanced clauses.[11] Quintilian complains that rhetors today "want every passage, every sentence to strike the ear by an impressive close. In fact, they think it a disgrace, nay, almost a crime, to pause to breathe except at the end of a passage that is designed to call forth applause."[12] The common use of epigrams as applause lines is apparent from Quintilian's complaint about rhetoricians who fill their speeches with florid commonplaces and epigrams designed only to provoke applause from the audience.[13]

The elder Seneca recounts a story that indicates how much style overwhelmed content in the mind of some audiences. Porcius Latro set a trap for his audience to show them how carelessly they listened. In one declamation, he concluded a particularly passionate passage with the solemn declaration, "*Inter sepulchra monumenta sunt!* (among the tombs there are tombstones)." Though it meant absolutely nothing, the impressive-sounding passage was met with shouts of applause.

Latro then turned on his audience and castigated them for their foolishness.[14]

We find a much more positive view of epigrams in Tacitus' *Dialogue on Orators*. Aper, who defends the modern style in that dialogue, justifies the frequent use of epigrams because of their memorable form. Young men, he says, want not only to hear a speech but also to bring home something remarkable and worthy of recollection. If some thought has glittered because of a concise and striking saying, or a passage has shone because of its careful poetic dress, they pass it on among their acquaintances and often include it in letters written to their own communities and provinces.[15] Cicero himself suggested using such epigrams as a means of rescuing oneself from a negative reaction by the audience. The crowd's love for such phrases would divert them from their bad feelings toward the orator or his cause.[16]

Epigrams in the Gospels

To be sure, Mark would not be considered a master stylist by the rhetorical writers. His language is often rough, but the words of Jesus tend to stand out as well-wrought epigrams. Some of these passages can stand with the best of the rhetors' epigrams and are likely, especially with a sympathetic and less sophisticated audience, to have evoked the same sort of admiration. Cicero, who paid close attention to the rhythms of his speeches, indicates that rhythm can occur naturally from certain figures of speech:

> Moreover, there are certain figures of speech which involve such a symmetry that rhythm is the necessary result. For when clauses are equally balanced, or opposite is set against opposite, or words are matched with words of similar endings, whatever is elaborated in this way generally has a rhythmical cadence.[17]

Jesus' speech in the Gospel tradition often makes use of these types of figures.[18] Quintilian's discussion of types of epigrams includes many figures to be found in the Synoptic sayings, including those drawn from contraries, those that make use of implied meanings, those that gain their effect from surprise, those that double a phrase, those that contrast opposites, those that apply a quotation to a different saying, and those that play on words.[19]

Quintilian links the use of epigrams with authoritative speakers. Although epigrams can be used in argument, they generally make claims without argumentation. Epigrams laying claim to a universal application, Quintilian says, are best suited to speakers whose own authority and character would lend weight to the words. "For who would tolerate a boy, or a youth, or even a man of low birth [such as Jesus?] who presumed to speak with all the authority of a judge and to thrust his precepts down our throats?"[20] For the most part, Jesus alone speaks in epigrams in the Gospel. He has such authority with the audience that his statements require no proof. John the Baptist, another figure of authority, also speaks in epigrams in Mark (both 1:7 and 1:8). The connection between this form of speech and authority makes even more striking the Syrophoenician woman's willingness to challenge Jesus' epigrammatic dismissal of her entreaty with a challenging epigram of her own (Mark 7:27–28).

Delivery of Epigrams

First-century audiences were ready to applaud vocal gymnastics of many kinds. Epigrams were ideal applause lines because they combined the perceived virtues of clever verbal arrangement with a display of impressive vocal delivery. Quintilian indicates that it was common to deliver epigrams in a particularly impressive style. He disapproves of rhetors who overuse epigrams to divide their speeches or to make arguments, "the only qualification necessary being that it come toward the close of the period and be impressively delivered."[21] He complains about the frequent pronouncement of quivering and passionate epigrams to induce applause.[22] The epigrammatic delivery was distinct enough that Quintilian can castigate speakers "who not merely deliver many such epigrams, but utter everything as if it were an epigram."[23]

The use of epigrams to mark every pause in the flow of an oration led, probably inevitably, to further manipulation by speakers. Quintilian reports, with disapproval, that many orators paused in their speech to induce applause.[24] There is a necessary connection between applause and a momentary interruption in one's speaking, since a speaker cannot be heard clearly over loud applause. Quintilian gives directions for dignified ways of filling "the extravagant pauses imposed by the plaudits of the audience," indicating that it was appropriate to walk back and forth, even though Cicero warned against it.[25] Pausing to induce applause, however, he considered unacceptable.

There were other forms of delivery that won applause from the audience as well, but it is much harder to determine whether and in what places such forms of delivery would have been used in Gospel recitations. Plutarch mentions audiences being carried away by harmonious and gentle modulations of the speaker's voice.[26] Quintilian complains about speakers who fall into a chant, and in the late second century Lucian satirizes speakers who chanted at every opportunity and turned everything into song.[27]

Applause Markers in Mark

Audiences are not completely predictable in their applause, but from a number of factors it is possible to identify passages that would probably elicit applause. First, audiences are likely to applaud when their side (Jesus) defeats the opponents. "Give to Caesar what belongs to Caesar, and give to God what belongs to God!"[28] "Amen!" "Preach it, brother!" "Yes, Jesus!" "Truly, the Son of God!" "Jesus rules!" Conversely, they are likely to indicate disapproval at the odious behavior of Jesus' opponents. "And as soon as they left, the Pharisees were plotting with the Herodians how to kill him"[29] "Slime balls!" "Scum!" "Murderers!" "May God strike them down!" Or, if the audience is partial to Luke, "Forgive them, Father!"

Second, since audiences often applauded for verbal effects, especially when delivered in an extravagant vocal style, a conjunction of verbal effect with other indicators of possible applause points increases the possibility of applause at those points. Well-wrought epigrams, in particular, were likely to induce applause in the late first century.

Third, since applause interrupts the story, intended applause lines most likely coincide with pauses in the narrative. Since most authors recited their works before releasing them in written form, it is unlikely that the Gospel would have passed into circulation before it had been recited and adapted to the responses of audiences.[30] Where Mark expects applause, he builds a pause into the narrative.

The episodic style of Mark is well structured to accommodate interruptions for applause. There are natural breaks between episodes, which allow for applause and might even, like the orators' pauses criticized by Quintilian, encourage audience response. Many episodes exhibit great works done by Jesus or show him defeating opponents in debate. Both are types of actions Christians might well applaud. Episodes that end with a pithy saying, called "sayings *chreiae*" in the schoolbooks, are ideally suited for applause.[31] These episodes relate a short narrative, often including a question put to Jesus or the attack of an opponent, and conclude with a saying. Such sayings are among the most artistic lines of the Gospel. Since sayings *chreiae* present a confluence of decorative verbal form and a natural pause point in the narrative, we expect applause at these points. Those episodes that present a saying in a debate or dispute format add the further delight of hearing Jesus defeat his opponents, often in a way that casts odium upon them.

Applause Marker in Mark 2:15–28

If we look at the series of such episodes in Mark 2:15–28, for example, we can see how the form creates natural applause points where the audience might respond. The first episode ends with the following pronouncement:

> *ou chreian echousin hoi ischuontes iatrou all' hoi kakōs echontes;*
> Not need have the strong of doctor but the [ones] problems having;
> *ouk ēlthon kalesai dikaious alla hamartōlous.*
> not I came to call righteous but sinners.
> It is not the strong who need a doctor, but those who have problems; I came not to call the righteous but the sinners. (2:17b, author)

Both halves of the saying are antitheses with the contrasting members separated by the conjunction *alla* or its contracted form *all'* (but). As Cicero observes, antitheses tend to set up rhythmic patterns of repetition, and doubling the pattern adds to the effect. To increase the impact, the saying is crafted so that words in the first part of the saying repeat many of the same sounds: *hoi ischuontes, hoi kakōs echontes.* Since *ou chreian* contains the same harsh guttural *chi* (Greek χ is pronounced more like the German "ch" than the English) sound as the two contrasting members of the antithesis, *iatrou* (doctor), with its softer sounds, stands out in contrast. Because *iatrou* (of a doctor) is separated from *chreian* (need), the word to which it connects, and placed in the middle of the clause (Greek word order is quite flexible), the sentence is balanced in sound as well as in thought. The sound perfectly reflects the meaning. Both the strong and those with problems share the same harsh sounds, while the doctor stands soothingly in the midst of both.

The second part of the saying repeats the pattern of the first: the initial *ouk ēlthon* produces the same rhythm and sounds as *ou chreian*, and *alla* ("but," the same as the contracted form *all'* in the first part) separates the contrasting sides of the rhyming antithesis. As the natural word order is retained in the second member, however, this part of the saying creates movement toward the end rather than the careful balance of the first member. Here the just and the sinners are not treated the same in terms of rhythm and sound. The sinners are preferred, and the saying comes to a rest with that preference for the sinners. Again, the choice of sounds perfectly reflects the meaning. The first part of the antithesis, "*oukēlthon kalesai dikaious* (I came not to call the righteous)," continues the same harsh gutturals found in the first member. Their absence in *hamartōlous* (sinners) sets the sinners apart. The doctor and the sinners are both separated from the harsh guttural noise of the world. This looks like an applause line in terms of its verbal form.

The line is emotionally satisfying as well. The books on rhetoric emphasize the importance of arousing feelings of hatred, or odium, toward one's opponents.[32] This episode shows Jesus' opponents to be self-righteous. They are uncomprehending and stand in the way of God's will as expressed through Jesus. The saying makes them look foolish (at least to those of us who share Jesus' view of the world). It excludes Jesus' opponents (and not incidentally, ours as well) from the kingdom of God and extends the call of salvation to us who are willing to accept the term *sinner* as an appropriate description. We are raised up from our humble estate (*ischuontes* and *kakōs* can mean strong and weak or base in general, not only in reference to health), so we can sneer with contempt at those who think themselves our betters. All that and clever phrasing as well! Even the most tepid listener should raise her hand for that one. I myself will jump from my seat and yell, "Divinely inspired!" "Hosanna!" or whatever we yell in our church. As the Gospel performer takes a moment to pause, indicating the beginning of a new episode, I can applaud to my heart's content.

Sometimes the verbal signs of possible applause points do not correspond to the subject matter. We may find beautifully crafted sayings, but no plausible emotional reaction to induce applause. In the very next episode, the dispute about fasting, is a case in point. We have another sayings *chreia*. Jesus' opponents challenge him because his disciples do not fast. Jesus responds with another well crafted saying. The opponents are shown up. Our position is vindicated. The situation looks quite ripe for applause, but I find it hard to applaud the pronouncement "The days are coming when the bridegroom is taken from them, and then they will fast, in that day" (2:20, author). Even if the audience understands the absence of Jesus as the unfolding of God's plan, it is not appropriate to applaud. This saying helps to develop another emotional current, the pity and fear the audience feels as a result of the mistreatment and death of Jesus. At this point in the narrative that current is carefully kept within its banks. At the end of the Gospel, it is allowed to overflow. I do not applaud at the crucifixion, no matter how well crafted the scene, nor when the women flee from the tomb.

The emotional tone in this dispute section of the narrative is rather complex. On the one hand, Jesus always wins. He vindicates us in our practices. He makes our mutual enemies look like fools. There is a lot to feel good about. On the other hand, the crucifixion keeps rearing its ugly head. The healing of the paralytic (2:1–12), which is the hinge episode between the healings and the disputes, contains the charge of blasphemy, for which Jesus is eventually condemned to death. In the fasting dispute, the bridegroom unexpectedly disappears just when I am prepared to applaud. After the synagogue healing, the Herodians and Pharisees plot to kill Jesus. Mark uses the disputes narratively to make the crucifixion plausible or even inevitable. It is written in the plot as well as in the Scriptures. This is an interesting narrative strategy because it subverts the audience's expectations. The genre of the sayings *chreia*, like that of the healing story, is inherently triumphalistic. A saying *chreia* is intended to show the wit and the wisdom of the protagonist. Mark subverts the genre by using these episodes to prepare the way of the cross. This section of the Gospel is quite effective because Mark works against audience expectations to build awareness of the coming crucifixion. There are other places where Mark builds toward an applause line and gives us something else. It is in keeping with the Markan view of the world that appearances are deceiving, or at best incomplete.

At this point in the narrative, however, we do not want to get too bound up with the cross. Applause has its value here. We want to involve the audience emotionally. Our position must be vindicated now so that when we get to the crucifixion, we know that death has been overcome. Death and departure are only allowed to disturb us for a moment. "No one sews a patch of new cloth on an old cloak. . . . No one puts new wine in old wineskins" (2:21–22, author). Applause comes easily now. We can share in feeling the superiority of our position. We can laugh at the Pharisees' being compared to a raggedy old cloak and brittle, useless wineskins. There is satisfaction in thinking of our opponents bursting apart in a great flood of wine. High marks for another well-turned phrase. The performer has natural points to pause. It is likely that these sayings are received with applause.

Vocal Effects in the Beginning of Mark

The beginning of any performance is quite important for the success of the rest of the work. If we do not catch the audience in the beginning, it is much harder to win them over later. A Christian audience would be relatively well disposed toward a Gospel performance. Nevertheless, a good author and performer will pay particular attention to the beginning. If I can win some applause in the first few minutes, I am well on my way to success. We have seen that vocal effects made a strong impression on ancient audiences. In this chapter, we will take a look at the vocal effects that Mark uses in the beginning of the Gospel. In the next chapter, we will return to the beginning again to examine how Mark interacts with the audience to win them over to a sympathetic hearing of the Gospel.

The beginning of the Gospel sounds particularly impressive. Cicero says that the conjunction of words with similar endings produces a strong rhythmical quality, and we find just such a strong rhythm in the first verse of the Gospel.

> *Archē tou euangeliou Iēsou Christou huiou theou.*
> The beginning of the joyous proclamation of Jesus Messiah Son of God. (1:1, author)

The transliteration of Greek letters into the English alphabet does not correspond to the actual pronunciation. The line is pronounced more like this:

> Ar-khay tou you-ang-ge -lee-ou Yay-sou Khrees-tou whee-ou the -ou (*th* as in thin, *g* as in girl).

The rhythmical quality caused by the rhyming "ou" endings sounds important to first-century ears. The rhythm is stressed by the tonal quality of the line. Remember the singing delivery of orators that some writers complained about? First-century Greek was a tonal language. This means that accents were not purely a matter of stress, as in English, but were pronounced with a different musical tone.[33] Some accented syllables were pronounced with a tone that rises from the ordinary tone. Others were pronounced with a tone that falls from the ordinary. A third type of accent, called a circumflex, is pronounced with a rising and then falling pitch. This is the type of accent found on most of the "ou" endings in the opening line. The line ends with repeated circumflexes: *Iēso͡u Chisto͡u huio͡u Theo͡u.* It has natural chantlike quality, and we have seen how much first-century speakers and audiences loved an impressive chanting delivery.

The line also sounds impressive because of the number of long syllables. In the pronunciation of Greek, long and short syllables refer to the length of time that it takes to pronounce a syllable. Length of syllables is determined by whether the vowel is long or short and the number and type of consonants following the vowels. Rhythm in Greek poetry was based on the distribution of long and short syllables, not on the distribution of stress accents, as it is in English. First-century audiences were still closely attuned to the length of syllables. An accumulation of long syllables slows delivery, which gives a more impressive and dignified effect. An accumulation of short syllables speeds delivery and sounds more lively. The opening line has a great number of long syllables. It scans as $--$ $-$ $--\cup\cup-$ $--$ $--$ $--$ $\cup-$ ($-$ being long syllables, $\cup$ short syllables). Since I want an impressive beginning, I would draw out the long "ē" "ou" sounds a little extra and exaggerate their rising-and-falling tone. If I deliver the line with enough aplomb and have a well-disposed audience, I can expect to be greeted with shouts of praise. "Preach it, Brother Mark!" Nothing increases goodwill in the first century like a gratuitous display of vocal gymnastics.

As a formula for the citation of Scripture, the second line produces a weighty effect as well:

Kathōs gegraptai en tō Ēsaia tō prophētē.
Just as has been written in Isaiah the prophet.

Here I have some long "ō" and "ē" sounds to draw out, and I can give a little extra roll to the circumflex accents on both occurrences of "tō." Next comes a "reading" of Scripture:

1 *Idou*
2 *apostellō ton angelon mou pro prosōpou sou,*
3 *hos kataskeuasei tēn hodon sou;*
4 *phōnē boōntos en tē erēmō ,*
5 *hetoimasate tēn hodon kuriou,*
6 *eutheias poieite tas tribous autou.*

"Look!
I am sending out my messenger [or angel] before your [sg.] face,
who will prepare your [sg.] way.
A voice of one crying in the wilderness,
'Prepare the way of the Lord!
Make straight his paths!'"

"*Idou*" is a wonderful word to play with vocally. You can draw out the "ou" forever. Aging baby boomers may remember Bob Dylan's version of the "Freight Train Blu-ooooooooooooooooooooooooooooo-hou-hues." That is excessive; I would stretch it out for about three seconds. It is like being able to extend your arm to the horizon when you point. "Looooooooooooooook! This is really impooortaant!" "*Idou*" has a falling accent (called a grave) on the "ou," and you can keep the tone falling as you drag out the "ou": "Idou ↘↘↘ ou." The shift from the exaggerated low tone of my drawn-out "ou" to the mid-tone with which "*apostellō*" begins provides an acoustic jolt to catch the listeners' attention. Scripture may have been chanted in the synagogues of the first century. If so, I am certainly going to chant this passage to give it scriptural weight. If not, I will adopt some weighty "quotation" style to indicate "The Word of the Lord."

The passage from Scripture is a composite of three passages from the Law and the Prophets (Isa 40:3, Exod 23:20, Mal 3:1). The composite is brilliantly constructed for vocal effect. Look at all the "ou" sounds. I have my wonderful drawn-out "*Idou*" in line 1. Lines 2, 3, 5, and 6 all end with rhyming "ou" sounds. Mark has added the "sou" (you) to the end of line 3, both for added audience involvement and to create the rhyming pattern. Lines 3, 5, and 6 are of approximately the same length. Line 2 is longer, but it has an internal "ou" rhyme to break it up.

Line 4, occupying the middle of the composite, gives a strong contrast. The line has a wonderful onomatopoeic effect. Look at all the long vowel sounds in "*phōnē boōntos.*" The accent gives me a nice falling tone on the "*ē*" of "*phōnē* ↘ *ē* ," which I can extend to produce a falling-off-a-cliff effect. Then I have this superb forever "o" sound in "*boō͡ ōntos*," with a rising-and-falling circumflex tone just at the right place. "*phōnē* ↘ *ē boō͡ ōntos.*" It sounds just like shouting off the side of a mountain. Then I receive a magnificent echo back with a repetition of the "*ē*" and "*ō*" sounds in "*en tē͡ ē erē↗ᵉmō.*" The echo works on a number of different levels. The mixture of short and long syllables gives a mirror effect: −−U−UU−U−−. The pitch tones also mirror each other: →↘→͡→ →͡→↗→ (→ equals a neutral tone).

"*Phōnē* ↘ *ē boō͡ ōntos en tē͡ ē erē↗ᵉmō.*"

Praise Jesus! Does that ever sound like crying out in the wilderness! In line 5, "Prepare the way of the Lord!" "*Hetoimasate tēn hodon kuriou*" begins with an accumulation of short vowels and short syllables: U−UUU. Thus the first word is pronounced more quickly, conveying urgency: "I do not want you to be laggards when you are preparing the way."

Other Applause Points

In response to healings and discourses of Jesus, the acclamations of the crowds correspond to natural applause points. Plutarch gives an account of stories that were told by a guide at the temple in Delphi, and he says that the listener was amazed at the account of the marvelous events.[34] The performer of Mark would want to achieve the same effect. The miracles are essential in Mark for understanding who Jesus is. The narrated amazement of the crowds at the conclusion of healings stories suggests the proper response of the audience as well. It works like the applause of the paid claque. If the people in the narrative are oohing and ahing, it encourages me in the audience to ooh and ah as well.

The ending of the synagogue scene in Mark 1:21–28 is an excellent example. The words reproduce the buzz of an active audience response. The earliest Greek text has no punctuation, so the passage can be performed to indicate an excited discussion by dividing the response into the greatest number of individual speakers. "Who is this?!" "A new teaching!" "With authority!" "He even commands the unclean spirits!" "And they obey him!" This is the first of the miracles of Jesus and the most elaborate of the audience responses. As a performer, I want my applause sign to blink most forcefully here so I can get the audience involved in the miracles. The narrative claque functions as an applause sign, so Mark works the claque as much as he can in the first scene.

On the other hand, some of the healings in Mark end not with acclamations but with commands to silence (1:44; 5:43; 8:26). These commands to silence undermine the audience's tendency to applaud the miracles of Jesus. In these cases, the natural pause between episodes follows the request for silence. The audience is not likely to applaud a command to keep quiet. That is not nearly as exciting as a healing. The command to silence even occurs in an impossible situation. When Jesus brings Jairus's daughter back to life, the whole village is outside the door, mourning (5:43). How is Jairus supposed to keep the healing a secret? Since secrecy is impossible in the narrative world, the command must be directed at those in the performance world, to control the applause of the audience. Applause increases the level of emotional reaction and signifies communal validation of the reaction. By undermining applause for the healings through commands to silence, Mark guides the audience's emotional response away from acclamation of Jesus as a healer. Yes, Jesus is a great healer and wonder-worker (so Mark encourages us to applaud some healings), but there is more to him than that (so Mark refuses to let us applaud others).

Applause points might be indicated as well by places in the discourses of Jesus where a new saying is introduced by a formula such as "and Jesus said." The quotation formula allows the speaker to resume the narrative and provides a transition from the audience's applause. Speakers often resume speaking before applause has completely died down, and the quotation formula is a throwaway phrase that can be lost in the receding applause without ill effect. It is especially valuable when the next line is an applause line as well, since the speaker can move on to the next applause line before the audience's enthusiasm has been diminished. Since applause has interrupted the flow of the narrative, it will not immediately be clear who is speaking when the narrator resumes, whether it is Jesus, some other character, or the narrator in his own voice. By indicating that Jesus is still speaking, Mark keeps the audience oriented within the flow of the narration.

The quotation formula is found, for example, at the end of the discipleship discourse in 8:34–9:1. The preceding statement may well be an applause line: "For those who are ashamed of me and *my words* in this *adulterous* and *sinful* generation, the *Son of Man* will also be ashamed of *them* when he comes in the glory of his Father with the holy angels!" (8:38, emphasis added). Clearly the Son of Man coming in glory is exciting. This is as triumphalistic as Mark gets. *We* are not ashamed of Jesus, so Jesus' shame is not aimed at us. We agree with the condemnation of "this generation," and condemning others always feels good. If the audience applauds here, the performer needs to regain everyone's focus for the next line, which is the climax of the discourse. "And he was saying to them" gets the audience quieted. "Amen! I say to you" tells them it is really important. "There are some of those standing here who will *not* taste death until they have seen that the kingdom of God has come with power!" (9:1, author). Thunderous applause. That is even more exciting than condemning others.

Peter's Confession

There is a very important place in Mark where we might expect applause from the shape of the narrative, but the absence of applause markers suggests that applause was not intended. Since Mark begins his Gospel by identifying Jesus as the Messiah, we might well expect to applaud when Peter identifies Jesus as the Messiah in 8:29. The construction of the episode, however, does not encourage applause. First of all, Peter's statement, "*Su ei ho Christos* (You are the Messiah)," is quite short and is given no verbal embellishment. Usually applause lines are given extra verbal weight. Second, there is no natural pause point. The following passage is a command to silence: "And he rebuked them so they would tell no one about him" (8:30, author). As in the miracle stories, the command to silence is used to control applause. If I start applauding before the performer pronounces the command to silence, I am going to be cut off and look foolish. Thus it is likely that the intended delivery would connect Peter's answer and Jesus response into one continuous sentence. Rather than allow the listeners to congratulate themselves on their own knowledge of Jesus as the Messiah, Mark uses the confession primarily to introduce the passion prediction. Applause lines do follow in the discourse about discipleship (8:34–9:1).

The situation is much different in Matthew's Gospel, where Peter's confession is crafted to induce applause. The confession (Matt 16:16) is expanded to give it more weight and verbally embellished with the repetition of endings and "ou", "o", and "s" sounds: "*Su ei ho Christos ho huios tou theou tou zōntos* (You are the Messiah, the Son of the living God)." Applause at this point does not interrupt the flow of the narrative at all, and in fact enhances the meaning of the following line: "And Jesus answered and said to him, 'Blessed are you, Simon bar Jonah, for flesh and blood did not reveal this to you, but my Father in heaven'" (16:17, author). By applauding the confession, the listeners express their own recognition of its truth and earn for themselves a share in the blessing that follows. Each of the statements in verses 17, 18, and 19 is independent enough to allow for applause following each. The whole structure is ideally suited for allowing the church to congratulate itself on its divinely inspired insight and the power that has been granted to it in the person of Peter.

Consideration of the audience's interaction with the Gospel performer helps us to recover the intended meaning of a passage. I, for one, have long thought that audiences would have closely identified with Peter's recognition of Jesus as the Messiah. Peter applies one of their own confessional titles to Jesus. I would expect them to react with a mixture of pleasure at hearing their belief expressed and relief that the lack of recognition in the narrative was finally broken. Such a reading is often encouraged by the typography of modern Bibles. Frequently, a heading such as "Peter's Confession" is placed above this episode, and another heading such as "Jesus Foretells His Death and Resurrection" over the following passion prediction. By undercutting applause for the confession, however, Mark subordinates the confession to the following material about the death of Jesus and the impending death (or the threat of death) of his followers.

Notes

1. Cicero includes a discussion of history as rhetoric in *De or.* 2.12.51–2.15.64.

2. Richard A. Burridge has some insightful comments about applause in reaction to sophists' performances; see "About People, by People, for People: Gospel Genre and Audiences," in *The Gospel for All Christians: Rethinking the Gospel Audiences* (ed. R. Bauckham; Grand Rapids: Eerdmans, 1998), 141.

3. Lucian, *Pro imag.* 4.

4. Seneca, *Ep.* 108.8–9 (adapted from Gummere, LCL).

5. Quintilian, *Inst.* 12.9.8.

6. Cicero, *De or.* 3.50.196.

7. Cicero, *Or. Brut.* 50.168; 63.214. Folker Siegert has argued for a sophisticated use of prose rhythms by Luke, who is, of course, a much more sophisticated writer than Mark ("Mass Communication and Prose Rhythm in Luke-Acts," in *Rhetoric and*

the New Testament: Essays from the 1992 Heidelberg Conference [ed. S. E. Porter and T. H. Olbricht; JSNTSup 90; Sheffield: Sheffield Academic Press, 1993], 42–58). For rhythm in Mark, see E. Ilif Robson, "Rhythm and Intonation in St. Mark I–X," *JTS* 17 (1916): 270–80; G. Lüderitz, "Rhetorik, Poetik, Kompositionstechnik im Markusevangelium," in *Markus-Philologie* (ed. H. Canzik; WUNT 33; Tübingen: Mohr, 1984), 165–203.

8. On the use of *sententiae* in rhetoric, see Paul A. Holloway, "Paul's Pointed Prose: The *Sententia* in Roman Rhetoric and Paul," *NovT* 40 (1998): 32–53; A. D. Leeman, *Orationis Ratio: The Stylistic Theories and Practice of the Roman Orators, Historians and Philosophers* (Amsterdam: Hakkert, 1963), 219–42, 260–83. The importance of *sententiae* in eliciting applause is also mentioned by Burridge, "About People, by People," 141.

9. Quintilian, *Inst.* 8.5.3.

10. Quintilian, *Inst.* 8.5.2.

11. Plutarch, *Rect. rat. aud.* 41d.

12. Quintilian, *Inst.* 8.5.13–14 (Butler, LCL); cited by Holloway, "Paul's Pointed Prose," 38.

13. Quintilian, *Inst.* 5.13.42.

14. Seneca, *Controversiae* 7.4.10.

15. Tacitus, *Dial.* 20 (Benario); cf. *Dial.* 22.

16. Cicero, *De or.* 2.83.340.

17. Cicero, *Or. Brut.* 45.220; cf. 49.164–50.167, where Cicero provides examples.

18. For an excellent study of the nature of Jesus' sayings in the Gospels, see Robert C. Tannehill, *The Sword of His Mouth: Forceful and Imaginative Language in Synoptic Sayings* (SemeiaSup 1; Philadelphia: Fortress, 1975).

19. Quintilian, *Inst.* 8.5.

20. Quintilian, *Inst.* 8.5.8 (Butler, LCL).

21. Quintilian, *Inst.* 8.5.3.

22. "*Vibrantibus concitatisque sententiis,*" Quintilian, *Inst.* 12.9.3.

23. Quintilian, *Inst.* 8.5.31 (Butler, LCL).

24. Quintilian, *Inst.* 11.3.121. The rhetorical use of the pause to induce applause is observed by Burridge, "About People, by People," 141.

25. Quintilian, *Inst.* 11.3.126 (Butler, LCL); Cicero, *Or. Brut.* 18.59.

26. Plutarch, *Rect. rat. aud.* 41d.

27. Lucian, *Rhet. praec.* 19.

28. Mark 12:17, author.

29. Mark 3:6, author.

30. E.g., Suetonius, *Poet.: Vita Verg.* 33; Pliny, *Ep.* 3.18; 5.3.7–11; 7.17. For audience input into written composition, see F. Gerald Downing, "Ears to Hear," in *Alternative Approaches to New Testament Study* (ed. A. E. Harvey; London: SPCK, 1985), 97–101.

31. Theon, *Prog.* 3.22–70 (Butts edition). The literature on the *chreiae* (which are called by a number of other names in scholarly discussions) in the Gospels is vast. Among important works that address the *chreiae* from a rhetorical point of view are Ronald F. Hock and Edward N. O'Neil, eds., *The Chreia in Ancient Rhetoric: Volume I. The "Progymnasmata"* (SBLTT 27; SBLGRRS 9; Atlanta: Scholars Press, 1986); Vernon K. Robbins, ed., *Ancient Quotes and Anecdotes: From Crib to Crypt* (FF; Sonoma, Calif.: Polebridge, 1989); Burton L. Mack and Vernon K. Robbins, *Patterns of Persuasion*

in the Gospels (FF; Sonoma, Calif.: Polebridge, 1989); Vernon K. Robbins, ed., *The Rhetoric of Prounouncement, Semeia* 64 (1994); Willi Braun, "Argumentation and the Problem of Authority: Synoptic Rhetoric of Pronouncement in Cultural Context," in *The Rhetorical Analysis of Scripture: Essays from the 1995 London Conference* (ed. S. E. Porter and T. H. Olbricht; JSNTSup 146; Sheffield: Sheffield Academic Press, 1997), 185–99.

32. E.g., Cicero, *De or.* 2.51.208.

33. For the pronunciation of Greek, see W. B. Stanford, *The Sound of Greek: Studies in the Greek Theory and Practice of Euphony* (Berkeley: University of California Press, 1967); W. Sidney Allen, *Vox Graeca: A Guide to the Pronunciation of Classical Greek* (2d ed.; London: Cambridge University Press, 1974); A. M. Devine and Laurence D. Stephens, *The Prosody of Greek Speech* (New York: Oxford University Press, 1994).

34. Plutarch, *Pyth. orac.* 8, 397e; cited by John J. Winkler, *"Auctor" and Actor: A Narratological Reading of Apuleius's "Golden Ass"* (Berkeley: University of California Press, 1985), 235.

CHAPTER NINE
Including the Audience

In oral presentation the words of the narrative exist simultaneously in two worlds. The first is the imagined story world of the narrative. The second is the social world in which the narrative is taking place, roughly what some people might call the "real world." The words present the events of the story. They also exist as the address of someone to the group hearing the story, as direct address to the audience. A silent reader of a book interacts with an artifact representing words abstracted from any particular social situation. Those listening to the recitation of the same text hear the words as part of an event within their social ("real") world.

Hearing the words of a story one's social world has a particularly strong effect on how one hears dialogue. A silent reader perceives dialogue as taking place within the story world of the text. Listeners simultaneously hear dialogue within their social world as well. All dialogue in orally performed narrative is addressed at one and the same time to a character or group of characters in the story world and to listeners in the social world. This leads to a partial collapse of the distance between the narrative dialogue and the audience. The effect is much more strong in narrative than in drama because of this element of direct address. In drama, we watch performers enacting dialogue on the stage. While dialogue in a play often carries a great deal of emotional power, the audience is primarily a spectator, overhearing dialogue between others. The distancing of staged dialogue is lost in oral narrative because the performer addresses the narrative to the audience. Thus words of the dialogue are addressed to the audience, not to another performer on the stage.

Many types of oral performance play with the effect created by collapsing the two worlds or forcing a switch from one world to another. It is a common effect in jokes. My youngest daughter used to be fond of a knock-knock joke:

Daughter: Knock! Knock!
Dad: Who's there?
Daughter: What??!! Have you forgotten *your own daughter??!!*

The joke is funny, at least to a child, because my line, which I presume to be part of the story world of the joke, is treated as being part of real world of our social interaction.

An equally unsophisticated example of the effect is found in a camp skit I remember from my boyhood. The drama takes place on an exotic tropical island. Unfortunately, the group performing the skit does not have enough players and is forced to draft an extra from the audience. Generally a camp counselor is chosen because they are willing to be helpful, and everyone enjoys making authority figures look foolish. The extra is given a few simple lines. He or she is to repeat the names of the gods of the island, accompanied by histrionic kneeling and bowing. The first god is named "Whadda," the second "Silligu," and the third "Siam." The extra is then led through a brief rehearsal, bowing and repeating the three exotic names until they blend into the nonstory-world statement, "What a silly goose I am."

The folklorist Richard Bauman has described several ways storytellers make use of the effect to comment on the narrative or the storytelling event. A storyteller may break completely out of the narrative world to comment on the story directly: "I don't blame y'all if you don't believe me about this tree." He or she may also provide explanations. "You know, we all put a X on a bee tree, for a brand. Which is a pretty good idea, to brand anything, you know, to kinda own it." One may also comment on the story through dialogue within the story world. In a tall tale that has become thoroughly unbelievable, one character comments to another, "Buddy, you got the foolishest notions I ever heard of. Your imagination just runs wild with you."[1]

Audience Inclusion in Ancient Literature

The effect of audience inclusion was well known in the ancient world and was used in many forms of composition. The author of *On the Sublime* cites direct address to the audience as a figure of speech creating a lively effect:

Change of person gives an equally vivid effect, and often makes the listener feel set in the thick of the danger:

... You would say that unworn and with temper
    undaunted
Each met the other in war, so headlong the rush of
    their battle.

And Aratus's line:
  "Be you in that month in the midst of the surge of
    the ocean."

Herodotus does much the same: "You will sail up from the city of Elephantine and there come to a smooth plain. And when you have passed through that place you will board again another ship and sail two days and then you will come to a great city, the name of which is Meroë." You see, friend, how he takes you along with him through the country and turns hearing into sight. All such passages with a direct personal application set the listener in the centre of the action. By appearing to address not the whole audience but a single individual—

Of Tydeus' son you [sg.] could not have known with
which of the hosts he was fighting—

you will move him more and make him more attentive and full of active interest, if you rouse him by these personal appeals.[2]

Obviously, Longinus makes use of the effect in this passage, so that his description of the technique is an example of its use.

Ancient playwrights found a number of ways of blurring the boundary between the narrative and performance worlds.[3] In Greek and Roman comedy a character might break through the boundary and address the audience directly, either to provide information or for comic effect. One method is the aside, in which a character takes the audience into his confidence, though he is unheard on the stage:

Simo: Do you think I believe your story that she has born Pamphilus a son?
Davus: I see his blunder: that shows me how to act.
Simo: Why don't you answer me?[4]

In this case Simo's response indicates to the audience that the aside is not heard in the narrative world of the stage. We also find double asides, with two characters competing for the audience's confidence:

> *Gnatho:* But what do you think of this for a slave?
> *Parmeno:* She's not amiss, certainly not.
> *Gnatho:* It's heart-burn to the fellow.
> *Parmeno:* How he's taken in![5]

To complicate matters, a second character can comment on the aside with a remark such as "Why are you talking to yourself?"[6] The existence of an aside makes no sense in the narrative world of the play, since there is no audience in that world. By commenting on the performance convention, the second character adds to the confusion between the narrative and social worlds.

Characters comment on other stage conventions as well. A character in one comedy turns to the audience and points out that the money he is holding is stage money.[7] In another comedy a character refers to the distinctive costume by which the stock characters of comedy could be recognized. The speaker is one such shopworn type, a parasite who sponges off the wealthy for dinners and other favors: "There are two sorts of parasite, Nausinicus: one the common one, *ridiculed* in comedy, ones who wear black, *like us*. I am seeking the other sort."[8] By calling attention to his dress, the character steps momentarily into world of the audience, watching costumed players on the stage.

The dialogue form, commonly used for expository writing in the Greek and Roman world, provides the most blatant examples of speech addressed to the listening audience. The dialogues of Plato served as a model for later writers. Platonic dialogues often feature characters that are complex and true to life, since Plato wanted to portray the process through which ideas arose and developed. By New Testament times, however, the dialogue framework is usually a flimsy excuse for the presentation of an author's ideas. The dialogues on oratory by Cicero and Tacitus—familiar to you by now, good reader, from frequent citation—are good examples. In these dialogues characters may present different points of view, but their speeches sound more like professorial lectures than conversation between friends. In spite of the mutual congratulation and occasional disagreement that punctuate the speeches, it is clear that everyone is addressing the audience of the dialogue rather than other characters in the narrative world.

Prologues

Direct address to the audience is quite common in the prologues to plays. The prologue provides a transition into the narrative world of the drama, and the audience can be directly addressed before the narrative world is constructed. The prologue to Terence's comedy *The Lady of Andros* ends with a direct appeal to the audience to give the play a fair hearing:

> [The playwright] begs of you the favour to sit through his play with impartial minds and due attention that you may see for certain what your hopes are for the future, whether his coming plays are to be worth your attendance or to be damned without a hearing.[9]

Terence had good reason to be concerned about his listeners' attention. We saw in our discussion of audience response that his hearers preferred tightrope walkers and gladiatorial combats to comedies. There is a similar appeal in the prologue of Plautus's *Amphitryon*. Here the prologue is spoken not by an actor in his own voice but by the god Mercury:

> According as ye here assembled would have me prosper you and bring you luck in your buyings and in your sellings of goods, yea, and forward you in all things . . . [and on and on for seven more lines], keep still while we are acting this play and all be fair and square judges of the performance.[10]

A comic effect is produced by the god suddenly stepping out of character to demand the audience's attention, an action quite unbecoming to a god. If I am directing the play, the actor's demeanor and delivery will suddenly change from the pompous to the schoolmasterish to make the joke apparent to those munching on bread in the back rows.

A similar use of direct address is found in prologues to many types of writings. Readers of the New Testament will be familiar with the direct address in the prologue of Luke: "Since I followed everything carefully from the beginning, it seemed good for me to write an

orderly account for you, most excellent Theophilus, so that you may
see that the words which you heard are faithful and true" (Luke 1:3–4,
author). Apuleius plays with the convention of direct address in the
prologue to his novel *The Golden Ass*.[11] He begins with a promise that
his tale will appeal to the audience. "But I would like . . . to caress your
ears into approval with a pretty whisper, if only you will not begrudge
looking at Egyptian papyrus inscribed with the sharpness of a reed
from the Nile." Then he introduces himself. "I begin my prologue.
Who am I? I will tell you briefly." The short description tells us that
his native tongue is Greek and he learned Latin later in life. This leads
to a humble appeal for tolerance. "So, please, I beg your pardon in
advance if as a raw speaker of this foreign tongue of the Forum I commit any blunders." This line is complicated by the fact that the actual
speaker of the line is not the author, but the reader. The reader may or
may not be a native speaker of Latin. The shift from one language to
another is compared to his tale, a Greek story told in the Latin
tongue. He ends the prologue with an appeal to pay attention, "We
are about to begin a Greekish story. Pay attention, reader, and you will
find delight." After concluding the prologue, he continues to speak in
the first person, but now, as we soon realize, the first-person speaker is
no longer Apuleius but the fictional narrator of the story. "I was traveling to Thessaly, where the ancestry of my mother's family brings us
fame. . . ."[12] Just like the unfortunate protagonist, who later turns into
an ass, the narrative "I" changes into another being.

Direct Address in Mark

In a number of places Mark provides explanations to his listeners. He
translated foreign words (5:41; 7:34; 14:36; 15:22; 15:34), provides
"explanations" of Jewish practices (7:3–4), comments on the emotional cause of actions ("for they were frightened," 9:6; "for they were
afraid," 16:8), a natural cause (there are no figs on the tree because "it
was not the time for figs," 11:13), and an occupational reason for
action (Simon and Andrew were "throwing nets in the sea—because
they were fishermen," 1:16).

Mark breaks more completely out of his narrative in the apocalyp-
tic discourse. "When you see the abomination of desolation standing
where it should not be, *ho anaginōskōn noeitō* (usually translated "Let
the reader understand"), then let those in Judea flee into the mountain"
(13.14, author). Sometimes this comment is proposed as evidence that

Mark intended his Gospel to be read by single readers. As we saw in an earlier chapter, however, "reader" in the ancient world often meant those listening to someone else performing a work of literature. As a performer of the Gospel, I would understand "reader" to refer to the individual members of the audience, not to myself. The phrase would be more accurately translated, "Let the one whom I am addressing understand." That would include both individual readers and listening "readers." More idiomatically, it could be translated, "Understand this carefully." The clause is often understood as advising the audience to look for the hidden meaning of the "abomination of desolation." Coming as it does between the when and the then clauses, however, it can refer both backward and forward. It may emphasize the urgency of the direction that follows, to flee immediately from Judea, as well as suggesting a deeper meaning for the preceding phrase. It may be successfully performed either way.

Mark uses the singular "addressee" in order to include each reader or listener individually. As we learned from *On the Sublime*, the singular form of address involves the audience more fully than does the plural.[13] Mark usually puts third-person imperatives ("Let so-and-so do such-and-such") in the singular for this reason. The closest analogy to the "understand carefully" passage is the stereotyped phrase with which many of the parables end, "Let one with ears to hear, hear!" (4:9, 23; 7:16).[14] Mark also uses the singular in these passages, although the entire crowd is addressed. Jesus must hope that more than one person in the crowd can hear the parable! He is simply being a good rhetorician and addressing each member of his audience individually.

Audience-Inclusive Dialogue

Mark frequently takes advantage of the overlap between narrative and social worlds to address his audience directly through the dialogue of the Gospel. Remember that narrators presented dialogue in character, with full emotional inflection. Performers were encouraged to feel the emotions they sought to convey. They were expressive in their voice and gesture. For a moment the performer becomes the character in the presentation of the dialogue. This means that when I, as the performer of the Gospel, relate the words of Jesus, I momentarily become Jesus and perform his words with the inflection and gesture I imagine Jesus using within the story-world situation.

To *you* [pl.] has been given the mystery of the kingdom of God,
    But to *those outside*, everything is taking place in parables
(Mark 4.11, author).

In my own performance of this passage, I gesture with a broad
sweeping motion of one or both hands toward the entire audience
during the words "to you." This indicates Jesus including his own
audience in the promise. "To those outside" is accompanied by pointing with the right hand to the side away from the audience. Those
watching the performance become unpaid extras in the drama. They
are, for a time, playing the role of Jesus' audience. The gesture of
Jesus including *his* audience in the promise simultaneously includes
the *performer's* audience within the contemporary social world. The
importance of gesture in the first-century performance style accentu-
ates the inclusive effect of the dialogue. "To you has been given the
mystery of the kingdom of God!"*Amen!* The man is talking to *me!*

Every mention of "you" in the narrative may have a double reference. "You" is heard in the story world as overheard dialogue between
characters. Because the narrative is addressed to me in the audience,
however, I can also hear "you" within the social world as addressed to
me. The extent to which I hear the "you" as addressed to me depends
on a number of factors, including how much I identify with the
addressee in the story world and how much I recognize the words as
appropriately addressed to me. If, as is probable, the Gospel performer is someone I know and consider authoritative, I am predis-
posed to hear the performer's words as addressed to me. In the
example just given, I think the audience would hear the promise as
addressed to themselves. If Mark's audience is a sectarian group that
understands itself as having been transformed by the mystery of the
kingdom of God, a mystery unknown or rejected by the outside
world, the fit would be close.[15]

Another place in the Gospel where the audience would welcome
inclusion is 3:34–35. "And looking around at those sitting in a circle
around him [I slowly turn my head from left to right to survey the
entire audience while simultaneously making a broad, sweeping gesture with my right arm], he said, 'Look! [I point at the audience] My
mother and my brothers! [I point at the audience with both hands, all
fingers extended] Whoever does the will of God [sweeping both hands
from the front to the sides to indicate the audience] is my brother
[point] and sister [point] and mother [point]!'" Most audiences include

listeners of the right age and sex to be cast as family members. I figure any woman who brought a rosary is going to be flattered to be Jesus' mother.

Audience Inclusion and Performance Style

In part, the extent of the collapse depends on the performer's style. Some performers generally address dialogue to an imaginary dialogue partner on the stage. Such a style makes the dialogue more removed from the audience, more as it is in drama. That style is well adapted for fairly large audiences in churches and other spaces where both the social and architectural construction of the space has already created a separation between the performer and the audience. The opposite extreme is my own style of performing Mark. I have generally performed the Gospel in a classroom setting or with other small groups. In small groups of less than forty people, without a stage or other formal separation, I found myself automatically using specific members of the audience as silent dialogue partners. Various audience members in the front rows are healed, have demons thrown out of them, and so forth. Words addressed to groups are addressed to the audience as a whole. That narrative style clearly creates a more thorough collapse of story world and social world.

It is impossible to determine with certainty which style is more likely for a first-century performer. There are analogies to both styles in the ancient world. It is most likely, however, that the Gospel would be performed in a house-church setting. Even the largest houses of all but the top strata of society would put serious spatial constraints on a performer and the size of the audience. It is unlikely that I could pack more than fifty people into the biggest room available in our house of meeting. This is not St. Patrick's Cathedral. I am going to be close to my audience. The limited space would facilitate intimate interaction. The audience would not experience the distancing created by a stage or pulpit.

Peter's Confession

The audience-inclusive effect of dialogue can be increased by a more vehement delivery. A likely case is found in 8:33. "But turning and looking at his disciples, he rebuked Peter, and said, **'Get behind me, *Satan!*** For you are not thinking as God but as a human.'" The language fits the expulsion of an evil spirit. *Epitimaō* "rebuke," is a verb commonly used in exorcisms (1.25; 9:25) as well as of other forceful charges,[16] and the direct address to Satan suggests exorcism as well. Since the exorcist has to overpower the demon to drive him out, realistic delivery would be forceful and authoritative. A number of narrative clues suggest audience inclusion. There is the forceful second-person imperative and the continued second-person address ("you [sg.] are thinking"). The narrative includes a body gesture (turning, probably toward the audience) and suggests an eye or hand gesture (in this context, *idōn*, is more likely "looking at" than "seeing"). Within the performance, the audience is caught off guard. They are already included in the language and gesture before the delivery of the punch line and are caught by surprise when both they and Peter are unexpectedly addressed as "Satan!" The power of the scene in oral delivery comes partly through the rapid shift in tone, the triumphant "You are the Messiah!" in 8:29, the unexpected silencing of the disciples in 8:30, the prediction of death and suffering in 8:31, Peter's unexpected resistance to Jesus in 8:32, and finally the expulsion of Satan from Peter in 8:33. It is strengthened by the identification of the audience with Peter in two of the pivotal sayings. If the confession of Peter, "You are the Christ!" parallels confessions within the assembled church, the audience easily puts itself in the place of Peter making the confession. This natural response is cleverly strengthened by the structure of the passage. When the performer/Jesus asks about his identity, "Who do people say I am?" the listeners may be expected to answer correctly within their own minds. The wrong answers of the people strengthen the listeners' right answer. By the time Peter answers correctly, he is only repeating the listeners' mental response. Then, after identifying so closely with Peter, the listeners suddenly find themselves addressed as "Satan!"

Mark moves immediately into Jesus' discourse on discipleship (8:34–9:1). This discourse is addressed directly to the Gospel audience. Mark supplies only the weakest pretense of a narrative frame. Jesus is on the road in the middle of nowhere, far from his normal haunts in Galilee. He has just concluded a private conversation with his disciples. Still he is able to muster a considerable crowd for the discourse: "If any of you want to follow me [using the open-handed proclamation gesture as in the cover illustration, with a little vibration since it comes in the middle of an emotional passage] . . . " Even though Jesus has just yelled at us and called us Satan, we still want to be included in that group. ". . . then *deny* yourself [with the emphatic pointing-down gesture] and take up your cross [lifting open hands upward—the lifting gesture ends in the supplication gesture for added effect] and follow me [pointing with the hand to your chest]." Coming on the heels of the passion prediction, the exhortation works quite well rhetorically. Since the crowd did not hear the passion prediction, they may be a bit confused.

In the last chapter we saw that Mark crafted Peter's confession to discourage applause at that point. In contrast, the discipleship discourse is designed to encourage applause. It is formed from a series of maxims or *sententiae*. There is a significant amount of verbal decoration, including sentences constructed in parallel and paradoxical constructions. Although each sentence builds on the preceding one, each is independent enough to allow for a pause. In fact, a pause improves the delivery quite a bit. It allows time for each sentence to sink in; it also allows for applause. Antithetical parallelism—such as "If you want to save your life, you will lose it. If you lose your life . . . , you will save it"—is perfect for inducing applause. If I applaud the first line, I get to applaud again for the second. The restatement of the idea in its opposite form validates my applause. So I am likely to applaud the second line with more fervor. As a performer, I am going to deliver the whole discourse as a series of quivering epigrams. The audience is bound to love that.

As the rhetorical handbooks indicate, such maxims are not effective arguments. If I agree, I applaud; but if I disagree, I am not convinced. Maxims are most effective when used to summarize in a memorable way a position already held by the audience. Thus such a discourse addressed to a crowd who has not heard such teaching before would be totally ineffective. The Gospel audience, however, knows the meaning of the crucifixion for those following Jesus. For them, the narrative-imbedded discourse provides an effective summary of their own understanding.

The Crucifixion

Mark's crucifixion scene (15:21–41) is an absolutely brilliant example of audience inclusion. His passion is not triumphalistic or heroic, as are the parallel accounts in John and Luke. Nor does it describe in excruciating detail the physical torments of Jesus' death, as do the martyrdom scenes in the books of Maccabees. Instead, the suffering of Jesus is expressed through the mockery and the cry of dereliction.

The crucifixion is one place where following the rules of rhetorical delivery has transformed my performance. The rules of delivery do not allow me to perform the scene as I originally felt I ought to present it. What I wanted to do was to express sympathy for the pain of Jesus and my own sorrow at his death. The discussions of pathos in the rhetorical handbooks lead me to expect that a first-century performer would adopt the same approach. When I first performed the Gospel, that is what I did. I would choke up a little and get misty-eyed and present the scene as if watching it from afar, perhaps from the vantage point of the women who are mentioned. The rhetorical handbooks, however, say that in the presentation of narrative, one should try to present a scene as realistically as possible, and speech should be done in character. If I follow those rules, the scene changes radically.

The cry of dereliction, I enjoy. I have one line to express the suffering of Jesus. I muster up every ounce of pain I have felt in my life and cry in a loud voice, **"Eloi! Eloi! Lema sabachthani?"** Then I get to repeat it in English: **"My God! My God! Why have you forsaken me?"** (15:34). It is very cathartic for me, though it may be disconcerting for the audience. The mockery is transformed by doing it in character. My understanding of mockery in character is extremely nasty. I overdo it a little and make the mocking sound like third-graders on the playground, with lots of "Naaah naah na naaah naah!" in my tone of voice. "Hey *Messiah!* King of *Israel!* Come on down from the cross so that *we* might see and believe!" The childish tone is appropriate since we are supposed to despise those who mock Jesus in his pain.

When I read the mockery silently, I usually think of the cleverness of Mark's irony. When I perform it, I think about how nasty the mockery is. Much of the crucifixion scene consists of mockery. About halfway through, it begins to feel a little strange to perform. This is the foundational narrative of Christianity. It is the climactic scene around which the whole narrative is built. I am standing there, insulting Jesus. The audience is sitting there, listening to me abuse Jesus. What a strange way to celebrate the Son of God! If I wanted to hear someone ridicule Jesus, I could go out on the street and find a Pharisee or some Roman soldiers.

It is this mockery that involves the audience so deeply in the crucifixion. Mark has focused on the one part of the suffering of Jesus that I can experience. If the performer describes the physical agony of crucifixion, it remains something external to me. I sympathize with pain of that sort. If the performer describes the mental anguish of

Jesus, it is still external to me. My reaction is still sympathy. If the performer yells insults at Jesus, I experience that directly. That "dinglewort" is insulting *Jesus*. That "dinglewort" is insulting *me*. Mark puts me in the place of Jesus in the one way I can feel directly.

Mark has developed the earlier scene of Peter's denial (14:66–72) with similar insight into audience psychology.[17] The abandonment of Jesus is quite stark in Mark's Gospel. The crowds abandon Jesus. The disciples abandon Jesus. Even God abandons Jesus. None are left except a few women watching from afar. How can I induce a listener surrounded by fellow Christians in a familiar home to feel alone and abandoned? I cannot. The whole Gospel experience develops comradery through the shared expression of common feelings and beliefs. But I can do the next best thing: I can involve the audience in the abandonment of Jesus. As a listener, Peter is the disciple I identify with at this point. I felt revulsion for Judas. I felt rather uncomfortable about that naked man fleeing for his life (14:52). Peter is my one hope. At least he has not completely abandoned Jesus. He took the risk of following into the courtyard of the high priest. The slave girl of the high priest sounds suspiciously like the folks down the street in their accusations of Peter. "You [pointing] also [pointing] were with [pointing] the Nazarene [pointing]" (14:67). The performer is pointing at *me!* Like Peter, I have to respond. If I recognized that earlier passage about brother betraying brother to death (13:12), I may, like Peter, begin to squirm a little. In any case, I have thoroughly identified with Peter, and I cannot avoid being implicated in his response. Peter is a hero of the church. Do I think I am going to do any better? We are caught in Peter's guilt. The abandonment of Jesus becomes real for us because we participated in Peter's abandonment of Jesus. For a while we feel estranged from Jesus. For a moment I am alone in my guilt.

The Beginning of the Joyous Proclamation of Jesus, Messiah, Son of God

It was generally agreed that emotional appeals should be most concentrated in the two parts of a speech, the introductory section (called the *exordium*) and the conclusion (called the *peroratio*). The prologue of Mark (1.1–16) serves much the same function as an exordium, the opening portion of an oration. In all forms of performance, whether poetry, Gospel, or oratory, the opening needs to accomplish the same purposes. Quintilian himself praises the opening lines of Homer's epics as having established the law that governs the composition of exordi-ums.[18] As both history and encomium were considered forms of epi-deictic rhetoric,[19] it is reasonable enough to analyze the opening of Mark in terms of the teaching of the rhetorical handbooks concerning the opening of a speech.

We can find rules for composing a proper opening in *De inventione*, a rhetorical handbook written by Cicero in his early years. The pur-pose of the introductory section, he tells us, is to put one's listeners in the right frame of mind to receive the speech. One wants listeners who are well-disposed, attentive, and receptive.[20] The introductory section must be crafted to fit the predisposition of the audience. Pre-suming a Christian audience, the Gospel performer would have a gathering that is already well disposed. In such a case, Cicero says I can dispense with the introduction altogether or use the introduction to increase the audience's goodwill.[21] I can increase goodwill by bring-ing my opponents into contempt, praising my own subject, or men-tioning the good deeds of my listeners. I can make my audience attentive if I show them my subject is important, novel, or incredible. Important subjects are those that concern humanity as a whole, the listeners in the audience, illustrious men, the immortal gods, or the general interest of the state."[22]

Mark makes use of a number of these techniques to increase audience goodwill in the prologue of the Gospel:

> The beginning of the joyous proclamation of Jesus, Messiah,
>   Son of God, just as has been written in Isaiah the prophet.
> Look! I am sending out my messenger [or angel] before your
>   [sg.] face, who will prepare your [sg.] way.
> A voice of one crying in the wilderness,
>   "Prepare the way of the Lord!
>   Make straight his paths!" (1:1–3, author)

Look how much Mark gets his audience involved at the very begin-ning! A Christian audience already thinks the glad announcement of Jesus Messiah is both important for the world and important to them. Mark adds more weight to it by linking it to Scripture, emphasizing the narrative's importance to God as well. The Scripture takes the form of a direct address from God to each of us in the audience. The second "you" (in "your way") is not in Scripture, but Mark is re-pre-senting the quotation in a form that emphasizes the direct address.

Most commentators suggest the "you" refers to either John or Jesus. In performance, however, it is rather clear that "you" means you, the listener. Mark is addressing the audience before beginning the narration, much as an actor might in the prologue of a play. Gesturing adds to the effect. How else does one indicate you other than pointing to "you" in the audience?

The voice in the wilderness also gives us something to do. "You all! Prepare the way of the Lord! You all! Make his paths straight!" These imperatives are imbedded in a short narrative describing the messenger. So we hear it at two levels. In the mininarrative of the messenger, God's herald cries in the wilderness to anyone there, "Prepare the way of the Lord!" I can also hear the command as addressed to myself. Mark has nicely paralleled "you" with the Lord. The messenger comes to prepare "your way (*tēn hodon sou*)." The messenger proclaims, "Prepare the Lord's way (*tēn hodon kuriou*)." There must be some connection between my way and the Lord's way! I always knew it! I am greatly flattered and quite well disposed to hear the Gospel.

John appears on the scene, preaching "a baptism of repentance for the forgiveness of sins" (1:4). Here Mark is indulging in additional flattery of the audience. Christian listeners have already been baptized or soon intend to be. We recognize the narrative as relating to ourselves. The baptism has something to do with preparing the way of the Lord. *We* are doing it! *We* are doing the right thing! *Everyone* came out to the wilderness (1:5). This is an important event. They were confessing their sins. We recognize ourselves again, doing the right thing. John proclaims: "A greater one is coming after me" (1:7). This is important. "I am not worthy to untie his shoestrings." This is really important. And incidentally, you who follow him are really important.

"I have baptized you with water, but he will baptize you with the Holy Spirit!" (1:8). Here is another point where the dialogue collapses the narrative and social worlds completely. The first half of John's proclamation is addressed to those listening to John in the narrative world. It is unlikely any of us in the audience were baptized by John. The second half erupts from the story world into the present. Nobody in John's audience was baptized with the Holy Spirit. Within the Gospel, Jesus does not baptize anyone with the Holy Spirit. It is only in the post-story-world reality of the Christian audience that Jesus baptizes with Holy Spirit. For the narrative-world audience of John, the promise is largely hypothetical. He will baptize you with Holy Spirit, later on, if you accept him. From the perspective of Mark's largely Gentile audience, it is clear that few of John's listeners did accept Jesus and were eventually so baptized. For Mark's Christian audience, however, the promise is a certainty. We have indeed been, or soon expect to be, baptized with Holy Spirit. A few of us in the audience may break out in tongues at the very thought. John addresses us in the audience to confirm the validity of our religious experience. The narrative-world audience of John has no way to understand baptism with Holy Spirit. Mark wisely skips over their reaction. If we subvert Mark's intention and consider the reaction of the audience in the narrative world, we must suspect that they were completely befuddled. This is the first reference to Jesus in the narrative world. John's proclamation tells me how to understand Jesus. All John tells us is that Jesus is important and he will baptize us with the Holy Spirit. So I am to understand Jesus and the Gospel in the context of my own baptism, specifically my baptism with the Holy Spirit.

Jesus comes out and is baptized (1:9). Again I recognize my own baptism. A voice comes from heaven (1:11). Usually, God speaks only on important occasions. "You are my beloved Son. In you I am well pleased." In the story world, God commends Jesus as very important. How we hear that in the social world depends on our understanding of baptism. If we are adopted as children of God in baptism, then the words identify us with Jesus.

Jesus is tempted by Satan (1:13). He preaches: "The time is fulfilled! And the kingdom of God has drawn near! Repent! And have faith in the joyous proclamation!" (1:14–15). This is Jesus preaching. I as the performer have to do my best Jesus imitation. In the narrative world, there is no one for Jesus to address, but proclaiming implies a crowd. I need to be loud so the crowd can hear. I need to be excited so that the crowd cares. I need to gesture in a way that indicates they ought to care. You who are hearing are placed in the role of the audience. We are coming to the end of the prologue. Mark is summing up the significance of the Gospel for us. He gives us short, forceful sentences, ideal for applause.

Now as we transition from the exordium to the body of the narrative, we have the double call story (1:16–20). Here Jesus has dialogue partners in the text. They do not have speaking parts, but they do have some individuality, and they perform important actions. How do I as the Gospel performer inflect Jesus' line, "Come after me, and I will make you into fishers for people!"? As Jesus, that is the only line I have to convince Peter and Andrew to turn their whole life upside down. Can I make it sound that convincing? I cannot. It is not a really convincing argument. Luckily, that does not matter, because my audience is already convinced of the importance of following Jesus. They just need to be told. They will project their own feelings into the story and identify with the disciples' response. As a listener, I am ready to respond, "Yes, Jesus! Here I come!" before James and John are able to get out of the boat. This is a brilliant rhetorical strategy, since Mark gets us to reconfirm our commitment to Jesus before the narrative ever gets going. What better frame of mind is there for hearing and responding to the Gospel? In that way the first call stories serve as a continuation of the prologue. You in the audience, listening to my story about Jesus, should hear it as one who has left your nets, your family, and your hired hands to follow him. I do not have to harangue you about that. If I embed my direction within the narrative itself, I can rely on the inclusive dialogue effect. I know all you good Christians in the audience will respond. I can expect at least mild applause for the disciples as well. "Uh huh! That's right!" As a listener, I have responded as the disciples. By applauding them, I get to applaud myself. That is always a good feeling.

The Ending of the Joyous Proclamation

The ending of the Gospel fits well with the prescription for ending a speech with a strong emotional appeal. Advocates are instructed to develop pity for those they represent and odium for their opponents. The trial and crucifixion scenes (14:53–15:47) are ideally suited for arousing those emotions. Jesus is shown to be abandoned and suffering even though innocent. His opponents are shown to be malicious, devious, and spiteful. Throughout the crucifixion scene the use of irony underscores their stupidity as well. We always like to think of our opponents as stupid and malicious. These two emotions are induced entirely through the portrayal of the scene, without resort to the direct appeals to the emotions that are typical of most rhetoric.

Judging from the evidence of the different texts, the more original version of Mark ended with the scene at the tomb (16:1–8). This scene is another brilliant example of the use of dialogue to involve the audience. There are two pieces of dialogue in the scene. In the first, the women ask each other, with some bewilderment, "Who will remove the stone from the door of the tomb for us?" (16:3). That line remains within the story world. I am not going to volunteer to help the women move the stone. After all, I know the stone is gone. I can feel smugly superior. I know the good news even before the women do. The dialogue emphasizes the miracle of the moved stone. More importantly, it makes me anticipate the resurrection before we ever reach the tomb. Because I have already told myself the story, Mark can present it in a condensed fashion.

The mysterious young man's lines are all in second-person address, directed to me. "And he says to them" (16:6–7, author). Mark has shifted from the past tense to the present. The immediacy of the present tense increases audience involvement. This does not merely happen in the past. It happens now, before my eyes. "Do not be amazed! [emphatic pointing-down gesture]." This is a clever variation on the crowd's acclamations that accompany the healings. By showing me the amazement of the crowd, Mark tells me to be amazed. Here Mark tells me to be amazed by telling me not to be amazed. He would not have to tell me not to be amazed if I was not already amazed. As a dutiful listener, I respond with amazement. "You are seeking [I use a semiembracing, semipointing, open-handed gesture with both hands toward the audience] Jesus [moving my hands slightly toward a different part of the audience] the Nazarene [moving again] who was crucified [pointing off toward the Place of the Skull]." The man speaks in the present tense. He makes me present in the tomb. I too seek Jesus.

"He has been raised [with raised hands]. He is not here [with hands lowered toward the side—after all, he is here with us]." Then we hear imperatives. "Look! [pointing emphatically to a spot to my side]. The place where they placed him [pointing to the same spot with an open hand]." This works wonderfully. The young man shows us that Jesus has been raised: "Do not rely on my word. Look and see for yourself." As a listener, I automatically follow the performer's command and look where he points. I become the women as I repeat their action. I can see for myself that Jesus is not there. Hallelujah! Jesus is raised! We participate in verifying the resurrection.

"But go! [emphatic pointing gesture]. Tell his disciples [pointing at the audience] and Peter [pointing]." The impertinent young man continues to order us around. I cannot tell Peter anything. He is dead and gone. But the command increases our identification with the following promise because we have been told to repeat it. It creates a much greater degree of audience involvement than would a simple proclamation of the same promise. "He is going [pointing at the audience] before you [pointing again] into Galilee [pointing to Galilee, off to the side of the room]. There [openhanded pointing] you will see him, just [pointing at the audience with both open hands] as he told you [spreading my hands to a more embracing gesture]." I may not see Jesus in Galilee, but the young man promises me that I *will* see him. I am being promised that he is going before me. Perhaps to prepare my way. Just as he told us. That sounds familiar. "I am sending my messenger before your face to prepare your way." "Just as it is written in Isaiah the prophet." "Just as he told you." We have returned to the beginning. It must be the end.

As a performer you rely on the promise to bring the Gospel to closure. But Mark does not want us to feel comfortable closure. If I am feeling good about the promise I have received, I am not feeling amazed. I am not appreciating the miracle that happened before my eyes. Once again, Mark shows his brilliance. He draws us to participate in the amazed befuddlement of the women by deliberately confusing us. The closing lines overcome us with a sudden emotional shift. "And going out, they fled from the tomb [rushing the delivery]! For they were seized with terror [hands pulled in toward my chest, confining myself—wide-open, terrified eyes] and beside themselves. And they said nothing to anyone [leaning forward toward the audience, hands and eyes open in amazement], because they were afraid." And I sit down.

What kind of ending is that? We do not grasp the resurrection if we are not shocked. We have heard the story too often to be shocked by the empty tomb. I never stop being shocked by the fleeing women. After all, the impertinent young man gave us the order. I am all prepared to go and tell someone. I am totally identified with the women, and then they run off like fools. I have the rug pulled out from under me. Just like the women. For a while I am not sure what to say either. I am still waiting for a real ending. Mark is already sitting in the audience with the rest of us.

Notes

1. Richard Bauman, *Story, Performance, and Event: Contextual Studies of Oral Narrative* (CSOLC 10; Cambridge: Cambridge University Press, 1986), 98–101.

2. Longinus, *[Subl.]* 26.1–3 (adapted from Fyfe, LCL)

3. Walther Kraus, "*Ad spectatores* in der römischen Komödie," *WS* 52 (1934): 66–83; David Bain, *Actors and Audience: A Study of Asides and Related Conventions in Greek Drama* (Oxford: Oxford University Press, 1977).

4. Terence, *Andr.* 496–500 (Sargeaunt, LCL, stage directions removed).

5. Terence, *Eun.* 273–74 (Sargeaunt, LCL, stage directions removed).

6. With various phrasing in Terence, *Haut.* 200; Plautus, *Aul.* 190; *Most.*512, 551; *Trin.* 567. Citations from Bain, *Actors and Audience*, 156-57.

7. Plautus, *Poen.* 597. Citation from Bain, *Actors and Audience*, 211.

8. Alexis, *Kybernētēs* (fragment 116). Citation and translation from Bain, *Actors and Audience*, 213-14 (emphasis added).

9. Terence, *Andr.* Prol. 24–27 (Sargeaunt, LCL).

10. Plautus, *Amph.* Prol. 1–15 (Nixon, LCL).

11. For a full analysis of the prologue, see John J. Winkler, *"Auctor" and Actor: A Narratological Reading of Apuleius's "Golden Ass"* (Berkeley: University of California Press, 1985), 180–203.

12. Apuleius, *Metam.* 1.1–2 (Hanson, LCL).

13. Longinus, *[Subl.]* 26.3.

14. Not all texts include 7:16, and most modern translations consign the verse to a footnote, but I judge it to be the "original" reading, whatever that means when texts are as fluid as in the first century.

15. See the discussion in Whitney Taylor Shiner, *Follow Me! Disciples in Markan Rhetoric* (SBLDS 145; Atlanta: Scholars Press, 1995), 243–51, for the fit between the so-called parable theory and the probable social situation of Mark's audience.

16. Silencing demons, 3:11; silencing the storm, 4:39; silencing Bartimeaus, 10:48; preventing the disciples from speaking, 8:30; disciples stopping people from bringing children, 10:13; Peter to Jesus, 8:32.

17. For another analysis of this scene as oral performance, see Thomas E. Boomershine, "Peter's Denial as Polemic or Confession: The Implications of Media Criticism for Biblical Hermeneutics," *Semeia* 39 (1987): 47–68.

18. Quintilian, *Inst.* 10.1.48.

19. For history as epideictic, see Cicero, *Orat.* 37, 207. Encomium, as a species of praise was included in the definitions of epideictic from the time of Aristotle.

20. Cicero, *Inv.* 1.15.20.

21. Cicero, *Inv.* 1.15.21

22. Cicero, *Inv.* 1.16.22–23 (Hubbell, LCL).

CHAPTER TEN
Conclusion

Our modern world has lost has lost much of the sense of the power of the spoken word as it was understood in the ancient world. For the ancients, speech had creative power. For the Jews, God created by the word. Demons could be expelled through the word. Words give the speaker power over another. Adam is given power over animals when he uses words to name them. Demons seek to gain power over Jesus by naming him. Jesus in turn gains power over the demons called Legion by securing their name (5:9). In the Jewish tradition, the sacred word that names God must not be pronounced because one cannot control God. In the traditions of magic that flourished in this era, the name of the Jewish God was often pronounced in an effort to gain that control over God's power.[1]

This perceived power of the word is derived from the basic nature of oral communication. The spoken word is not abstracted from life. It is the stuff of life. In large part our common life is created by the word. We create relationships by our words. We create common meaning by our words. To a significant extent we create ourselves through our shared words, through which we define who we are. The spoken word is never separated from the speaker. My authority, or my powerlessness, inheres in my words. The centurion says, "I am a man under authority, with soldiers under me. I say to one, 'Go,' and he goes, and to another, 'Come,' and he comes" (Matt 8:9, author).

In contrast to the written word on a page, the spoken word involves the entire body. Even with God, the divine speech was understood in quasiphysical, bodily terms. The *pneuma* of God is both God's breath and God's spirit since the word combines both meanings. When it enters a prophet, the human vessel speaks the words of God through the breath of God. Breath, spirit, life, and speech are closely connected. Speech had power even apart from meaning because it embodies the breath. Magical texts from the ancient world

191

abound in meaningless words with magical power. Particularly potent are the extended lists of vowels that magicians chanted as part of their spells. Vowels have primordial power because they are most closely associated with the *pneuma*, the spirit or breath.

Embodied speech involves not only the breath but also the whole body. We have seen the importance of gesture in ancient performance. The speaker paces back and forth, points with his finger, waves his hand, and strikes his thigh. The listeners respond with their whole body as well, raising a hand or leaping to their feet in approval, shouting out praise and condemnation.

Because of the embodied nature of speech, it is the perfect vehicle for the emotions, which involve visceral reactions of the whole body. When the performer of Mark points right at you and shouts in your face, **"Get behind me, Satan!!"** there is nothing intellectual about your reaction. The demons quake within you. More than one chosen stand-in for Peter has been still recovering from the shock when the Gospel draws to a close. The ancients understood the power of emotion in creating our world. What we feel with our entire body, we believe much more deeply than what we think in our mind.

The rhetoricians of the Greek and Roman world understood the intense power that could be generated by the embodied word. They studied carefully how to create the desired effects. They practiced constantly to perfect the power of their presence. They also understood how to use the power of the embodied word to bring into the present the events that happened, or that might have happened, in another time and place. The performed word creates events right before your very eyes and makes you feel them as if you were there.

This is the power that a performer of Mark would have harnessed to make the Gospel present. The Gospel was not a story. It was an event. "Were you there when they crucified my Lord?" I was there. And because I was there, I was frightened and I was transformed. And still "it causes me to tremble, tremble, tremble." And when they mocked him, they mocked me. When they questioned Peter, I was weak and afraid. And I heard Jesus promise me the kingdom. And he told me to take up the cross. And he said I was his mother. And I could not find him at the tomb. And I was confused. And if I died with him, surely I will be raised with him also (Mark 8:34–35).

The performance of the Gospel makes Jesus powerfully present. It allows me to participate in his life and his death. The Gospel event embodying the life and death of Jesus is transformative. Transformative because it lifts me out of ordinary existence. It creates a new reality. Something in me dies. Something in me is born. It is no longer I who live. The Pauline language describes the intended effect of the Gospel event. I participated in the faithfulness of Christ. It continues to live in me.

Notes

1. For a collection of ancient spells, see Hans Dieter Betz, ed., *The Greek Magical Papyri in Translation, Including the Demotic Spells* (2d ed.; Chicago: University of Chicago Press, 1992).

BIBLIOGRAPHY
For Further Reading, Looking, and Listening

If you are interested in the general issues raised in this book, the following works provide excellent introductions. Readers seeking more detailed information on specific topics may find resources in the notes.

Orality and Literacy

Havelock, Eric A. *Preface to Plato*. Cambridge: Harvard University Press, Belknap, 1963. A pioneering study of how writing transformed classical Greek culture.

Lord, Albert Bates. *The Singer of Tales*. Cambridge: Harvard University Press, 1960. 2d ed. Edited by S. Mitchell and G. Nagy. Cambridge: Harvard University Press, 2000. A study of oral composition in Homer and twentieth-century epic poets in the Balkans.

Ong, Walter J. *Orality and Literacy: The Technologizing of the Word*. London: Methuen, 1982. The best introduction.

Ancient Rhetoric

Kennedy, George A. *A New History of Classical Rhetoric*. Princeton: Princeton University Press, 1994.

Orality and Literacy in Mark

Bryan, Christopher. *A Preface to Mark: Notes on the Gospel in Its Literary and Cultural Setting*. New York/Oxford: Oxford University Press, 1993.

Horsley, Richard A. *Hearing the Whole Story: The Politics of Plot in Mark's Gospel.* Louisville: Westminster John Knox, 2001.

Kelber, Werner H. *Oral and Written Gospel: The Hermeneutics of Speaking and Writing in the Synoptic Tradition, Mark, Paul, and Q.* Philadelphia: Fortress, 1983.

Markan Narrative from the Perspective of Its Oral Presentation

Boomershine, Thomas E. *Story Journey: An Invitation to the Gospel as Storytelling.* Nashville: Abingdon, 1988.

Malbon, Elizabeth Struthers. *Hearing Mark: A Listener's Guide.* Harrisburg, Penn.: Trinity Press International, 2002.

Rhoads, David, Joanna Dewey, and Donald Michie. *Mark as Story: An Introduction to the Narrative of a Gospel.* 2d ed. Minneapolis: Fortress, 1999.

Orality and Literacy in the New Testament World

Dewey, Joanna, ed. *Orality and Textuality in Early Christian Literature. Semeia* 65 (1995).

Silberman, Lou H., ed. *Orality, Aurality and Biblical Narrative. Semeia* 39 (1987).

Video Performances

Watching a video is much different from participating in an oral performance, but a video does show how voice and gesture give meaning to words.

McCowen, Alec. *St. Mark's Gospel: King James Version.* Videotape. Produced by Arthur Cantor Films, 2112 Broadway, Suite 400, New York, NY 10023. Distributed by the American Bible Society, 1865 Broadway, New York, NY 10023.

McLean, Max. *Mark's Gospel as Told by Max McLean.* Videotape. Produced by Fellowship for the Performing Arts, P.O. Box 230, Convent Station, NJ 07961–0230. http://www.bibleonstage.org.

Rhoads, David. *Dramatic Presentation of the Gospel of Mark.* Videotape. Distributed by SELECT, c/o Lutheran Seminary, 2199 E. Main Street, Columbus, OH 43209; 614–235–4136; http://www.elca.org/dm/select.

For More Advanced Study

The following New Testament scholars have written extensively on orality and literacy. Some of their works have been cited above.

Boomershine, Thomas E. "Biblical Storytelling in Education." *Journal of Christian Education* 36 (1993): 7–18.

———. "Jesus of Nazareth and the Watershed of Ancient Orality and Literacy." *Semeia* 65 (1995): 7–36.

———. "Mark 16:8 and the Apostolic Commission." *JBL* 100 (1981): 225–39.

———. "Mark, the Storyteller: A Rhetorical-Critical Investigation of Mark's Passion and Resurrection Narrative." Ph.D. diss., Union Theological Seminary, New York, 1974.

———. "Peter's Denial as Polemic or Confession: The Implications of Media Criticism for Biblical Hermeneutics." In Lou H. Silberman, ed., "Orality, Aurality, and Biblical Narrative." *Semeia* 39 (1987): 47–68.

———. *Story Journey: An Invitation to the Gospel as Storytelling.* Nashville: Abingdon, 1988.

Boomershine, Thomas E., and Gilbert L. Bartholomew. "The Narrative Technique of Mark 16:8." *JBL* 100 (1981): 213–23.

Botha, Pieter J. J. "Greco-Roman Literacy as Setting for New Testament Writings." *Neot* 26 (1992): 195–215.

———. "The Historical Setting of Mark's Gospel: Problems and Possibilities." *JSNT* 51 (1993): 27–55.

———. "Letter Writing and Oral Communication in Antiquity: Suggested Implications for the Interpretation of Paul's Letter to the Galatians." *Scriptura* 42 (1992): 17–34.

———. "Living Voice and Lifeless Letters: Reserve towards Writing in the Graeco-Roman World." *Hervormde Teologiese Studies* 49 (1993): 742–59.

———. "Mark's Story as Oral Traditional Literature: Rethinking the Transmission of Some Traditions about Jesus." *Hervormde Teologiese Studies* 47 (1991): 304–31.

———. "Mark's Story of Jesus and the Search for Virtue." Pages 157–84 in *The Rhetorical Analysis of Scripture: Essays from the 1995 London Conference.* Edited by S. E. Porter and T. H. Olbricht. JSNTSup 146. Sheffield: Sheffield Academic Press, 1997.

———. "Mute Manuscripts: Analysing a Neglected Aspect of Ancient Communication." *Theologia Evangelica* 23 (1990): 35–47.

————. "οὐκ ἔστιν ὧδε . . . : Mark's Stories of Jesus' Tomb and History." *Neot* 23 (1989): 195–218.

————. "Paul and Gossip: A Social Mechanism in Early Christian Communities." *Neot* 32 (1998): 267–88.

————. "Schools in the World of Jesus: Analysing the Evidence." *Neot* 33 (1999): 225–60.

————. "The Social Dynamics of the Early Transmission of the Jesus Tradition." *Neot* 27 (1993): 205–31.

————. "The Verbal Art of the Pauline Letters: Rhetoric, Performance and Presence."Pages 409–28 in *Rhetoric and the New Testament: Essays from the 1992 Heidelberg Conference*. Edited by S. E. Porter and T. H. Olbricht. JSNTSup 90. Sheffield: Sheffield Academic Press, 1993.

Dewey, Joanna. "From Oral Stories to Written Texts." In *Women's Sacred Scriptures*, in *Concilium* 1998 (no. 3): 20–28. Edited by Kwok Pui-Lan, E. Schüssler Fiorenza, and L. S. Cahill. London: SCM Press, 1998.

————. "From Storytelling to Written Text: The Loss of Early Christian Women's Voices." *Biblical Theology Bulletin* 26 (1996): 71–78.

————. "The Gospel of Mark as an Oral-Aural Event: Implications for Interpretation." Pages 145–63 in *The New Literary Criticism and the New Testament*. Edited by E. S. Malbon and E. V. McKnight. JSNTSup 109. Sheffield: Sheffield Academic Press, 1994.

————. "Mark as Aural Narrative: Structures as Clues to Understanding." *Sewanee Theological Review* 36 (1992): 45–56.

————. "Mark as Interwoven Tapestry: Forecasts and Echoes for a Listening Audience." *CBQ* 53 (1991): 221–36.

————. "Oral Methods of Structuring Narrative in Mark." *Interpretation* 43 (1989): 32–44.

————, ed. *Orality and Textuality in Early Christian Literature. Semeia* 65 (1995).

————. "Textuality in an Oral Culture: A Survey of the Pauline Traditions." *Semeia* 65 (1995): 37–65.

Kelber, Werner H. "Die Anfangsprozesse der Verschriftlichung im Früchristentum." Pages 362 in *ANRW*, part II, vol. 26. Edited by Wolfgang Haase and Hildegard Temporini. Berlin/New York: Walter de Gruyter, 1992.

————. "Apostolic Tradition and the Form of the Gospel." Pages 24–46 in *Discipleship in the New Testament*. Edited by Fernando F. Segovia. Philadelphia: Fortress, 1985.

———. "The Authority of the Word in St. John's Gospel: Charismatic Speech, Narrative Text, Logocentric Metaphysics." *Oral Tradition* 2 (1987): 108–31.

———. "The Bible in the Book Tradition." Pages 592–600 in *Medienwissenschaft: Ein Handbuch zur Entwicklung der Medien und Kommunikationsformen*. Handbucher zur Sprach- und Kommunikationswissenschaft, Band 15.1. Edited by Joachim Felix Leonhard, Hans-Werner Ludwig, Dietrich Schwarze, and Erich Strabner. Berlin: Walter de Gruyter, 1999.

———. "Biblical Hermeneutics and the Ancient Art of Communication: A Response." *Semeia* 39 (1987): 97–105.

———. "The Birth of a Beginning: John 1:1–18." *Semeia* 52 (1990): 121–44. Reprinted as pages 209–30 in *Gospel of John as Literature: An Anthology of Twentieth-Century Perspectives*. New Testament Tools and Studies 17. Edited by Mark W. G. Stibbe. Leiden: Brill, 1993.

———. "In the Beginning Were the Words: The Apotheosis and Narrative Displacement of the Logos." *JAAR* 58 (1990): 69–98.

———. "Incarnations, Remembrances, and Transformations of the Word." Pages 111–33 in *Time, Memory, and the Verbal Arts: Essays on the Thought of Walter Ong*. Edited by Dennis L. Weeks and Jane Hoogestraat. Selinsgrove: Susquehanna University Press, 1998.

———. "Jesus and Tradition: Words in Time, Words in Space." *Semeia* 65 (1995): 139–67.

———. "Mark and Oral Tradition." *Semeia* 16 (1979): 7–55.

———. "Modalities of Communication, Cognition, and Physiology of Perception: Orality, Rhetoric, and Scribality." *Semeia* 65 (1995): 193–216.

———. "Narrative as Interpretation and Interpretation of Narrative: Hermeneutical Reflections on the Gospels." *Semeia* 39 (1987): 107–33.

———. "New Testament Texts: Rhetoric and Discourse." Pages 330–38 in *Teaching Oral Traditions*. Edited by John Miles Foley. New York: Modern Language Association, 1998.

———. *The Oral and the Written Gospel: The Hermeneutics of Speaking and Writing in the Synoptic Tradition, Mark, Paul, and Q*. Philadelphia: Fortress, 1983. Reprint, Bloomington, Ind.: Indiana University Press, 1997.

———. "The Quest for the Historical Jesus from the Perspective of Medieval, Modern, and Post-Enlightenment Readings, and in

View of Ancient Oral Aesthetics." Pages 75–115 in John Dominic Crossan, Luke Timothy Johnson, and Werner H. Kelber, *The Jesus Controversy: Perspectives in Conflict*. Harrisburg, Penn.: Trinity Press International, 1999.

———. "Sayings Collection and Sayings Gospel: A Study in the Clustering Management of Knowledge." *Language and Communication* 9 (1989): 213–24.

———. "Walter Ong's Three Incarnations of the Word: Orality—Literacy—Technology." *Philosophy Today* 23 (1979): 70–74.

Index

201